IN THE
SHADOWS
OF THE NET

"This is the book we've all been waiting for on cybersex. It explains what computer sex is all about and how to get help if it becomes a problem. The personal stories are excellent for assisting clients in relating to this issue."

—Joseph M. Amico, M.Div., C.A.S., C.S.A.C.
President, National Council on Sexual Addiction and Compulsivity

"The authors provide a simple, effective guide for self-evaluation and recovery if cybersex is causing problems."

—Pia Mellody
Author, *Facing Codependence* and *Facing Love Addiction*
Coauthor, *Breaking Free*

"A much needed resource for professional and lay audiences. An important and timely book about a contemporary problem that is escalating and causing enormous personal, family, and professional distress. The authors are to be commended for clearly articulating how this problem behavior develops and presenting methods for therapeutically addressing it."

—Christine A. Courtois, Ph.D.
Author, *Healing the Incest Wound* and *Recollections of Sexual Abuse*
Clinical director of the CENTER: Posttraumatic Disorders Program, Psychiatric Institute of Washington

"Once again, Patrick Carnes, with the help of David Delmonico and Elizabeth Griffin, is pushing the frontier of our knowledge of trauma and emptiness, manifesting in addictions. Cybersex addiction is the latest of a myriad of sexual behaviors in our culture where courtship so often goes awry. The authors' gentle approach to the newest compulsive users and their families is realistic, thorough, knowledgeable, practical, and helpful to all who read it, including those whose Internet use is not a problem. Since sexuality is so very powerful an issue, we must learn to use it wisely, safely, and with discretion, lest it destroy us. *In the Shadows of the Net* gives us a way to approach it with integrity."

—Martha Turner, M.D.
Medical director of the STAR (Sexual Trauma and Recovery) Program

IN THE

SHADOWS

OF THE NET

*Breaking Free of
Compulsive Online Sexual Behavior*

PATRICK CARNES, PH.D.
DAVID L. DELMONICO, PH.D.
ELIZABETH GRIFFIN, M.A.
with JOSEPH M. MORIARITY

 **HAZELDEN**®

Hazelden
Center City, Minnesota 55012-0176

1-800-328-0094
1-651-213-4590 (Fax)
www.hazelden.org

Library of Congress Cataloging-in-Publication Data

In the shadows of the net : breaking free of compulsive online sexual behavior / Patrick
Carnes ... [et al.].
       p. cm.
   Includes bibliographical references and index.
   ISBN 1-56838-620-6
     1. Sex addiction. 2. Computer sex. I. Carnes, Patrick, 1944–

   RC560.S43 I52 2001
   616.85'83—dc21

                                                                            00-054049

05   04   03   02   01   6   5   4   3   2

Authors' note
Every story in this book is true; however, each has been edited for clarity. Names, locations, and other identifying information have been changed to protect confidentiality.

Editor's note
The Twelve Steps are reprinted and adapted with permission of Alcoholics Anonymous
World Services, Inc. (AAWS). Permission to reprint and adapt the Twelve Steps does not
mean that AAWS has reviewed or approved the contents of this publication, or that
AAWS necessarily agrees with the views expressed herein. AA is a program of recovery
from alcoholism *only*—use of the Twelve Steps in connection with programs and activities which are patterned after AA, but which address other problems, or in any other
non-AA context, does not imply otherwise.

Interior design by Elizabeth Cleveland
Typesetting by Stanton Publication Services, Inc.

Contents

Illustrations

Figures

$\mathcal{P}reface$

The remarkable and far-reaching impact of the Internet revolution continues to permeate our society in ways few of us imagined. So much is possible through the Net, including sex—and for an ever growing number of men and women and those who love them, cybersex has become a problem.

We have written this book to help you understand problematic Internet sexual behavior: how it starts, how it develops such strength, and how it can even become addictive. In this book, we also offer a plan for successfully dealing with problematic cybersex activities, one that can enable you to regain control of your life and your relationships. This hope-filled guide is designed and written to support your efforts to grow and heal. We extend our thanks to all those individuals who have graciously allowed us to share their stories in this book.

PATRICK CARNES, PH.D.
DAVID L. DELMONICO, PH.D.
ELIZABETH GRIFFIN, M.A.

I

The Shadow Side
of the Net

THE INTERNET. THE WORLD WIDE WEB. We speak of it with such awe and reverence that you would think it was a divine being coming to rescue and deliver us into a new and perfect world, an entity so powerful that it will transform—for the better, of course—our businesses, our interactions with others, the way we communicate, the way we shop—every aspect of our lives. Nothing will be the same again, and everything will be better, faster, easier.

Whatever we want—information, goods, connections—we can find it or do it whenever we want via the Internet. Yes, everything . . . even sex. We can have sex on the Internet whenever we want with exactly the kind of person we want.

Sometimes that creates a problem. The opportunity is too enticing, alluring, fulfilling, immediate, and powerful. So much is available. There are so many options, ones we've only dreamed of—or have yet to dream of! So much opportunity and stimulation is available that it's difficult to control. And hard to stop. For some it is seemingly impossible to stop.

No, the Internet isn't all sunshine and progress. There is the shadow side to the Net. For some people, the pull of cybersex can be so powerful that, like alcohol or other drugs, it's hard to put down and control. The shadowy world of cybersex is overtaking and overwhelming far too many people, undermining careers and upending relationships. And the problem is growing. Worse, it is becoming clear that for some, cybersex becomes a compulsive or an addictive disorder. No one could have forecast that cybersex would have had such an impact.

KEVIN'S STORY

Kevin, a married thirty-seven-year-old manufacturing company executive with two children, gives his account of what it's like to be hooked on cybersex:

It is 3:30 A.M. and I'm still online. Pornographic images of men, women, and children stream through my phone wires and onto my computer screen. Earlier tonight, after putting my two kids to bed, I watched the evening news with my wife, Jeneen. Since my wife was tired after a long day at work, she soon went to bed. Though I, too, was exhausted, primarily from too many late nights on the computer, I, as usual, told her I was still not tired and would stay up late and read for a while.

Once I was sure that Jeneen was asleep, I turned off the bedroom light and headed for the den and the family computer. "OK, tonight I'm just going to stay online for an hour," I promised myself. "It'll be midnight when I'm done, and that's enough time. I really just can't stay up half the night again. Today at work I actually caught myself nodding off during Alan's important sales plan presentation. I haven't been able to really focus lately, either."

Once I sat down, I arranged my chair and the screen so that if Jeneen should awaken and come in, I'd have a moment to switch the screen view over to a work-related document. I'm more careful now, since a few months ago my wife surprised me and saw the photo of a naked woman I was viewing.

I talked myself out of that embarrassing situation with the excuse that while trying to finish a work project, I'd opened an e-mail from one of my colleagues. In it was a link to a site that the guy had said I would find interesting. It was a porn site, and I told my wife that I'd never seen anything like it and was just looking at it out of curiosity.

I remember only too well how I'd felt at that moment. Heart pounding in my chest. My mouth instantly parched. Feelings of fear, shock, embarrassment, and panic coursing through my body as, in those very, very long moments, I searched for a plausible explanation. I didn't ever want to go through that again. Besides, I knew there would be no good excuse if my wife caught me again.

I'd actually sworn off porn sites after that night. I deleted the bookmarks and told myself that it wasn't worth it. I realized that I loved my wife and children and didn't want to jeopardize these relationships over some nude photos.

That promise was broken in less than a week. After a particularly hard day at work, I told myself that I deserved a reward. I'd take just thirty minutes to masturbate, and then I'd go off to bed with Jeneen.

For several evenings, I kept to this thirty-minute ritual. Feeling more confident now with my control over my Internet usage, I decided to give myself an hour each evening. A few weeks passed, and before I knew it, I was online for hours on end again each evening—until two, three, even four o'clock in the morning. I just didn't know where the time was going. What felt like an hour just suddenly turned into three or four. I was searching for just the right woman, just the right look to masturbate to before going to bed. At times, I felt like this Internet thing was spiraling out of control.

I felt extreme anticipation and excitement when I first went online in the evening, the concentration and thrill increasing as I searched various Web sites and found new ones. But after I masturbated, I felt awful. I had so many harsh feelings and was angry for wasting so much time. I felt ashamed and guilty that I had done this again. And worst of all, I felt helpless and full of despair because I realized I didn't know how or when I would be able to stop. Exhausted and beaten down, I quietly slipped into bed, wondering how I was going to make it at work again on just three hours' sleep.

CAN YOU RELATE TO KEVIN'S STORY?

Kevin isn't alone in his problems with sex and the Internet. Countless others, men and women alike, also find themselves in what seems to be a futile struggle with online sexual behavior. Mostly they struggle alone and in silence, too embarrassed or guilt-ridden to seek help, not knowing where they can find help, believing that no one else would really understand anyway. Just like Kevin, they experience a roller coaster of emotions each day. Perhaps you are in a similar predicament. Have you ever done any of the following?

- kept sexual activity on the Internet a secret from family members
- carried out sexual activities on the Net at work

- frequently found yourself erasing your computer history files in an effort to conceal your activity on the Net
- felt ashamed at the thought that someone you love might discover your Internet use
- found that your time on the Net takes away from or prevents you from doing other tasks and activities
- found yourself in a kind of online trance or time warp during which hours just slipped by
- frequently visited chat rooms that are focused on sexual conversation
- looked forward to your sexual activities on the Net and felt frustrated and anxious if you couldn't get on it when you planned
- found yourself masturbating while on the Net
- recognized the girls in the interactive online video while they recognized your screen name when you signed on
- had sexual chat room friends who became more important than the family and friends in your life
- regularly visited porn sights
- downloaded pornography from a newsgroup
- had favorite porn sites
- visited fetish porn sites
- taken part in the CuSeeMe sexual video rooms
- viewed child pornography online

Discovering the Net's potential for sexual activity may have at first felt very exciting. After all, a new world was opening up for you, ready for exploration. It may have seemed like a harmless one in which to play, to fulfill fantasies, to occasionally find sexual gratification. It may have felt like a dream come true. But eventually you may have found, as Kevin did, that there was a downside—a very powerful one that seemed difficult, if not impossible, to control. Even as resolutions are made to limit or stop using the Net for sex, they are rendered hollow by the echoes of previous vows and promises. "How could this be happening to me?" you may wonder. Again, you are not alone in these feelings. The power and attraction of the Internet in general, and its use for sexual activity in particular, has entered and permeated our culture subtly and with blinding speed.

A DIFFERENT WORLD

It's almost impossible to imagine it now, but only five short years ago, most of us knew little, if anything, about this mysterious creation for communication called the Internet. Today, however, its burgeoning growth and wide accessibility are altering patterns of social communication, business activity, and interpersonal relationships. An estimated nine to fifteen million people access the Internet each *day* at a rate that is growing by an estimated 25 percent every three months. Internet users spend an average of 9.8 hours per week visiting the more than two hundred million Web sites now in existence.

Given the dramatic pace at which this remarkable and powerful technology has entered our lives, few of us are aware that the Internet has profoundly changed many aspects of our lives. Telephones, computers, and television, once separate technologies, are merging. Our schools, work environments, and even our social lives are becoming more and more centered around computers. Five years ago, you probably could not have imagined doing your holiday shopping online, sending an RSVP to a wedding invitation via e-mail, being able to send letters and photos in seconds to a friend on the other side of the world, or "chatting" online with five, fifty, or five hundred people simultaneously. That these activities now seem commonplace indicates just how quickly we adapt to and take for granted technologies that a few years ago lived only in the realms of science fiction.

While it's not difficult to recognize technological changes, anticipating how pervasive and profound an effect they will have is a far greater challenge. Numerous authors, including Lynn White in a classic book on the Middle Ages, *Medieval Technology and Social Change,*[1] and Alvin Toffler in *Future Shock,* have argued that new technological developments can actually create changes in human thinking patterns and in how we see the world—changes that are known as paradigm shifts. Who would have imagined when the Wright brothers discovered how to build an airplane that only seventy-five years later, national and international flight would be commonplace? That a world without electricity, telephone, radio, and television is almost unimaginable today is testimony to the profound effect these technologies have had on the human race in less than a century. Our world is absolutely dependent on them. Yet at the time of their discovery, these inventions seemed little more than oddities developed by eccentric inventors.

What effect has the Internet had on society since it came into use by the general public in the early 1990s? It's difficult to know now, but the speed at which it has penetrated our culture is an indication of its power. As you know, sexuality is one important aspect of our lives that is being dramatically affected by the Internet. Mention "cybersex" and the response you'll receive will be, more often than not, a chuckle and a lewd comment. Such reactions do not, however, come from anyone who is familiar with the reality of sex and the Internet. Access to the Internet, and more specifically sex on the Internet, is on the rise in America. Access to these sex-related Web sites by children and teens also appears to be on the rise—and is illegal. Hundreds of thousands of adult-oriented Web sites are readily accessible to online users by simply typing the word "sex" in one of the many search engines available to Internet users. In fact, the word "sex" is one of the most frequently typed words in search engines. (The only words more common than "sex" are "and" and "the.") Without parental control, a young boy or girl can be exposed to unsolicited e-mails inviting the subscriber to an adult-oriented Web site.

The statistics are as remarkable as they are surprising:

- As of January 1999, there were 19,542,710 total unique visitors per month on the top five *pay* porn Web sites, and there were 98,527,275 total unique visitors per month on the top five *free* porn Web sites.
- In November 1999, Nielsen Net Ratings figures showed 12.5 million surfers visited porn sites in September from their homes, a 140 percent rise in traffic in just six months.
- Nearly 17 percent of Internet users have problems with sex on the Net.
- A profile of severe problems with sex on the Net exists for 1 percent of Internet users—and 40 percent of these extreme cases are women.
- Most of all e-porn traffic, about 70 percent, occurs weekdays between the hours of 9:00 A.M. and 5:00 P.M.
- There are 100,000 Web sites dedicated to selling sex in some way—this does not include chat rooms, e-mail, or other forms of sexual contact on the Web.

- About 200 sex-related Web sites are added each day.
- Sex on the Internet constitutes the third largest economic sector on the Web (software and computers rank first and second), generating one billion dollars annually.
- The greatest technological innovations on the Web were developed by the sex industry (video streaming is one example).

It is easy to categorize online sexual behaviors as either all good or all bad. The Internet, however, is a communications tool that is inherently neither good nor bad. It is, rather, the interaction of the content offered by its creators (those who host Web sites, post to newsgroups, organize chat rooms, and so on) and the ways Internet users of these electronic meeting sites react and respond to these messages, images, and sounds that result in "good" or "bad" outcomes.[2] Some social scientists have noted the educational potential of the Internet, citing the greater availability of information about sexuality and the potential for more candid discussions of sexuality online. The Internet can also offer the opportunity for forming online or virtual "communities" in which isolated or disenfranchised people can communicate with one another about sexual topics.

Far more often, however, an increasing and rapidly growing number of people find that using the Internet for sexual purposes is fraught with risks and, at the very least, interferes with many aspects of their lives, including family relationships, work life, and financial security.

Three people share their experiences here. (Please note that while the stories used in this book are true, they have been altered as needed to protect individual anonymity.)

Carl, a parole officer, tells his story:

I had worked for several years as a parole officer and recently I'd been seeing more sex offenders, some of whom had been using the Internet in their crimes. I hadn't really known of or thought about the Internet's potential for sexual activity or encounters until I talked with my clients and their caseworkers. Curious about the cybersex scene, I went online a few times at work just to see what sexual content was actually available on the Net. My superiors were aware of my sex activities on the Net and accepted them as necessary for my job. After a few months passed, I was still surfing sex-related sites at work. What's more, the time I spent online had been inching up. One day, I'd been online exploring sex-related sites for nearly an hour. My boss noticed and commented to me about it. I reiterated that it was work-related and that I needed to know what my guys were doing. My boss said, "OK," but suggested that maybe I was spending a bit too much time doing this, I'd best watch myself more closely, and I'd better make sure none of my other responsibilities were being neglected.

Jake, a wealthy twenty-five-year-old single man, narrowly escaped being arrested:

I seemed to have it all: a well-off family, hot new car, and nice apartment. But I had never really taken charge of my life; supported by my parents, I was unemployed, spoiled, a heavy drinker, and lacked ambition. However, I did have one area of expertise—computers. My computer knowledge developed as a young adult while being holed up in my bedroom at home as punishment for my many transgressions. I had spent endless hours on the computer during this time and was truly skilled at programming, games, and surfing the Net.

I discovered chat rooms fairly quickly, and eventually I decided that I wanted to set up sex with a young girl. Soon, I was regularly in online conversations with a particular fifteen-year-old girl. Thanks to my superior computer skills, however, I discovered that there was another older guy who was also trying to arrange to have sex with this girl. I e-mailed this man and asked him how it was going with her. By maintaining regular communications with him, I eventually discovered that the girl had finally agreed to meet him to have sex.

I discovered that the two had arranged to meet at a restaurant in town. Since I knew the time and place and was curious to see what the two looked like, I decided to anonymously observe the rendezvous, but not participate. By this time, I had given up my frequent online conversations with this girl.

On the appointed evening, I was sitting in my car in a parking lot adjacent to the restaurant where I expected to have a great view of the action. Soon, the other man showed up—and seemingly out of nowhere three police squad cars and a half dozen FBI agents appeared. Before the man knew what had happened, he'd been arrested, handcuffed, and dumped in the back of a police car.

My heart was in my mouth, pounding like a jackhammer. I could hardly breathe. I couldn't move a muscle. I'd heard of guys being busted for trying to hook up with teen girls for sex, but I thought I was clever enough to avoid such a trap. Now I knew how close I had come to being in the back of that squad car on the way to jail. I realized I had a problem, and I sought help the very next day.

Marcy, a middle-aged social worker, with a history of relationship infidelity:

I had been married thirteen years—and unfaithful the whole time. In fact, when I married, I was actually having an affair with one of the groomsmen in my wedding party. My husband never had a clue about what was going on. Finally, I started going to counseling, as my behavior began to bother me. Very soon into therapy, my therapist told me, "I think you have a problem with sex addiction." My response, however, was that the real problem was a "problematic marriage."

At this time, I discovered the Internet—more specifically, chat rooms. My husband regularly went to bed around 9:30 or 10:00 P.M. That's when I would get on the computer and head straight into one of my favorite chat rooms, where I would converse with various men. These "chats" became increasingly sexual and seductive, and eventually I was staying up very late, until three or four in the morning. I realized that my Internet use was getting out of hand, and each night I promised myself that I'd be in bed by eleven. But I just couldn't meet that goal. Despite my efforts at control, I became even more infatuated with my online life. The conversations became more and more sexual and tantalizing. Eventually, I became more and more daring. I began giving out my phone number to men I'd met online. They would call me and then together we would have phone sex. All the while, my husband was asleep in an adjacent room.

Finally, I encountered a guy who seemed irresistible, and crossing yet another boundary, I arranged an in-person meeting for sex with a guy who lived in Dallas. We agreed to meet at a Dallas hotel. We had sex, and then I was attacked, beaten unconscious, and left for dead. I awoke days later in a hospital with no clue as to where I was, how I'd gotten there, or how much time had passed. The hospital staff had no way to identify me, since my purse had been stolen along with all my identification and money. And my husband? He knew nothing about what had happened. Since I was not at the hotel I claimed to be staying at, he was frantic with worry and had called the police to file a missing persons report.

When I was finally able to use a phone at the hospital, my first call was to my therapist. I said, "OK, you're right. I have a problem. I need help."

WHAT IS CYBERSEX?

Internet sex can be accessed and experienced in many different ways. Each has the potential to cause users problems and to lead them into risky or dangerous situations. In the following section, we outline these new avenues of sex to give you an idea of the breadth of the cybersex world.

The term "cybersex" has become a catchall to address a variety of sex-related behaviors when using your computer. They fall into three general categories:

1. ACCESSING ONLINE PORNOGRAPHY, AUDIO, VIDEO, AND TEXT STORIES

The kind of pornography available on the Internet varies widely, just as it does in the noncyber-world, ranging from photographs of models posing in bathing suits or lingerie to young children being sexually abused. It can be found in various forms, including photos and audio, video, and text stories. Its variety and ease of access, however, is much greater than offline access since many of the sexual content and activity laws that exist in the United States are difficult to enforce or don't apply in other countries (which can be easily accessed via the Internet).

Pornographic materials can be found on personal and commercial Web pages, with access just a mouse click away. Pornographic pictures, video, audio, and text can also be exchanged via e-mail and discussion or newsgroups. These forums allow participants to use their e-mail to post stories, ideas, photographs, or software related to the topic of the group. These messages can then be stored for other group participants to read or retrieve. Literally thousands of sex-related newsgroups exist on the Net and as such accommodate the highest volume of traffic of all newsgroups—so much so that they are often excluded from Internet statistics because of their extremely high usage.

2. REAL TIME WITH A FANTASY PARTNER

The second form of cybersex takes place in what is known as "real time"—though time may be the only aspect of the interaction that is "real." Real-time chatting can be likened to a computerized version of citizens band (CB) radio. Internet chat rooms resemble CB channels in that they offer varying numbers of people the opportunity to listen to and discuss specific topics. The number of CB radio channels are relatively small and are limited to available broadcast frequencies. At any one time on the Internet, however, there are typically about ten to twenty thousand "channels" available to "join." In addition, while Federal Communications Commission (FCC) laws limit the types of communication that can take place over the airwaves, most of these laws do not apply to international cyberspace.

After reviewing the chat room topic areas, it is not difficult to understand how one may engage in sexual conversation with others online. Advanced technology has also provided ways to exchange images and files online during a live conversation. In addition, "virtual locations" exist in which you can engage in online chatting with others. You may, for example, start in the virtual "dining area" and talk with someone over "virtual coffee" and later be invited to a "virtual bedroom" where "one thing often leads to another."

Current technology also allows for the exchange of voice and video images via the Internet. By simply providing a credit card number, you can take advantage of live video cameras that capture and transmit images of males or females engaged in everything from everyday activities to explicit sexual acts. Though a fee is common, some of these sites can even be accessed for free. Some live video sites accept requests for specific sexual behaviors from online users, thus enabling an individual to create and fulfill personal fantasies. Thanks to live video feed technology, it is even possible to chat online while viewing pornography. Such virtual video booths are steadily growing in number and allow cybersex users to have nearly complete control over the "object" at the other end of the phone line, even though the "object" happens to be a human being. For a relatively small fee, you can also link to X-rated video feeds without any interaction or, with CuSeeMe software and camera, watch others masturbate or engage in other sexual activities while they watch you do the same.

3. MULTIMEDIA SOFTWARE

The final category of cybersex does not take place online at all. With the invention of more sophisticated multimedia systems, people can play X-rated movies, engage in sexual games, or view the latest issues of erotica magazines on a desktop or laptop computer. Compact disc read-only memory (CD-ROM) technology allows companies to release software titles with sound and video clips. Such multimedia productions can also include erotic information. Studies estimate that erotica CD-ROMs account for 20 percent of all CD-ROM business, with sales in 1994 reported at $260 million. Others report that the CD-ROM market has turned X-rated cyberspace into a billion-dollar-plus business.

WHY CYBERSEX?

With all the various forms of media available in our culture, what is it that attracts people to the Internet to engage in sexual activities in such a high-tech fashion? Five factors play a part in making the Internet enormously appealing for someone seeking sexual arousal and fulfillment. These are accessibility, isolation, anonymity, affordability, and fantasy.

ACCESSIBILITY

Before the Internet, access to various forms of sex-related materials and sexual experiences had limitations. Most strip clubs and XXX-rated theaters are not open twenty-four hours a day. Buying porn magazines requires getting to a store that sells them, and most stores aren't open all the time. Another limitation is distance. Stores, theaters, strip clubs, and areas where prostitutes ply their trade cannot be conveniently found in every neighborhood of every city and suburb or rural community, requiring those who wish to access them to have time and transportation to get there. The Internet changed all of this. It offers incredibly broad and easy access to sex of all kinds. Twenty-four hours a day, seven days a week, anyone with access to a computer with an Internet connection—be it at work; a cybercafé; a public library, school, or university; or at home—can choose from literally millions of sex-related Web sites offering whatever type of sexual experience is desired.

ISOLATION

Perhaps the most powerful component of cybersex is isolation: it provides a perfect opportunity to separate yourself from others and to engage in whatever fantasy you prefer without risk of sexually transmitted infections or the distraction of reality. Separated from the outside world, users can create the justifications and rationalizations needed to convince themselves and others that their behavior is both victimless and harmless.

Guy, a married corporate executive in his early fifties, had just sold the company he founded for a great profit. After the pressure and excitement of the months leading up to the sale, however, Guy felt let down and depressed. Not in the mood for much of anything, he stayed at home and began playing on the computer. One of his favorite activities was to create various personae and then advertise for dates while portraying them in online personal columns. Given the multitude of responses, Guy turned this into an enormously entertaining game, one that he spent hours and hours playing. Days merged into nights and nights into days. Time blurred. Weeks passed unnoticed. After a fairly short time, Guy was barely speaking to his wife and was ignoring his work completely. His life existed almost solely in cyberspace.

ANONYMITY

Not only is Internet access to sex-related sites and activities easy for anyone, twenty-four hours a day, every day of the year; it also provides the most anonymous form of obtaining and using pornographic materials or interacting sexually with another person. You don't have to walk into a store to buy a magazine or be present at a strip club where someone might recognize you. No need to minimize the risk of arrest in an undercover prostitution sting. As long as no one walked into the room where they were online, the actions of Guy and Jake, for example, were completely anonymous. No one with whom they interacted really knew who they were, their age, their gender, where they lived, or anything else about them. What's more, software is now available that has been specifically designed to increase access anonymity, making it possible, for example, to post to newsgroups anonymously.

Affordability

For anyone on a budget, cybersex provides a low-cost alternative means to a sexual high. Hard-core pornography magazines may run fifteen to fifty dollars. However, for the cost of Internet access (ten to twenty-five dollars per month), anyone can find hundreds of photographs, stories, chat channels, and more. In addition, the user can choose to retrieve and view only the information that is of interest; there's no need, for example, to purchase an entire magazine full of mostly unwanted advertisements and articles.

Sex: what you want, when you want it, at low cost, minus the "messiness and hassles" of a person-to-person relationship, and with complete anonymity. It should not be surprising that the number of sexually related Web sites and activities are exploding along with the number of people accessing and using them.

Fantasy

Finally, cybersex provides a perfect opportunity for people to develop sexual fantasies and objectify others without the fear of rejection. In fact, the CD-ROM versions of adult sexual material often let the user choose the ideal partner and ideal situation—one step beyond noninteractive magazines. Computer users may choose a partner's gender, age, hair, skin, body type, and eye color, as well as whatever sexual scenario they want to engage in. Other titles are disguised in the form of a game. Perhaps a sexual mystery must be solved or an adventure taken in which users have to solve puzzles or find clues that lead them to their next sexual "conquest." The common factor among all cybersex material is that the user is free to become part of the fantasy without responsibility, consequence, or rejection. What's more, the variety of possibilities on the Internet is truly mind boggling; whatever kind of sexual activity or depiction you can think of you can likely find on the Net.

Jason, in his late twenties, had long fantasized about watching another couple having sex, but he'd never found a way to make this actually happen. One evening while browsing sex sites on the Net, Jason stumbled across a link to a site that offered live video streaming. Clicking into the site, he discovered that, among other options, he could choose to actually watch men and women have sex. A number of cameras located around the room provided any view of the action he wanted. Elated at his discovery, Jason soon found himself spending twenty to thirty hours per week online fulfilling his fantasy.

These five factors also seem to increase the chances that the Internet will become a problem for those who already struggle with sexual compulsivity and for those who are emotionally or psychologically vulnerable to such sexual availability.

While research in the area of cybersex usage is only beginning, a recent survey by Al Cooper, David L. Delmonico, and Ron Burg of 9,265 Internet users describes three categories of people who use the Internet for sexual pursuits:[3]

- Recreational users, who access online sexual material more out of curiosity or for entertainment purposes and are not typically seen as having problems associated with their online sexual behaviors.
- At-risk users may never have developed a problem with online sexuality if not for the availability of the Internet. These individuals use the Internet a moderate amount of time for sexual activities, and if their pattern of use continues, their use could become compulsive.
- Sexually compulsive users, due to a propensity for pathological sexual expression, use the Internet as a forum for their sexual activities. For people in this group in particular, the power of isolation, fantasy, anonymity, and affordability interacts with certain underlying personality factors to increase their use of the Internet for sexual activities to the point where it becomes difficult, if not impossible, for them to control it. We also want to note here that compulsion is a sign of an addictive disorder. In the addiction field, one of the signs of addiction to alcohol or another drug is that someone uses the substance compulsively.

The study also found that while 84 percent of the respondents did not meet criteria for cybersex compulsivity, 6 percent of all respondents scored in a way that suggested cybersex compulsivity. A third group of approximately 10 percent of the entire sample also emerged as those "at-risk" users who may not be exhibiting all signs of cybersex compulsion, but who are in a potentially dangerous stage with their behavior. According to a July 2000

Nielsen survey, there are 148.8 million Internet users in the United States alone. (International Data Corporation reports that the number of Internet users worldwide exceeds 200 million.) Extrapolating from the cybersex use percentages in the study by Cooper, Delmonico, and Burg, approximately 8.9 million people in the United States (6 percent of 148.8 million) need intervention for their sexually compulsive use of cybersex. In addition to these 8.9 million, there are 14.8 million individuals (10 percent of 148.8 million) who are using cybersex moderately and show beginning signs of sexual compulsivity. Their continued use can predictably be a significant danger to many of them. It is also important to note that the above approximations are thought to be extremely conservative estimates.

There is little doubt that use of the Internet will continue to explode. As people spend more time online and look to the Internet to fulfill an ever increasing number of sexual needs and fantasies, the problems associated with online sexuality will become increasingly important.

2

Do I Have a Problem
with Cybersex?

IN THIS CHAPTER, we will help you examine your own use of sexually explicit material on the Internet. You may have many questions about when
or even if using the Internet for sex is a real problem for you. By reading the
stories of others, you'll be able to look more closely at your own Internet
behavior and determine whether it's a problem or not.

In chapter 1, we looked at the many ways people use the Internet for sex.
Reading about these people may have left you wondering about how you and
others view your use of the Internet. You might now be asking yourself, "Do
I have a problem with my sexual use of the Internet?" "How would I know if
there's a problem?" "Am I at risk for sexually problematic behavior on the
Internet?" or "Just what *is* 'problematic' sexual behavior on the Internet?"

Let's take a moment to clarify our use of the word "problematic." When
a particular behavior or a set of behaviors begins to interfere with other aspects of your life, psychologists, psychiatrists, and counselors call them
problematic. This simply means that these behaviors are causing problems
and jeopardizing important areas in your life. Let's say, for example, that
you've been using the Internet for sex more than ever lately. You've gone
online with the intention of staying there for thirty minutes only to suddenly realize that two or three hours have slipped by. On more than one
occasion, this "slipup" had some consequence—once you missed an important business appointment and another time you were late picking up your
daughter from soccer. Perhaps you learned of some consequence only later.
It's not unusual for people to be unaware of the consequences their actions
are having in their own and in other people's lives.

When isolated instances like this occur, they probably are not an indication of a problem. However, if they continue or increase, it may be a signal to pay more attention to what is happening. As these behaviors increase and we become aware of them, we may try to avoid or minimize consequences by attempting to control the problematic behavior. Unfortunately, during this time it also becomes more and more difficult to clearly see what is happening to us and more difficult to control our behaviors.

INDICATORS OF PROBLEMATIC BEHAVIOR

Three criteria are often used as indicators of problematic behavior. They are compulsivity, continuation despite consequences, and obsession.[1] A detailed description of each follows.

COMPULSIVITY

This is the loss of the ability to choose freely whether to stop or continue a behavior. In our daily lives, we establish habit-forming routines. We often get up at the same time every day, brush our teeth in the same way, keep a workbench or cupboard arranged in a particular order, put the same arm into a shirt first when getting dressed, or shop at the same grocery store week after week. We repeat many behaviors, often to the point where they become habits. We could even say that habits serve a useful function in that they free us from having to actually think about what we're doing all the time. Imagine if every single time you put on your shirt or brushed your teeth, you had to think about how you were going to do it.

Compulsive behavior is altogether different from simple daily or rigid habits. It is out-of-control behavior marked by deeply entangled rituals and obsessions along with overwhelming feelings of frustration, self-blame, powerlessness, and hopelessness. Sean experienced these feelings and shares his story about what life is like when using cybersex compulsively:

> I had long fantasized about going to a strip club, but had never followed through because I was worried about being recognized by someone I knew when entering or leaving the club. I knew I would die of embarrassment if my wife or friends found out. One day at home, I was surfing porn sites when I discovered a link to a site that offered live

video feeds from a strip club—twenty-four hours a day, no less! Here was the answer to my dreams.

That first time, I stayed online for a couple hours . . . until I heard the garage door opening when my wife and kids arrived home. Forced to quickly jump offline, I was already wondering when I could find a way to get back to "the club."

That opportunity came the following evening when everyone in my family was tired after a busy weekend and headed to bed. Though I was tired, too, I made an excuse about needing to finish a report for work and headed into my home office, where I again logged on to the live feed from the strip club. Riveted to the screen, I watched for hours until I could no longer stay awake. The next day at work, I began obsessing again about this new discovery and decided that perhaps during my lunch hour, I could just jump on to that site for a few minutes—which I subsequently did.

Soon, I found myself visiting "the club" more and more often. So often, in fact, that I became concerned about the amount of time I was spending online. I was staying up at night more and more often. I was "visiting" more and more often at work, and for longer periods of time. So I made a promise to myself that I'd just set some rules up for my use. I made a commitment to stop "visiting" while at work altogether and "visit" at home only every other day for thirty minutes.

That promise to myself was broken only two evenings later when I was online at home for two and a half hours. I rationalized by saying, "Well, everyone is gone, so what difference does it make?" Slowly, my time online at the strip club steadily increased. It became an obsession for me. I just couldn't stay away from it.

Continuation despite Consequences

It is common to continue the behavior despite adverse consequences, such as loss of health, job, relationships, marriage, or freedom. All behaviors have consequences—some positive and some negative. At a relatively basic level, if we brush and floss our teeth regularly, we'll have a more positive experience at the dental office. If we neglect our teeth, the consequences will include painful dental procedures and costly dental bills. We learn how to work cooperatively and meet expectations on the job, thus avoiding being fired. Most of the time, we are able to look at our behavior and make the appropriate changes to reduce negative consequences. Unfortunately, this isn't always the case.

At first, Sean didn't see any negative consequences resulting from his Internet use. But it was only a matter of time before he was discovered.

> One weekend afternoon my wife and kids were out visiting my wife's sister. Not expecting them home for a couple more hours, I was deeply engrossed in a new online strip club I'd recently located and I never heard her car pull up in the driveway. Walking past my home office window, my wife inadvertently glanced in and saw me sitting at the computer screen masturbating. She bolted into the house and said, "Sean, my God, what were you doing? What if one of the children had seen you? How often do you do this? Whenever I'm not around? And why? Why?"
>
> I made up a string of apologies and promised to behave myself in the future. I didn't dare visit the online strip club at home anymore. Instead, I began spending more time at work visiting sexually explicit sites. One day, however, a company memo was circulated warning all employees that our Internet usage was now being monitored during work hours and that visiting porn sites was expressly forbidden. I knew that the company was serious. In fact, I'd heard of another employee who'd been caught surfing porn sites and he was warned that if he did it again, he'd be fired on the spot.
>
> Realizing I'd better be careful, I decided that I'd only go to "the club" before or after hours when almost no one was around and I'd only stay online for ten or fifteen minutes. I convinced myself that I wouldn't really be violating company policy if I wasn't surfing the porn sites during actual working hours. After a week, I found this regimen too difficult and began trying to find a way to go to my "club" more often. I started believing that maybe visiting during my lunch hour would be safe. I sincerely thought that by now enough time had passed since my wife discovered my computer activity and it was OK to start visiting the "club" again on my home computer, too, as long as I was careful.

Despite Sean's attempts at control and potentially dire consequences, he continued his behavior and no longer thought about how he could stop it.

Instead, he tried to find a way to visit his "club" without incurring any negative consequences. Sean's experience also reveals the indirect consequences of his behavior—and how he is unaware of them. By calculating the number of hours Sean spent online in his "club" at work and multiplying that by his hourly wage, it is easy to see that his employer lost thousands of dollars in productivity. What might have—or should have—Sean accomplished for his company in the hours he was "missing" at work?

OBSESSION

Obsession means being so preoccupied, you focus exclusively on a particular behavior (in this case, sex) to the exclusion of other parts of your life and without care for the consequences of that behavior. You are obsessed with something when you just can't stop thinking about it. It occupies much of your mental energy most of the time. In our example, Sean had become obsessed with using the Internet to visit particular Web sites, particularly the strip clubs.

By this point, Sean really lived in one of three states of mind: planning his next visit to an online strip club, being online, and coming down from a visit. In one way or another, online strip clubs were always on Sean's mind. When he was at work in a meeting, for example, Sean was thinking about how long it was going to last. He was trying to figure out whether he'd have ten minutes or so during a break to go online.

Sean became very creative about finding additional time for cybersex activities:

> One day, a great idea came to me. Occasionally, my wife and I would have wine with our dinner. This usually made her pretty tired and she'd go to bed earlier than usual and sleep pretty soundly on those nights. So, I fabricated a story about how I had decided we ought to try some better wines and have them with dinner more regularly, "like the Europeans do." Shelly agreed and was actually quite excited about this. Pretty soon, we were drinking a bottle of wine with nearly every dinner, and as a result, my wife was often in bed and sound asleep by nine. Looking back, I'm embarrassed to say that I was proud of myself for coming up with this idea and actually carrying it out.

TEN CRITERIA OF PROBLEMATIC ONLINE SEXUAL BEHAVIOR

Earlier we talked about the difficulty in deciding how to determine whether a given online sexual behavior is actually problematic. Taking into consideration Sean's account of his online sexual behavior, do you think he has a problem? To help you evaluate your own online behavior, we've developed the following set of ten criteria. As you read through them, pay close attention to those that seem to apply to your life.

1. Preoccupation with sex on the Internet
This is more than just thinking about online sex; it's not being able to *not* think about it. At some level, these thoughts are always with you. You find yourself regularly wondering how you can orchestrate your life in ways that will allow you time online. You think about past online sexual experiences or about what future online experiences will be like. You can't seem to get away from thoughts about online sex. You may even find yourself dreaming about sex on the Internet. It's there in both your conscious and unconscious life.

2. Frequently engaging in sex on the Internet more often or for longer periods of time than intended
When you look at the amount of time you're spending online, you see that it has been increasing. You decided, for example, to go online for sex for just an hour, but when you looked at the clock, you realized you'd been on for more than two hours. You don't know where the time went. Perhaps you told yourself you could be online for just two hours from midnight to 2:00 A.M., but suddenly you discover it's 4:00 A.M. and you're still online. You had originally been going online for sex-related activities a couple days a week. Now you're on daily and not just once, but four, five, six, or more times per day. You keep track of your time for a few days and discover that you're actually spending five hours a day online for sex-related activities.

In a sense, you are developing a "tolerance" to Internet usage. The concept of tolerance is common in the field of drug and alcohol addiction. When people begin drinking, for example, they may feel intoxicated after only one or two beers. Over time, however, their bodies develop a tolerance to alcohol and they find that they need six, eight, or twelve bottles of beer to achieve that same high. The concept applies to Internet sex too. Many people have discovered that they have a psychological need to be online more and more over time to achieve the same high.

3. Repeated unsuccessful efforts to control, cut back on, or stop engaging in sex on the Internet

Once you realized that the amount of time you'd been spending for sex online was excessive, you decided to set some limits. Perhaps you promised yourself that you would go online only once a day or week and only for thirty minutes at a time. Or maybe you decided to quit cold turkey for a week or to go online only on weekends. But whatever promise you made to yourself, you couldn't keep it. Maybe your attempts at control worked for a few days, a week, several weeks, or even a month, but eventually "something" happened and you "needed" to go back online. No matter what you tried, you eventually returned to the Internet for sexual activities.

4. Restlessness or irritability when attempting to limit or stop engaging in sex on the Internet

When you've attempted to stop or limit your online sexual activity, you find that you become nervous and irritable. If you haven't noticed this yourself, think about what others who know you—family members, friends, work colleagues—would say if you asked them about this. Often these people will recognize changes in your behavior before you yourself can see them. Do you know someone who has recently quit smoking? If so, how did this person act in the first days and weeks without a cigarette? Is this similar to how you act when you try to stop or limit your online activities?

5. Using sex on the Internet as a way of escaping from problems or relieving feelings such as helplessness, guilt, anxiety, or depression

Everyone has feelings of helplessness, sorrow, worry, depression, and anger. There are many ways to address or cope with these feelings. When you are just feeling down and would like a little boost or pick-me-up, do you turn to the Internet for a sexual release so you can feel better and function at home or work?

6. Returning to sex on the Internet day after day in search of a more intense or higher-risk sexual experience

Your expectations of what you want out of the Internet continue to increase and become more elaborate. You might hope to find your true love via the Internet. At first, you may drop into chat rooms, remaining anonymous, just to see whether you could find a potential mate online. Eventually, being anonymous no longer does it for you. Your search of various chat rooms becomes more intense and frantic and time-consuming. After connecting with one man in particular, you begin corresponding privately with him via e-mail. Eventually, you arrange a meeting with him for sex in a hotel. The excitement and hope you feel in your search lead to more risky behavior both on and off the Internet.

What have you been looking for on the Internet? How has that changed from when you first started going online? Are you moving into areas you once told yourself you'd never explore?

7. Lying to family members, therapists, or others to conceal involvement with sex on the Internet

In our culture, most people are secretive about their sex lives, regardless of whether their behavior is normal or problematic. What is of concern is being dishonest about it when asked. When Sean was questioned by his wife about his late nights on the computer, he regularly answered by saying that it was a work-related project with a tight deadline. When initially confronted about his use of the Internet for sexual purposes, Sean lied to his wife and told her it was his first time.

Have you lied about using the Internet for sex-related activities? Have you downplayed your involvement or failed to be honest about your involvement to a spouse, partner, boss, or therapist? Have you used the "just curious" excuse?

8. Committing illegal sexual acts online (for example, sending or downloading child pornography or soliciting illegal sex acts online)

Certain activities on the Internet have been declared illegal in many, if not all, states. As people use the Internet for sex-related activities, and as they increase their time on the Net, some also move closer and closer to engaging in illegal behaviors. A forty-year-old male who'd fantasized about having sex with a teenager for several years eventually began visiting a teen chat room. He engaged in a conversation with a thirteen-year-old female for some time before moving the relationship to a point where he asked where he could meet her to have sex. Soliciting sex acts with minors online is illegal, just as sending, exchanging, or downloading child pornography is illegal. These are felony offenses that, in many states, will result in mandatory prison time. Have you engaged in or are you thinking about such actions?

9. Jeopardizing or losing a significant relationship, job, or educational or career opportunity because of online sexual behavior

Online sex-related activities can have serious consequences. Ray downloaded a child pornography image to a chat room. As a result, he was arrested through an undercover operation. The shame of being charged with felony counts for sexual exploitation of a minor became overwhelming, and the consequences rippled through every aspect of his life. Because of escalating legal fees, he lost most of his savings and retirement funds. He was closing on his new home the day the search warrant was served. Consequently, he lived in his new home for only two days before he had to sell it as a result of this crime. He lost a well-paying, prestigious job with tremendous advancement potential in an excellent corporation. He endured house arrest and faced a potential prison term of 220 years. Ray had been respected in his community and was on numerous boards and committees. This all ended with his arrest.

What parts of your life are being affected by your online sexual behavior? Have you jeopardized or lost a significant relationship? What about a job, a career, or your health and well-being?

10. Incurring significant financial consequences as a result of engaging in online sexual behavior

While basic Internet access can be fairly inexpensive, many cybersex sites charge a monthly access fee. A thirty-two-year-old male client was shocked when he opened his credit card bill one day to find charges totaling more than twelve hundred dollars. He'd been registering to enter various cybersex sites and had completely lost track of how many he'd paid for. A twenty-three-year-old female client received an Internet server bill for hundreds of dollars. She'd spent six or so hours per day in chat rooms and had sailed miles past her free minute limit without having any idea of the charges that were accruing. Another male client spent forty thousand dollars in one month dating high-priced call girls and using cocaine. He'd arranged for both through an online prostitution service.

Have you felt the financial consequences of your time online? How many memberships are you paying for each month? What are your monthly Internet fees? Have you lost job or educational opportunities because of your time online?

WHAT IT MEANS FOR YOU

We assume that you are reading this book because you or someone who cares about you is concerned about your use of the Internet for sex-related activities. The most important step you can take now is to look honestly at your Internet behavior *and* the consequences of that behavior. Perhaps you're spending more time than you really want in sex-related Internet activities. This should sound an alarm indicating that something is out of balance and that you need to take action and seek help.

If you can relate to three or more of the ten criteria for problematic online sexual behavior, your online activities are probably a problem. This is not something you should ignore, and the sooner you act to make changes in your life, the easier it will be for you to overcome this problem.

Complete the following Internet Sex Screening Test to further examine your online behavior:

INTERNET SEX SCREENING TEST
Read each statement carefully and answer honestly. If it is true or mostly true for you, mark the blank with a T. If it is false or mostly false, mark the blank with an F. After answering all twenty-five questions, add up your score according to the formula listed on page 28.[2]

____ 1. I have some sexual sites bookmarked.
____ 2. I spend more than five hours per week using my computer for sexual pursuits.
____ 3. I have joined sexual sites to gain access to online sexual material.

___ 4. I have purchased sexual products online.

___ 5. I have searched for sexual material through an Internet search tool.

___ 6. I have spent more money for online sexual material than I planned.

___ 7. Internet sex has sometimes interfered with certain aspects of my life.

___ 8. I have participated in sexually related chats.

___ 9. I have a sexualized user name or nickname that I use on the Internet.

___ 10. I have masturbated while on the Internet.

___ 11. I have accessed sexual sites from other computers besides my own.

___ 12. No one knows I use my computer for sexual purposes.

___ 13. I have tried to hide what is on my computer or monitor so others cannot see it.

___ 14. I have stayed up after midnight to access sexual material online.

___ 15. I use the Internet to experiment with aspects of sexuality such as bondage, homosexuality, and anal sex.

___ 16. I have my own Web site that contains sexually explicit material.

___ 17. I have made promises to myself to stop using the Internet for sexual purposes.

___ 18. I sometimes use cybersex as a reward for accomplishing something like finishing a project or enduring a stressful day.

___ 19. When I am unable to access sexual information online, I feel anxious, angry, or disappointed.

___ 20. I have increased the risks I take online (for example, giving out my real name and phone number or meeting people offline).

___ 21. I have punished myself when I use the Internet for sexual purposes. For example, I've arranged a time-out from the computer or canceled Internet subscriptions.

___ 22. I have met face-to-face with someone I met online for romantic purposes.

___ 23. I use sexual humor and innuendo with others while online.

___ 24. I have run across illegal sexual material while on the Internet.

___ 25. I believe I am an Internet sex addict.

Total number of statements marked "true": _____
Total number of statements marked "false": _____

Scoring the Internet Sex Screening Test

Have you answered each question? Give yourself one point for each statement that you marked "true." Based on 935 people who have previously taken this test, we have found that if your score is nineteen or above, it is very likely that you have a problem with your online sex-related activities. You've taken an important, positive first step by beginning to read this book and showing a willingness to begin exploring and addressing the problem. Be assured that you can find help here to better understand and regain control over your online sex-related behavior.

On the other hand, you may not recognize yourself as having a problem. If you see a pattern in your Internet behavior that seems similar to the problematic behavior we've explored thus far, this may be an indication that you are at risk for problems and that you would do well to learn more about your behavior and your reasons for using the Internet for sexual activities. If you can relate to only some examples or feel that a partner might have a problem with online sexual behavior, read on.

Remember that no set of criteria or test is an absolutely accurate measure or indication of a problem. Tests do not deal well with individual differences and behaviors. Screenings are based on the behavior of many people; they are not capable of measuring individual differences or of addressing every kind of behavior. Scoring between nine and nineteen could indicate that you do have some behaviors that may be problematic or that will eventually become problematic.

Once again, if you are reading this book because you are concerned about your use of the Internet for sex-related activities, pay attention to that, regardless of your score on the screening test.

If you don't feel you have a problem and you scored below nineteen on the screening, but are reading this book at the suggestion of someone who cares about you, pay attention. As you likely know, those who know us can often see our lives and our behavior in ways we cannot. It's difficult to be objective with ourselves. It's important to realize that others may see you are having a problem that you do not see.

We also want to point out that sex-related activity on the Internet covers a broad range of activities, as indicated in chapter 1. Problematic behaviors lie on a continuum, from those that are relatively harmless to those that are compulsive or addictive and pose serious health, relationship, and legal risks.

In chapter 3, we will more closely examine problematic sexual behavior on the Internet. You'll learn more about why people use the Internet for sex, how problems develop and manifest themselves, and the potential consequences of sex-related behavior on the Internet.

3

Understanding Problematic
Sexual Behavior on the Internet

IN THIS CHAPTER, we will look in greater detail at the types of problematic online sexual behavior, and we'll show you how that behavior can become so compulsive that it seems impossible to control. Not everyone who is using the Internet for sexual activities does so for the same reason or to the same extent. We can divide those who are engaging in sexual behavior on the Internet into five groups. The diagram on page 31 illustrates these five groups. Recreational users of cybersex—both those in the appropriate and inappropriate user categories—as a rule have little, if any, problem with compulsive or addictive cybersex use. People in the discovery, predisposed, and lifelong sexually compulsive categories often end up using the Internet compulsively or addictively once they discover the availability—and the extent of—sex on the Internet.

RECREATIONAL CYBERSEX USERS

The category of recreational users can be divided into two categories: appropriate recreational users and inappropriate recreational users. The former seem to be able to explore sex on the Internet without any sign that their behavior is becoming problematic. They may, in fact, use cybersex as a way to enhance their sexual experiences in a positive way.

The latter group of recreational cybersex users includes individuals who do not have a compulsive or addictive problem with sex on the Internet, but who use what they find on the Net inappropriately. They may, for example, show an item or a site they discovered on the Net to others, such as their work colleagues, family members, or friends who are not interested in

Cybersex User Categories

Recreational Users

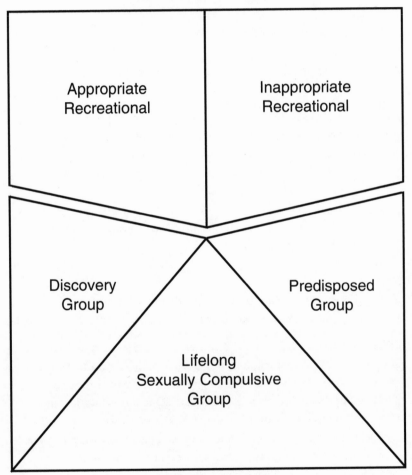

Appropriate
Recreational

Inappropriate
Recreational

Discovery
Group

Predisposed
Group

Lifelong
Sexually Compulsive
Group

Problematic Users

Figure 3.1

such information or are embarrassed by it. They do so not as a means of hurting or embarrassing others, but simply because they think such information is funny or because they like the feeling of shocking others. Recreational users who use cybersex inappropriately don't try to hide their activities either, whereas people who have a more serious problem with cybersex go to great lengths to cover up their cybersex activities from others in their lives.

PROBLEMATIC CYBERSEX USERS

People who have problematic sexual behavior on the Internet tend to fall into one of three groups:

1. Discovery Group: those who have no previous problem with online sex or any history of problematic sexual behavior
2. Predisposed Group: those who have had their first out-of-control sexual behavior on the Internet after years of obsessing over unacted-on sexual fantasies and urges
3. Lifelong Sexually Compulsive Group: those whose out-of-control sexual behavior on the Internet is part of an ongoing and severe sexual behavior problem

DISCOVERY GROUP
People in this group have no previous problem with online sex and no history of problematic sexual behavior. Shania's story is typical of this group:

> In my mid-twenties, I led quite a conservative life when it came to sex. I'd never had a sexual relationship, much less kissed anyone before. It wasn't that I didn't have an interest in men. I just hadn't found a good way to approach and meet eligible guys. One day while surfing the Net, I discovered the realm of Internet sex, and it rocked my world. I suddenly felt free to explore relationships and my own sexuality. I spent hours and hours online visiting sexually oriented chat rooms and writing ads for online personal columns. Soon I discovered I was attracted to men from other countries. After finding one seemingly very attractive man, I made arrangements to meet him on a cruise ship. How did it turn out? The cruise was fine, but the guy was anything but. He was

crude, physically not at all how he'd depicted himself, and he had the personality of a dead fish. But despite this and other so-so experiences, I've continued to rendezvous with other guys. I'm sure I'll find "Mr. Right" one of these times.

There is, in a sense, a healthy aspect to Shania's story in that she had wanted to have sexual relationships and the Internet freed her to do so. She discovered and explored her ideas about relationships and sexuality through the Internet. On the other hand, Shania became completely carried away with her online activities, spending countless hours at her computer and avoiding reality. By courting and meeting strangers about whom she actually knew nothing, Shania also put herself in great danger. She could have chosen instead to use one of the many dating services available that carefully screen their members.

Gerry is another person who had no history of problematic sexual behavior before discovering the realm of cybersex. He had had no previous arrests or any history of compulsive sexual behavior. In his mid-forties, Gerry came to treatment as part of a sentencing agreement after he had been arrested for trying to meet a teenage girl whom he'd first contacted online. Here is Gerry's story:

> I was a man whose children were grown up and out of the house. I was unhappy in my marriage and dissatisfied with my job. I felt that, given my age, I should have had more responsibility and been making more money in my career. One night, I stumbled upon a cybersex site. I began playing around just to see what was out there, and in a matter of weeks I couldn't stay away. Gradually, my Internet use increased from thirty minutes to an hour, then two hours or more every night. I began spending fifteen to twenty hours a week online, surfing porn sites and visiting chat rooms where I tried to hook up with young girls. Before I knew what had happened, I was obsessed with cybersex activities. After my arrest, I admitted that I knew the "girl" (who was actually an adult male FBI agent) I was trying to meet was under eighteen, but I was so flattered by the thought of her wanting to meet me that I arranged the rendezvous anyway. I knew I was taking a chance but just couldn't stop myself.

PREDISPOSED GROUP

This group comprises people who had never acted out sexually—though they had thought about it—until they discovered cybersex. They might have fantasized about exposing themselves or had the urge to see a prostitute or go to strip clubs. Until the arrival of cybersex they were, however, able to control those fantasies and urges. They might have been afraid of being recognized at a strip club or being busted in a prostitution sting. Perhaps they simply were healthy enough and possessed adequate coping skills to recognize and resist acting impulsively.

When it comes to Internet use, people in this group may use the Net for sexual purposes—perhaps looking at pornography, occasionally visiting a chat room or a voyeur site—but not too often . . . five, six, or seven hours a week at most.

They are, however, at risk for more problematic online sexual behavior. With the Internet, sex is just a click away. And at some point, they discover sexually explicit activities that they just can't resist. They may become attracted to live-feed strip clubs or live video of women having sex. At first, the consequences of doing these activities may seem minimal. After all, no one will see them or recognize them online.

Sharon's story is an excellent example of this behavior:

> I had often wondered about what it would be like to have sex with another woman. I was thirty-four, happily married with two children, and generally happy with my life. Over the past few years, I'd heard more about bisexuality and realized that I had bisexual tendencies. I didn't know how to explain the sexual feelings I'd have for other women as well as those for my husband. I was more curious than ever now, but I'd always been a little afraid to act on these feelings. And I didn't know, really, how I could go about meeting a woman who had similar feelings. Besides, I wasn't interested just in sex. I wanted a real relationship where I could feel some connection to her too. Since I'd occasionally visited chat rooms in the past, one night I decided to search for one focused on lesbianism. To my surprise, I found one quickly. I was instantly intrigued and began spending more time online in lesbian-oriented chat rooms. While my online explorations were initially positive experiences and helped me sort out my feelings, I began

to spend so much time online that other aspects of my life became affected. My work life suffered as a result of too many late nights on the computer. And I had less time and energy for my family too.

Don provides another excellent example of this behavior:

After twelve years of marriage, I felt that there just had to be more to a relationship. I'd never been unfaithful to my wife and didn't intend to because I felt that it was simply morally wrong. But I was becoming more and more frustrated with my marriage as time passed. Over the years, I had spent much time fantasizing about having affairs with other women. Almost by chance, I found a chat room in which there were others like me with similar feelings about their relationships. I "met" and began conversing with a woman, and soon we both found that we had much in common. Our conversations were fun, interesting, and progressively more sex-related. I loved how I felt after my time online—energized, happy, supported, and satisfied. Eventually, we began having sex online. Was I being unfaithful? I decided I wasn't because I wasn't really having actual sex with anyone. In fact, I wasn't even physically with this woman. I didn't even know her real name. After a few months, however, online sexuality wasn't fulfilling enough for me. I wanted to meet this woman I'd been conversing with online in person. She lived fairly close to me, as it turned out, so we met at a local hotel for dinner and sex—and in so doing, I crossed my own boundary into infidelity. Since I had already crossed the line, I had nothing more to lose by continuing this behavior. And it had all been so easy—easy to arrange meeting women online who were interested in sex; easy to meet them in person; and easy to have sex with them. My illicit liaisons increased in frequency. Before I knew what was happening, I was becoming involved with more and more women.

Part of the power of cybersex is that it's one step removed from reality. Having thoughts and urges and fantasies and then acting on them via the Internet seems different from acting on them in real time. We are not face-to-face, literally, with another human being. We can't look into their eyes, feel their touch, read their emotions, or in any other way physically interact with them. Cyber-interactions feel more remote, safer. The "other" is out there somewhere, at arm's length. We tend to view the computer as a magical place where everything is safe and secure. We can be whoever we want to be, with no apparent consequences.

This distance, this step apart, however, also makes it easier to cross lines that we would not otherwise cross—something that's not uncommon for people in this group. Don, for example, swore he'd never have an affair, but that is exactly what he was doing, albeit initially without actual physical contact. That "step apart" made it very easy for him to rationalize and excuse his behavior when meeting women in motels for offline sexual encounters. People in this group often have clear boundaries around their urges or fantasies—until they encounter the cyber-world where they feel OK about pushing beyond them. Once that boundary is stretched or breached, little may be left to control behavior.

LIFELONG SEXUALLY COMPULSIVE GROUP
People in this group have been involved in problematic sexual behavior throughout most, if not all, of their lives. They might compulsively masturbate, use pornography, practice voyeurism or exhibitionism, or frequent strip clubs and prostitutes. For these people, while cybersex provides a new option for acting out sexually, it fits within their already existing patterns of problematic behavior.

Gene's story is typical of people in this group:

> As a child, I was sexually abusive to my younger brother. During adolescence, I frequently exposed myself to others. This behavior began as a bit of a joke at first. I would "streak" through a sporting event or beach, for example. There was a dark side too. I had a history of molesting children, but in more discreet and subtle ways. I would invite a young child to sit on my lap and then fondle her—but always in the context of trying to move the child off my lap. During my mid-thirties, I was finally arrested for exposing myself to teenage girls. When I came into treatment, I revealed that I had a lengthy history of exposing myself at a well-known department store as well as a long history of using pornography and compulsive masturbation.
>
> As a skilled computer programmer, I discovered sex online before most people had even heard of the Internet. I primarily ventured into

cybersex while on the job. When I was at work, I couldn't expose myself and I couldn't have pornographic magazines lying around my office so I instead visited porn sites. I spent hours each day in nudist, exhibitionist, and voyeuristic sex sites, with a particular preference for nudist sites with pictures of children.

How was it that I was never caught? Since I provided computer and Internet tech support for employees, I arranged my computer in such a way that I could still talk on the phone and provide support and yet keep my computer monitor screen hidden from anyone who just happened by. I was very savvy at multitasking. I could be surfing sex sites and at the same time provide help to others over the phone. Thanks to my computer skills, I was able to thwart any site blockouts or attempts by my company's tech information services staff to monitor my online behavior.

My preferred behaviors were exposing myself and window peeping. I entered treatment after being arrested for exposing myself to two girls at a department store. I initially denied this behavior, and then claimed it wasn't sexual. The truth was that I used cybersex merely as a stopgap measure while I was at work because I didn't dare expose myself there.

Gene's story shows the intensity of what it's like to have an out-of-control sexual behavior and how it is fueled by accessing online sexually oriented Internet sites. There are three separate subgroups within the Lifelong Sexually Compulsive Group. First, there are those people who use the Internet as an additional way of acting out with the same behaviors they use offline. A person may have long used pornography and compulsively masturbated. The advent of the Internet now provides this person with a new source of pornography. Someone like Gene, who exposes himself regularly, can do so now on the Net using a Webcam with far less risk than doing so in public.

A second group of people includes those who see the Internet as a less risky way of acting out. Sean, whom we met in chapter 2 and who enjoyed frequenting live video feeds from strip clubs, could now spend time in teen chat rooms communicating with young girls. As long as he didn't try to meet them, he felt he was being safe with his behavior. Cybersex allows these people to feed their compulsion—in virtual anonymity—and receive the rush of doing so with less risk than if they were interacting face-to-face with another person.

The final group includes people whose sexual behavior is out of control already and who use the Internet to further increase the danger associated with their sexual behavior. Mark's fascination with young girls accelerated after using the Internet:

> I loved to cruise past school yards during recess and other places where children congregated, but I never went so far as to risk actually talking to any of them. Instead, I'd drive by and fantasize about stopping, picking up a young girl, talking to her, and fondling her. Through the Internet, I found that I could easily have personal conversations with young girls. By actually communicating with children online, I had unknowingly crossed a line into more dangerous territory. This moved me another step closer to illegal behavior. It heightened my arousal and excitement, because I was actually doing what I had been afraid to do all the years when I had only been cruising for children.

VIEWING A PROBLEMATIC SEXUAL BEHAVIOR AS AN ADDICTION

The people's stories contained in this book all involve a problem with their use of the Internet for sexual behavior, ranging from relatively minor to very serious. We would like to go one step further and help you to understand how these problematic sexual behaviors can, in some cases, actually be addictive behaviors.

A way to understand the behavior of someone like Gene is to compare his behaviors with those of alcohol and drug addicts. A common definition of alcoholism, for example, is that a person has a pathological relationship with this mood-altering chemical. The alcoholic's relationship with alcohol becomes more important than family, friends, and work. The relationship progresses to the point where alcohol is necessary to feel normal. To feel "normal" for the alcoholic is also to feel isolated and lonely, since the primary relationship he or she depends upon to feel adequate is a chemical, not other people.

A parallel pattern can be found among those people who have problematic sexual behaviors, including cybersex activities. Again, an addict substitutes a sick relationship with an event or a process for a healthy relationship with others. An addict's relationship with a mood-altering "experience" becomes central to his or her life. Gene, for example, routinely jeopardized all that he loved for the sake of his cybersex activities. His attempts to stop his behavior were lost against the power of his behaviors. According to this definition, Gene is addicted to cybersex.

Addicts progressively go through stages in which they retreat further from the reality of friends, family, and work. Their secret lives become more real than their public lives. Eventually, what other people know is a false identity. Only the person knows the shame of living a double life—the real world and the addict's world.

Leading a fantasy double life is a distortion of reality. Marcy, the middle-aged social worker whom we discussed in chapter 1, was so caught up in the thrill and fantasy of meeting men that she never considered the danger she was placing herself in until she was nearly murdered. An essential part of sanity is being grounded in reality. One thing is certain: addiction warps one's sense of reality.

THE ADDICT'S BELIEF SYSTEM

Addiction is a system, one with its own momentum. The more often you engage in the addictive behaviors, the more momentum your addiction has. The addictive system also has various component "parts," the first of which is a belief system. Addiction begins with delusional thought processes, which are rooted in the individual's belief system. That is, these people begin with core beliefs about themselves that affect how they perceive reality. This belief system is very important, and for now we will point out only its role in addicts' impaired thinking.

Each of us has a belief system that is the sum of the assumptions, judgments, and myths that we hold to be true. It contains potent family messages about our value or worth as people, about relationships, our basic needs, and our sexuality. It includes beliefs about men and women and having a secret life. Within it is a repertoire of what "options"—answers, solutions, methods, possibilities, or ways of behaving—are open to each of us. In short, it is our view of the world.

On the basis of that view, we plan and make decisions, interpret other people's actions, make meaning out of life experiences, solve problems, pattern our relationships, develop our careers, and establish priorities.

For each of us, our belief system is the filter through which we conduct the main task of our lives: making choices.

CORE BELIEFS

An addict's belief system contains certain core beliefs that are faulty or inaccurate and, consequently, provide a fundamental momentum of problematic behavior and addiction. Simply put, these are the four core beliefs:

1. I am basically a bad, unworthy person.
2. No one would love me as I am.
3. My needs are never going to be met if I depend on others.
4. Sex is my most important need (for an alcoholic, it would be alcohol).

Generally, addicts do not perceive themselves as worthwhile human beings. Nor do they believe other people would care for them or meet their needs if everything was known about them, including the addiction. Finally, those who have problems with sexual behavior believe that sex is their most important need. Sex is what makes isolation bearable. Their core beliefs are the anchor points of sexual addiction.

Our core beliefs are formed as we are growing up and are primarily developed within our families. Healthy families have the capacity to organize and reorganize as they grow and change. Children are supported and nurtured. Above all, children get the message that, despite mistakes and inappropriate behavior, they are worthwhile human beings who deserve love—and they are indeed loved.

In unhealthy families, however, children are abused and neglected. When parents don't nurture and support their children, these children make the assumption that they are not good human beings, that they are not worthy of love and affection, and they carry these attitudes into adulthood.

As adults, they do not perceive themselves as worthwhile, nor, again, do they believe other people would care for or love them. This extends into another core belief. Someone with this perception might state, "Since you will never love me anyway because of my innate badness, there's no reason for me to think you would want to do anything for me. I can't count on you to help, assist, support, or take care of me." This thinking destroys trust in others and leaves only one option: to survive you must be in control. An equation is created: an increased level of distrust equals more controlling behavior. Sex becomes a source of nurturing that they believe they have control over. Finally, these people come to believe that sex is their most important need.

These core beliefs have become the anchor points of what, by our definition, is sexual addiction. Sex is what makes their isolation bearable. They believe that sex will fill the loneliness and that it will make them feel good. They have, however, mistaken sex for intimacy, a true connection with another. What they want and need is intimacy, but what they seek instead is sex. Without intimacy, sex will never fulfill their needs, no matter how much they get.

THE POWER OF THE INTERNET

The Internet and cybersex can be so powerful because the actual online experience can reinforce unhealthy coping mechanisms learned in childhood. When children experience traumatic situations, they often cope by dissociating (mentally and emotionally detaching) themselves from the traumatic situation. For children in such circumstances, this can be a useful strategy.

Such childhood coping mechanisms can, however, easily be carried forward into adulthood. But that causes problems. If, as children, they never learned how to be in a relationship, they will lack the interpersonal skills to interact with others on an emotional level. Additionally, when people encounter situations that remind them, even unconsciously, of childhood trauma, they automatically switch off. In other words, they dissociate, and by so doing they are not really in the present any longer. When this happens in relationships, it creates distance and prevents intimacy.

The Internet is a way to interact with others while keeping a barrier between you and other people. It is especially useful if you never learned healthy ways to engage with or relate to other people or if you don't trust or feel safe with them. You can remain anonymous and distant and never have to reveal your true identity or anything else about yourself. Sex in "real time," no matter how impersonal, still requires some physical contact or proximity to another human being. For example, you have to tuck money into a stripper's G-string. Exposing yourself requires another person seeing you. Having some form of sex with a prostitute requires physical contact.

Cybersex provides the ultimate pseudo-connection with another person, the perfect impersonal personal relationship, with no hassles or demands or connection. Cybersex enables users to truly objectify the person on the other side of that computer connection. In real time, you are still forced to confront, at some level, the fact that you are interacting with a human being. He or she is there in front of you, moving, breathing, talking, and so on. On the Internet, nothing is really there, save a flickering image on a computer monitor.

In many ways, the Internet allows people to create a kind of cyber-dissociation. They remain detached from those with whom they are interacting. The ineffective coping mechanisms learned as a child can come into play seemingly without negative consequences. The cyber-world offers the ultimate form of detachment.

IMPAIRED THINKING

Out of the belief system—the set of interacting faulty beliefs—come distorted views of reality. Denial leads the list of ways addicts distort reality. They use many devices to deny to themselves and to others that there is a problem. Ignoring the problem, blaming others, and minimizing the behaviors are part of the addict's defensive repertoire. Consequences such as venereal disease, lost jobs, arrests, and broken relationships are either overlooked or attributed to factors other than their problematic sexual behavior.

> Arrest: "I wasn't really going to do anything with that girl; I just wanted to talk to her."

> Job loss: "My boss had it in for me anyway. Other guys were e-mailing hot pictures around, too, and nothing happened to them."

> Relationship: "She's been looking for an excuse to dump me for years."

When these people believe in the defensive *rationalizations*, the result is *denial* that a specific incident or behavior is part of an overall pattern.

Arguments, excuses, justifications, and circular reasoning abound in the person's impaired mental process:

"If I don't go online for sex every few days, the pressure builds up."

"I just have a high sex drive."

"What he doesn't know won't hurt him."

"If only my wife (or husband or partner) would be more responsive."

"We men are like animals—we're just more sexual than females."

"With the stress I am under, I deserve this."

"It doesn't hurt anyone because . . ."

"It's my way of relaxing."

"It's just on the computer."

"No one knows but me, and no one would care, anyway."

No matter what rationalization is used, people who use statements like these are further cut off from the reality of their behavior. The people who make a commitment to themselves and others to change, quit, or follow through on a behavior are often sincere in their intentions. They may even experience a great deal of emotion—painful tears, expressions of tenderness, or anger when someone doesn't believe in their good intentions. When their behavior simply doesn't match up to their commitment, they begin defending a lie that they believe is true. This is an example of seriously impaired thinking. For those caught up in addictive sexual behaviors, there is tremendous delusion, and that delusion is just part of a much larger rationalization they use to justify all their behaviors. For example, a man who has been confronted by his partner because he was not at work when he was supposed to be tells a lie regarding his whereabouts. His partner doubts he is telling the truth. The man becomes incensed at his partner's distrust. He assumes that she would act this way even if he were telling the honest truth. His emotions about her distrust are real, and he's even angrier now. His lies and sincerity become fused.

Making declarations of love just to seduce the other person, becoming incensed at the behavior of an arresting officer just to obscure your own behavior, and protesting that something "happened only once" to cover up—these all are types of delusion and rationalization.

Ironically, these people *know* that they are not really trustworthy. In their isolation, they are also convinced that most people cannot be trusted. Further, they are certain that if anyone found out about their secret life of sexual experiences, there would be no forgiveness, only judgment. To complicate matters, they have placed themselves in so many precarious situations that they live in constant fear of the eventual discovery that they are being untrustworthy. Suspicion and paranoia heighten their sense of alienation.

Blaming others for all their problems is another way they protect their secret life. Fault lies with others who are critical, self-righteous, and judgmental. There is no acceptance of personal responsibility for mistakes, failures, or actions. This appearance of integrity further insulates their world from reality. The blame dynamic provides further justification for their behaviors. Ungrateful children, demanding spouses, hard-nosed bosses create an unfair world in which they deserve a reward. To be honest about their limitations would bring the wall crumbling down and, in turn, jeopardize the one source of nurturing and care that can be counted on—their sexual behaviors and compulsions.

Each of these delusional thought processes—denial, rationalization, sincere delusion, paranoia, and blame—closes off an important avenue of self-knowledge and contact with reality for those struggling with problematic sexual behavior. Their world becomes closed off from the real world. Within their closed-off world the addictive cycle is now free to work.

THE ADDICTIVE CYCLE

The addictive experience progresses through a four-step cycle that intensifies with each repetition:

1. Preoccupation—the trance or mood wherein the person's mind is completely engrossed with thoughts of sex. This mental state creates an obsessive search for sexual stimulation.
2. Ritualization—the person's own special routines that lead up to the sexual behavior. The ritual intensifies the preoccupation, adding arousal and excitement.
3. Compulsive sexual behavior—the actual sexual act, which is the

end goal of the preoccupation and ritualization. The person is unable to control or stop this behavior.

4. Unmanageability and despair—the feeling of utter hopelessness and powerlessness the person has about his or her sexual behavior.

The pain felt at the end of the cycle can be numbed or obscured by sexual preoccupation that reengages the addictive cycle.

PREOCCUPATION

Sex addicts are hostages of their own preoccupation. Every passerby, every relationship, and every introduction to someone passes through a sexually obsessive filter. More than merely noticing sexually attractive people, there is a quality of desperation that interferes with work, relaxation, and even sleep. People become objects to be scrutinized. A walk through a crowded downtown area is translated into a veritable shopping list of "possibilities."

To understand the trancelike state of preoccupation, imagine the intense passion of courtship. We laugh at two lovers who are so absorbed in one another that they forget about their surroundings. The intoxication of young love is what these people attempt to capture. It is the pursuit, the hunt, the search, the suspense heightened by the unusual, the stolen, the forbidden, and the illicit that are so intoxicating to them. The new conquest of the hustler; the score of the exposer, voyeur, or rapist; or the temptation of breaking the taboo of sex with a child—in essence, they are variations of a theme: courtships gone awry.

People with addictive sexual behavior use—or, rather, abuse—one of the most exciting moments in human experience: sex. Sexual arousal becomes intensified. Their mood is altered as they enter the obsessive trance. The metabolic responses are like a rush through the body as adrenaline speeds up the body's functioning. The heart pounds and the person focuses on his or her search object. Risk, danger, and even violence are the ultimate escalators. One can always increase the dosage of intoxication. Preoccupation effectively buries the personal pain of remorse or regret. They do not always have to act. Often just thinking about it brings relief.

Their excitement-seeking parallels preoccupation found in other addictions. In that sense, there is little difference between the voyeur waiting for hours by a window for a minute of nudity and the compulsive gambler taking a hunch on a long shot. What makes those with sexual addictions different is that they draw upon the human emotions generated by courtship and passion.

Ritualization

The trance is enhanced by the sexual addict's ritualization. Professionals have often wondered why sex offenders use the same "MO" (modus operandi, or method) each time when it only makes apprehension easier. Why would someone visit sexually explicit Web sites while at work, knowing full well that all employee Internet activity is being electronically monitored, making his or her discovery inevitable?

The answer is simple: a ritual helps induce the trance. Like a yogi in meditation, people caught up in compulsive sexual behavior do not have to stop and think or disrupt their focus. The ritual itself, like preoccupation, can start the rush of excitement. In that moment, they have become oblivious to external factors, consequences, and environmental cues that say, "Stop, this is not the time." When you study techniques of meditation, one step is learning how to focus, how to avoid distractions. Online rituals put people into a trancelike state that has incredible focus. The ritual becomes another way to further distort perception and distance cybersex users from reality.

Sex addicts often talk about their rituals. The compulsive masturbator and his surroundings, the incestuous father and his elaborate preparations, the exposer's regular routes, the hustler's approach and cruising area, the cybersex user's favorite chair, lighting, time of day, and Web sites—all involve complex rituals. The rituals contain a set of well-rehearsed cues that trigger arousal.

The preoccupation trance supported by extensive rituals is as important as—or sometimes more important than—sexual contact or orgasm. The intoxication of the whole experience is what they seek in order to move through the cycle from despair to exhilaration. One cannot be orgasmic all the time. The search and the suspense absorb their concentration and energy. Cruising, watching, waiting, and preparing are part of the mood alteration.

The first two phases of the addictive cycle (preoccupation and ritualization) are not always visible. Those in the addictive cycle struggle to present an image of normalcy to the outside world. The public self is a false ego, since they know the incongruity of their double lives. Compulsive sexual behavior, the third phase of the cycle, however, leaves a trail despite the protective public image.

COMPULSIVE SEXUAL BEHAVIOR

As you may recall, chapter 1 included a story about Kevin. He promised himself and his wife that he'd stop going online for sex. Yet that promise was broken in less than a week. Kevin could not control his behavior even though he wanted to. Like Kevin, addicts are powerless over their behavior. They have lost control over their sexual expression, which is exactly why they are defined as addicts. The failure of their efforts to control their behavior is a sign of their addiction. Sexual addicts often describe the process of picking a day—a child's birthday, a change of jobs, a holiday—as "the last day." Usually, this marks a time when "it" will never happen again. Sometimes, addicts will set goals—a year, a month, or a week. It could be forever or a shorter period of time, but addicts betray themselves, buying into the delusion that they are in control of their behavior. When they fail, yet another indictment of self-control and morality is added to ever increasing shame. For recovering addicts who have acknowledged powerlessness, there is hope. They know that they might get through one day free from their addiction—with a lot of help.

The despair that addicts experience after being compulsively sexual is the "low" phase of the four-step cycle. The letdown combines the sense of failure at not having lived up to resolutions to stop with hopelessness about ever being able to stop. If the behavior was particularly degrading, humiliating, or risky, the addict's self-pity grows. If the behavior violated basic personal values or exploited them, the addict experiences self-hatred as well. Addicts often report suicidal feelings along with their despair and shame.

Standing in the wings, however, is the ever-ready preoccupation that can pull the addict out of despair. The cycle then becomes self-perpetuating. Each repetition builds upon the previous experiences and solidifies the reiterative pattern of the addiction. As the cycle fastens its grip on the addict, the addict's life starts to disintegrate and become unmanageable. The addict is similar to the hamster running around the wheel in a cage; he or she runs around and around through the addictive cycle, unable to escape and becoming more and more physically, emotionally, and mentally exhausted.

Unmanageability and Despair

Addicts are caught up in the task of keeping their secret lives from affecting their "public" lives. Even so, the consequences come: arrests, unmasked lies, disruption, unmet commitments, and attempts to explain the unexplainable. The addiction surfaces in addicts' inability to manage their lives. For a moment, mental process blurs reality with euphoric recall of sexual successes. They face yet again the ultimate seduction: a unique opportunity that, of course, will be "the last time."

This unending struggle to manage two lives—the "normal" and the addictive—continues. The unmanageability takes its toll. Family relationships and friendships are abbreviated and sacrificed. Hobbies are neglected, finances are adversely affected, and physical needs are unattended. The lifestyles of addicts become a consistent violation of their own values, compounding their shame. The impaired mental processes result in faulty problem solving in all areas of their lives. These decisions add to further unmanageability.

Nowhere is this clearer than in the workplace. Faulty problem solving and diversion of energy require the addict to devote extra time and effort to hold down a job. Extra hours at work further the unmanageability at home. Worse, if the addiction is connected with the work environment, it becomes even more precarious.

Addicts often point to the connection between their addiction and the stress of high-performance demands involving an important personal investment. Graduate school, for example, is often the time when people first encounter compulsivity. New jobs, promotions, and solo business ventures are also good examples. The stress of proving oneself in an area where every inadequacy is evaluated is a potent flash point for the ignition of problematic sexual behavior and sexual addiction. Unstructured time, a heavy responsibility for self-direction, and high demands for excellence seem to be the common elements that are easy triggers for compulsive or addictive behaviors. Procrastination becomes a daily nemesis for these addicts. Once ignited, the compulsion and addiction make work easy to put off. One of the worst consequences of such behavior is isolation. The intensity of the double life affects relationships with family and friends. The more intensely involved in compulsive sexual life addicts become, the more alienated they are from their parents, spouses, and children. Without those human connections, addicts paradoxically lose touch with their own selves. The unmanageability stemming from the addiction has run its course when there is no longer a double life. When there are no longer friends or family to protect or a job to hold or pretenses to be made—even though some things are valued enough to at least have a desire to stop—the addiction is at its most destructive and violent point. The addict's world has become totally insulated from real life. As we have already noted, the Internet and cybersex feed perfectly into the need for isolation. Even when online in a chat room or using a video feed, the addict is essentially still alone. The reality is that he or she is sitting alone in front of a computer monitor. No one else is there.

THE ADDICTIVE SYSTEM

As people move from healthy relationships to sexual compulsion and addiction, their internal processes combine to form an addictive system. The addictive system—as with all systems—contains subsystems that support one another. Often this support occurs in repetitive, predictable cycles.

To picture the addictive system with its subsystems, consider the human body. It is a complex system with many subsystems—the nervous system, digestive system, immune system, and so on. Clearly, when one subsystem, such as the digestive system, is upset, all the other bodily systems are affected and must adjust in some way.

The addictive system starts with a belief system containing faulty assumptions, myths, and values that support impaired thinking. The resulting delusional thought processes insulate the addictive cycle from reality. The four-phase addictive cycle (preoccupation, ritualization, sexual compulsivity, and despair) can repeat itself unhindered and take over the addict's life. All the other support systems, including relationships, work, finances, and health, become unmanageable. The negative consequences from the unmanageability confirm the faulty beliefs that the addict is a bad person who is unlovable. In turn, revalidated beliefs allow further distortion of reality. Diagrammed, the addictive system looks like this:

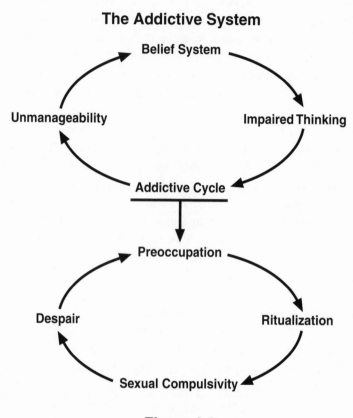

The Addictive System

Figure 3.2

Within the addictive system, sexual experience becomes the reason for being—the primary relationship for the addict. For the addict, the sexual experience is the source of nurturing, focus of energy, and origin of excitement. It is the remedy for pain and anxiety, the reward for success, and the means for maintaining emotional balance. Outsiders, especially those who care about the addict, witness the unmanageability and maybe even the behavior. They see the addict's personal loss, the self-degradation, and the abandoned hope and values. It would seem so simple to just stop, even for a while. For the cybersex user, for example, who may spend up to seven hours a day online and another four thinking about it, the task is not so easy. The addiction is truly an altered state of consciousness in which "normal" sexual behavior pales by comparison in terms of excitement and relief from troubles.

In the addict's world, there is an ongoing tension between the person's normal self and the addicted self. A Jekyll-and-Hyde struggle emerges. The addictive system is so compelling that the addict feels it would be deadly to stop it. Yet, as the system continues, the person's values, priorities, and loved ones are attacked. Sometimes, only a major crisis can restore perspective. Twenty-five years ago, one of the authors of this book, Patrick Carnes, first proposed the existence of the addictive system for sex addicts. Over the years, this hypothesis has been verified by literally millions of people who have used it to help them understand their recovery from sex addiction. The Internet has a profound effect on this system in that it dramatically intensifies the system, in turn making it all the more difficult to break and stop. The Internet is "the great amplifier." People who never experienced problematic or compulsive sexual behavior before now find themselves seemingly inextricably trapped. Such was the case for Kevin, whom you met in chapter 1. Kevin tells more of his story:

> I was a highly respected executive in my company. I was admired by my peers, and my innovative ideas regularly contributed to my company's success. I loved my wife and children dearly and made sure that my work demands did not take time away from them. But I had another, hidden side. My growing obsession with Internet sex was beginning to take its toll. I didn't really know why this obsession was so powerful. My productivity at work was beginning to suffer. Others hadn't noticed, but I knew. The time I wasted on the Internet bothered me, since I could have instead been spending time with my family. I began using work as an excuse to come home later in the day and for more late nights on the computer.
>
> My sexual behavior was also taking a toll on my health. I wasn't sleeping enough, and the stress of making excuses, of covering for work not completed, of keeping more and more of my life hidden was exhausting.
>
> I didn't like what I was doing. In the morning, looking at the trusting faces of my wife and children, I would feel the profound incongruity

of what I'd been doing late into the night. They were happy and loving, ignorant of my secret life. Still, I knew.

I finally asked for help with my sex addiction when I had an un-expected heart attack. The short nights and increased stress had been taking their toll on me. Finally, sitting in a hospital bed, I told my story to a chaplain. Amid deep sobs, I disclosed my loneliness and my love of family and work. Through my conversations with the chaplain, I ac-knowledged and took responsibility for what I'd been doing.

Kevin, like any other addict, lived in two worlds. One was a world of business challenges and accomplishments, family gatherings, and love for his wife and children. The other world was filled with isolation as he spent hours glued to a computer monitor, his face lit by dancing images of naked women. The coexistence of these two worlds continued until Kevin's body refused to live up to the strain.

All types of compulsive behavior can be woven into the scenario of ad-diction. Shoplifting, gambling, and spending are frequent counterparts. Sexually abused families often report that sexual addicts use physical vio-lence to release pent-up energy. The workaholic who gets high on the ex-citement of a new deal or a new breakthrough finds professional life even more exhilarating when coupled with sexual addiction.

By far the most common combination of addictions is when the sexual addict is also dependent on alcohol or another drug. Many people attribute sexual excesses and some instances of incest to the power of alcoholism. The reality, however, is that alcoholism is often a concurrent illness with, rather than the cause of, sexual addiction. Emotional illness also flourishes within the addict's world. Depression, suicide, obsessive-compulsive behavior, and paranoia are common companions.

GETTING HELP

Recovery from problematic sexual behavior or sex addiction is possible by reversing the alienation that is integral to the addiction. With the proper help, you can integrate new beliefs and discard dysfunctional thinking. Without the mood-altering insanity to insulate you from knowledge about your own self, you become a participant in the restoration of your own sanity.

All forms of addiction are vicious because they reinforce the inability to trust others. Yet without help from others, you cannot regain control because the addiction feeds itself. Sexual addiction is especially virulent because few forms of fixation or excitement are as supercharged with social judgment, ridicule, and fear. Consequently, seeking help is especially difficult for anyone with problematic sexual behavior.

One proven path to recovery, though by no means the only one, is the Twelve Steps of Alcoholics Anonymous. Many people suffering from compulsive disorders have translated the Steps for their own use, such as Overeaters Anonymous, Gamblers Anonymous, and Emotions Anonymous. This book proposes the Twelve Steps as one way for people with problematic sexual behavior to emerge from their double lives. Across the country, local groups have modified the Twelve Steps for the sexually compulsive. The Twelve Steps of Alcoholics Anonymous Adapted for Sexual Addicts is listed in the appendix (page 218).

Twelve Step programs can help people restore the living network of human relationships, especially in the family. The program asks addicts to first accept their problem by looking at their addictive cycle and the consequences of it. A first step is to admit that they are powerless over their sexual behavior and that their lives have become unmanageable. With that admission, the sexual addicts, called program members, are then able to start rebuilding relationships by taking responsibility for what they have done and by making amends where possible. Values and priorities are reclaimed. Throughout the program, members explore basic spiritual issues as a way of understanding and facing their anxiety. As members live by the program's tenets, the double life, with all its delusion and pain, can be left behind.

In chapters 7 and 8, we will talk in greater detail about various interventions, including the Twelve Step approach, therapy, medication, support groups, and spiritual guidance, that you can take to break out of the world of compulsive cybersex. In the next chapter, we will examine how we learn about sex, what makes people sexually aroused, and the impact the Internet is having on sexual stimulation.

4

What Turns You On?
The Arousal Template

WHAT AROUSES YOU SEXUALLY? Lingerie? Certain words or images? Role playing? Romantic dinners? Dancing?

Each of us has different preferences for what turns us on sexually, and this is what we call an arousal template—the total constellation of thoughts, images, behaviors, sounds, smells, sights, fantasies, and objects that arouse us sexually. While most of us, if we're asked, can describe what turns us on, we generally react unconsciously to these sexual stimuli. They are just a part of us.

Humans are pattern seeking and pattern creating. For example, when young children are learning how to speak English, they might use the wrong past tense for some verbs: "I see'd it" rather than "I saw it" or "I go'd to the store" rather than "I went." This mistake actually demonstrates that the child has discovered a pattern in English; generally past tenses are formed by adding "ed" to the present-tense form—"change" becomes "changed," "follow" becomes "followed," and so on.

Our tendency and ability to create patterns is why, for example, metaphors are such useful tools for conveying ideas. In a discussion about a problem at work, for example, a person might say, "Well, we'd been having trouble with our new online ordering system. We thought we had solved the problem, but today, more incidents cropped up and then, suddenly, the dam burst." The idea of a bursting dam created a visual image of an uncontrollable flow of water pouring through a gap and spreading chaos and destruction far and wide. With only three words, the speaker instantly conveyed the scope of the problem. Of course a dam didn't really burst in the office, but you can imagine, thanks to that image, the extent of the disaster. You recognize the "pattern" and respond to it. When encountering new situations or ideas, your brain immediately searches for connections, for ways to make that information fit within already existing structures. You will see how this process is important when we look at the influence of Internet sex on arousal templates.

Sexual arousal works on the same principle in that it is pattern based. You have an arousal template that is essentially a pattern you created unconsciously as you were growing up—one that determines what you find sexually arousing—whether or not you are now aware of its existence.

HOW AROUSAL TEMPLATES ARE FORMED

While it's not absolutely certain how arousal templates are established, we do know that their formation is a complicated process involving many factors, including

- physiology, biology, and genetics
- culture, including religious and ethnic background
- family history
- experiences of physical, emotional, or sexual abuse or exploitation, if any
- general life experiences
- sexual history

Much discussion exists within the scientific community about what determines an arousal template. Part of it is likely biologically hardwired, but even our brain may be less "hardwired" than originally thought. Until recently, brain scientists accepted as a matter of faith that the neurons, or brain cells, you were born with were all the brain cells you would ever possess. In 1998, however, neurobiologist John Gage revealed in a groundbreaking experiment that neurons are constantly being born, particularly in the learning and memory centers.[1] Gage now believes that changes in behavior—like exercising more—can affect the growth of brain cells and alter the brain's "wiring." He speculates that what you do can actually change the structure of your brain.

It's also clear that what humans find sexually attractive and arousing is affected by their environment, culture, and upbringing. Some cultures, for example, regard heavier women as extremely attractive. Others hold the opposite view. In cultures where women's bodies must be nearly completely covered, the glimpse of a wrist, a forearm, or an ankle is extremely erotic.

THE THREE PRIMARY EMOTION SYSTEMS

Helen Fisher, an anthropologist and research professor at Rutgers University, has done remarkable work studying the neurochemistry of sex.[2] Humans and other mammals, she says, have evolved three primary emotion systems: one for mating, one for reproduction, and one for parenting. The first to evolve was the sex drive (lust or libido). Characterized by a craving for sexual gratification, it is associated primarily with the estrogens and androgens. The sex drive evolved principally to motivate people to seek sexual union with any appropriate member of the species to continue the survival of the species.

The second emotion system is attraction, which we call passionate love, obsessive love, or infatuation. It is characterized by feelings of exhilaration, intrusive thinking about the object of our attraction, and a craving for emotional union with this partner or potential partner. Attraction is associated primarily with high levels of dopamine and norepinephrine and low levels of serotonin. This emotion system evolved primarily to facilitate mate choice, enabling people to select between potential mating partners, conserve their mating energy, and focus their attention on genetically superior individuals.

The third emotion system is attachment, usually termed "companion love" in humans. It is characterized in birds and mammals by mutual territory defense or nest building (or both), mutual feeding and grooming, staying physically close to one another, feelings of anxiety when separated, shared parental chores, and other affiliation behaviors. In humans, attachment is also characterized by feelings of calm, security, social comfort, and emotional union. Attachment is associated primarily with the neuropeptides oxytocin and vasopressin. This emotion system evolved to motivate people to engage in positive social behaviors and to sustain their relationships long enough to raise their children.

Fisher concludes that during the course of our evolution, these three emotion circuits—lust, attraction, and attachment—became increasingly independent from one another and have a physiological component.

The Internet can significantly affect these three emotion systems as well as the neurochemical reactions that underlie them. As "the great amplifier," the Internet allows you to quickly access and stimulate these emotions in a powerful way. "But," you may be thinking, "everything on the Net is virtual, so how could it really affect me physically?" Do you recall watching a particularly scary movie scene in a theater? What was going on in your body at that moment? Maybe your heart was racing, your stomach was in a knot, and you tightly gripped the arm of your seat. Why did you react this way? Nothing was "really" happening. You were just sitting in a comfortable seat in a large room with a lot of other people simply watching images projected on a large white screen accompanied by dubbed-in voices. What you were watching and hearing was completely fictitious, unreal, and virtual. It was created one scene at a time over a long period of time. Nevertheless, this "virtual" experience had a profound impact on your emotions and an obvious physical effect. This is also true of the Internet and cybersex.

Cybersex can produce a trancelike state, capturing you and drawing you in just as a good movie does. It becomes all the more powerful and captivating because you can control your experience. What you can do is virtually limitless. Interested in romance and relationships? Countless chat rooms are waiting just a mouse click away. Seeking sex and lust? Again, it's right there. While these experiences are virtual, they do affect you emotionally and physically (just like watching a horror movie). In addition, you have the opportunity to be exposed to activities you've never before engaged in or perhaps never even thought of. And you can do that repeatedly whenever you want and for as long as you want. As we have already seen, these seemingly wonderful experiences can, and often do, lead to dire consequences.

TRIGGERING THE AROUSAL TEMPLATE

Lingerie. A cute butt. Nylons and garters. Underwear. Small breasts. Large breasts. Full, wavy hair. Well-cut pecs and abs. An erotic message on your answering machine. There are situations, thoughts, actions, places, and images that trigger your arousal template. Often, however, you're not very aware of them, but you find yourself sexually aroused anyway. These triggers can and often do date back to your childhood and adolescence.

Identifying the Triggers

As a set of well-rehearsed cues that trigger arousal, the special routines we called rituals lead up to the sexual behavior and work together with triggers. Some actions may not initially seem to be sexual triggers, but they can become so under certain circumstances. For example, taking your dog for a walk could be an arousal trigger for you if you had been a voyeur who used to peep in other people's windows while walking your dog. Going into a bar was the trigger for Barry because he had, in the past, gone to bars to pick up a sexual partner and wouldn't leave until he'd found someone. For someone who regularly practices online sex, just the sound of a modem dialing and connecting, or touching the keyboard, could be an erotic trigger. For some people, watching young girls smoke is very erotic. Certain Web sites provide just these types of photos for that reason. Feelings such as anger and sadness can also become erotic triggers.

The Connection between Arousal and Childhood Abuse

It may seem impossible that sexual or physical abuse could be part of a person's arousal template, but it can and does happen. If as a child, for example, you felt both fear and pleasure during an act of sexual abuse, often you will have similar feelings as an adult—to the point of actually putting yourself in abusive relationships. In a sense, trauma becomes connected, even fused, to the arousal template. If you were abused as a child, then trauma, though painful, can become comforting too. Repeating the familiar trauma, you experience a complex biological reaction that includes a neurochemical component that is biologically the same as when you were a child. Jacquelyn's story helps to illustrate this:

> As a young girl, I became erotically aroused, scared, and filled with shame and contempt when my father had sex with me. In addition, however, I felt very powerful because he would do anything I wanted after he had sex with me. In my late teens, I ran away from home and ended up on the street as a prostitute. When I walked into the hotel room with a trick, I knew I had to gain control of the situation. I felt both shame and pleasure—the same feelings I experienced as a child

during sex with my father. In my mind, I was in control, too, because these guys paid me a lot of money. I felt strong and powerful as well because to me these men were contemptible scum.

The Role of Hierarchies

Arousal templates can include a variety of activities and situations. Not all parts of the arousal template are triggered every time. There is a hierarchy among the arousing activities and situations. In fact, many people with compulsive/addictive sexual behavior have very clear and changeable hierarchies out of which they operate. James, for example, travels often for business and is turned on by just walking into a hotel room—primarily because he has a long history of illicit sexual behavior in hotel rooms. Upon arriving at a new hotel, James first goes to the Yellow Pages to look for escort services or massage parlors. If the phone book is missing the Yellow Pages, he goes to option two—walks down to the hotel bar to see if any hookers are hanging around or perhaps even a lonely woman to hustle. If James strikes out again, he returns to his hotel room, opens his laptop computer, hoping to log on to the Internet and start searching for cybersex Web sites. Should he discover that his battery is dead, he locates a nearby bookstore where he buys a copy of the latest *Penthouse*. James has a set of sexual options—sex with a prostitute, sex with a woman he picks up, cybersex, and pornography—as well as a clear order of preference.

The "Erotic Moment"

Most people assume that the goal of sex is intercourse, orgasm, and ultimately intimacy. Often, however, this is not so. Many people instead seek what we call the "erotic moment." A stripper, for example, may find her erotic moment when she takes off her clothes and then watches the men pull out their wallets to give her money. She feels that she has humiliated them and that she is the winner in this exchange. Her arousal template is tied to aspects of sexuality that are related to money and power rather than to intercourse, orgasm, or intimacy.

Cybersex can become part of a person's arousal template. Many people find eroticism in the trancelike state previously mentioned. Internet chat rooms can be captivating, particularly for women, because they provide opportunities for romantic intrigue, manipulation, seduction, and power.

The erotic moment for these women is not found in actually physically having sex with men, but rather in seduction.

Teresa, a woman who grew up in an incestuous family, for example, will often find it very erotic to bring a man to the point of being sexually aroused—and then refuse to have sex with him. The act of flirtation is so powerful that it becomes her erotic moment. Internet chat rooms provide a perfect way for Teresa to create erotic moments at the expense of others, hence the incredible allure and power of cybersex for her.

There are many other examples of erotic moments being quite removed from the actual sex act or orgasm. Voyeurs can experience their erotic moments by finding on the Internet an endless supply of erotic pictures taken through windows or by small hidden cameras in locker rooms or department store dressing rooms.

In a sense, it's the chase rather than the actual capture that is arousing. Many cybersex users talk about the excitement of finding a sex site that has the particular images they really like. For others, the erotic moment comes as a given photo slowly downloads onto their screen.

The Internet is a perfect tool for supplying many kinds of erotic moments, and it can do so endlessly. Those moments are always there, just waiting to be called up. For the voyeur, the Internet creates a new opportunity. No longer is there any need to sit for hours outside the home of a young woman waiting for ninety seconds of nudity. His desires can be met for hours on end in the safety of his home.

Exploring the Forbidden

The Internet can also provide a way to explore long-held fantasies and discover unacknowledged parts of the arousal template. Clyde tells his story:

> I had long fantasized about watching in person two women have sex with one another. Since I'm a man who takes my marriage and religion seriously, I thought this fantasy would never come true. One day while messing around on my computer, I discovered an interactive pornography site where I could request just such a scenario. In no time, however, I was hooked on this fantasy. I'd spend countless hours watching women have sex with one another.

Most of us have a part of our sexuality that lies unacknowledged, unexplored, and without a voice, and the Internet offers a way to explore that sexuality. These sites, however, can quickly take on a larger role in people's lives. Some people, like Clyde, lose control once they enter the cybersex world. After years of suppression, the floodgates are opened and they don't know how to close them again.

The Greek myth of Pygmalion and Galatia provides a useful analogy for understanding the role of cybersex and the Internet in the fulfillment of sexual fantasies. In this myth (upon which the musical *My Fair Lady* was based), Pygmalion wanted to make over the young Galatia to match his idea of the perfect woman. This desire of men creating women who match their idea of perfection is deeply embedded in Western culture, and the Internet provides the opportunity for a reenactment of this ancient Greek myth. Thanks to live-feed video sites and interactive sex sites and their kin, it's possible to log on and describe the woman or man you want to see and what that person should be doing. It's a kind of "instant Galatia."

CHANGING AROUSAL TEMPLATES

Historically, the arousal template has been regarded as quite rigid and fixed, but in recent years, research has shown it to be more flexible and malleable, almost amoeba-like in its ability to grow and incorporate new information as time passes. Much of the original research and writing on arousal templates was based on work with pedophiles, people who were severely damaged as children and who, as a result, had rigid and narrow arousal templates that deviated dramatically from normal behavior. It is extremely difficult for these people to make significant changes in their arousal templates because the damage they suffered is so deep and came so early in life. Their behavior has been in a set groove for a long time.

SPONTANEITY, FLEXIBILITY, AND THE AROUSAL TEMPLATE

For the majority of people, however, arousal templates have a great deal of spontaneity and flexibility. Food can be used as an analogy to the arousal template. Your sexuality is, of course, far more complex than your relationship to food, but the analogy does have similarities that will help make our message clearer.

There are many sexual activities and arousal triggers from which you can choose, akin to a smorgasbord of foods. Consider some of the people in this chapter who have been damaged. Let's say they lived for many years with only hamburgers to eat. Maybe they've had lettuce and tomato on them sometimes, and perhaps an occasional side of French fries, but they've still never seen mashed potatoes and gravy or vegetables, let alone the dessert cart.

We first learn about food likes and dislikes as children in our families. All of us carry our food background, together with our likes and dislikes, into adulthood. As adults, we are exposed to a wider variety of foods. There are many people who, as adults, just aren't particularly interested in exploring new foods and tastes. They like what they grew up with and are content to stick with what they know.

We begin to learn about sex in our childhood, with the process intensifying as we enter our teen years. As a part of that process, we develop a sense—a "taste," if you will—for what turns us on sexually, and this becomes our arousal template. As we've said, its creation is influenced by physiological, biological, and genetic factors, our culture, our religious and ethnic background, and any experiences of physical, emotional, or sexual abuse or exploitation.

John Money has described the template as a kind of "love map."[3] We follow the trails and roads on our love map to sexual arousal. From our point of view, however, the arousal template is much more dynamic than a map. A map describes a territory that is basically unchanging, with set roads and trails. We see the template as more of a fluid matrix in which decisions are made regularly.

As adults, most of us begin to have more sexual experiences. We may, for example, have a partner who introduces us to oral sex, role playing, or sex toys. We may find this new experience erotic and pleasing and add it to our sexual repertoire. It then becomes part of our arousal template.

For many people, however, the arousal template seems to have a static quality to it because they never examine it. Most people never really think about what turns them on and why it does so, just as we don't really think about why we like certain foods and dislike others. In addition, until recently many of us simply didn't have the opportunity to explore the broader landscape of sexual possibilities. Because of the myriad sexual materials and activities available online, it's now possible to access the entire sexual landscape from home (or office or library) with the click of a mouse.

Through our research and work with people who are having problems with their sexual behavior, we see more and more people whose arousal templates are being altered as a result of cybersex experiences. We are also seeing obsessions forming—sometimes very quickly—that ultimately affect all aspects of their lives.

The Internet allows people to discover new sexual interests, as they find that the things that used to arouse them in the past no longer do so. The new interests often take on a power and a focus that have an almost obsessional quality. Thanks to the Internet, people are being sexually stimulated in ways that have nothing to do with culture or any of their previous experiences. Our arousal templates seem to be much more fluid than originally thought.

For centuries, humans have been looking at sex as though through a magnifying glass. We have focused on a small range of activities and ideas. This view has been further narrowed by the taboos fostered by religion and culture. Polygamy, for example, was more commonly practiced in Asia, Africa, and the Middle East many centuries ago than it is now. Some cultures forbade (and still do today) women to interact with men who were not their relatives. Public male or female nudity has long been unacceptable in many cultures. And sex before marriage has also been widely considered immoral for centuries. The Internet, however, acts like a wide-angle lens that instantly gives us a view of the whole sexual landscape.

We now have access to a worldwide sexual smorgasbord. Sex via the Internet is accessible, affordable, and anonymous—a powerful combination. These factors are changing arousal templates, and changing them rapidly.

The Internet allows a new and novel way for people to explore sexuality, and in some respects, this can be a positive experience. People can find other people who have similar tastes, no matter how unusual. Discovering that you are not alone in having a particular desire or fantasy can reduce shame and reinforce positive feelings about yourself, and it can offer a means for exploring these areas of sexuality.

We like to say that one of the best things about the Internet is that you can find others who have interests similar to yours. At the same time, one of the worst things about the Internet is that you can find people who have interests similar to yours.

Web sites can be educational, not only allowing people to learn about and experience particular sexual desires or fantasies, but also pointing the way to new and related areas. In areas and activities that are illegal or unhealthy, the Internet makes it possible for people to reinforce that undesirable behavior and strengthen an unhealthy arousal template.

The Internet also connects people, making it possible to compare notes and exchange materials. Child pornography is an example of illegal activity that is rampant on the Internet. An active and sophisticated child-porn black market exists there, one that has been difficult to infiltrate and control.

HOW CRAVINGS AND OBSESSIONS BEGIN

Given a look at the sexual smorgasbord available on the Internet, people may want to sample some of the new offerings they've seen. More and more people are experimenting sexually in areas that were previously unavailable to them—and not only do they like what they're finding; they now crave it. People can develop new sexual obsessions very rapidly. It is not unusual to see people become absolutely fixated on a new sexual idea—one they've never before imagined—literally within days of discovering it. It's amazing how suggestible people can be and how quickly a previously unknown behavior can become part of a person's arousal template. This reality further points out how complex our templates are.

There's yet another reason why cybersex can create such a powerful hold on people so quickly. When a person goes to a strip club, views a porn movie in a theater, or takes part in some other kind of voyeuristic or exposing activity, it's usually not possible to have an orgasm at the moment that the activity is taking place. People generally return to a car or their home and masturbate to the memory of the event. One of the attributes of the Internet that makes it so powerful is that it's possible to have an orgasm while watching a stripper or "spying" on a woman via a voyeur cam in the safety of your own surroundings. The sexual activity and orgasm suddenly become linked. In addition, the computer and its location become sexualized too. Going to the computer, turning it on, logging on to the Net, taking part in online sexual activities, and orgasm all become fused into a very powerful ritualized activity.

MODIFYING UNHEALTHY BEHAVIORS

The malleability of arousal templates runs the gamut of inflexible to fairly loose and free-floating. Depending on the person, it may be fairly easy or quite difficult to modify unhealthy behaviors in the template. Some individuals become obsessed with certain activities quickly while others seldom, if ever, do so.

Why do some people become hooked, or hooked so quickly, and others do not? A number of factors seem to play a role. One has to do with a person's innate resiliency. For example, in abusive families, we know now that it is not unusual for two children to have different responses to similar traumatic experiences. Often one will be much more damaged than the other. What seems to have the biggest influence in helping those healthier children keep bouncing back is having a healthy relationship with a kind and supportive adult—a teacher, neighbor, relative, or coach, for example, who takes the child under his or her wing. That kind of positive relationship can make an enormous difference in a child's life.

Stress—and the resources we have to cope with it—also play a significant role. One client, a successful businessman whose company was about to go public, was under tremendous stress the day of his company's initial public offering. How did he cope with the pressure? He went to his office and logged online to have cybersex for more than six hours. He took refuge in cybersex during the most critical moment in his company's history because he simply didn't have the resources to cope in a positive way with this level of stress. He used cybersex as a way to reduce it and to take his mind away from the situation. Fortunately, the initial public offering moved ahead without problems despite his lack of oversight.

Sometimes people break down despite having plenty of coping resources. For example, the death of a loved one or feelings of isolation can leave someone quite vulnerable. A person who is not normally interested in cybersex might under stress respond by trying to avoid the outside world and retreating into cybersex. Some might also use cybersex merely as a stopgap measure, but then not be able to turn away from it once the "excuse" for its use is gone. We find that there is no way to predict who will have a problem with cybersex. Those who do come from a broad range of ethnic, social, and economic backgrounds. They can be people who've had trouble with sex before and people for whom it's never been a problem. They may be people with healthy or unhealthy coping responses. This is one of the unique aspects of cybersex. In other sexual problems, it's possible to detect patterns or common points—such as childhood sexual or emotional abuse or a familial history of addictive disorders, for example—among the people who are struggling. Not so with cybersex.

TURNING OFF THE AUTOPILOT MECHANISM

Many people's attitudes toward sex and their arousal templates generally lie unexamined. The same is true for our response to stress—we often just react without thinking about why we did what we did. It's as though we are an airplane on automatic pilot. The Boeing 767 and the French Airbus are enormous machines that use complicated computer programming to monitor much of what is happening during takeoff, flight, and landing. The pilots don't actually do a lot of flying; instead they oversee the system. When everything is running smoothly, the pilots are hardly aware of all the complex adjustments that are being carried out automatically.

Our bodies are far more complex than any airplane, and much of what we do isn't monitored by our conscious mind. We fall into patterns and roles and continue them for years, not realizing that a process is being followed, one that we can both become aware of and change. One of the goals of this book is to help you become aware of some of your unrecognized habits, rituals, and responses to life's events.

You can examine, evaluate, and change the systems and responses you've been using throughout your life. There is hope. Just as the pilot can break in and override the autopilot, you, too, can take greater control over your life and the decisions you make. The first step, of course, is to acknowledge the existence of your unconscious programming and to become aware of its messages.

We have already mentioned the importance of having healthy relationships. One of the factors that consistently plays a role in all addictions, including cybersex addiction, is people's inability to develop and maintain healthy, positive relationships. One of the core components of the arousal template is our relationship and courtship experiences and skills. Our arousal template is connected to our relationship and courtship template. In this chapter, we have been looking at the broad picture of arousal. In chapter 5, we will specifically examine what happens during courtship and its connection to relationships and cybersex.

As we conclude this chapter, we would like to help you look more closely at what makes up your arousal template and how it may have been affected by your sexual activities on the Internet. The following exercise will help you do this. Keep in mind that there are no right or wrong answers; what you discover will help you better understand your own sexuality.

1a. List whatever it was that you found sexy *before* you became involved in cybersex:

b. Next, list whatever it was that you found sexy *after* you became involved in cybersex:

2a. List whatever it was that you found romantic *before* you became involved in cybersex:

b. Next, list whatever it was that you found romantic *after* you became involved in cybersex:

3a. List whatever it was that kept you attached in a romantic relationship *before* you became involved in cybersex:

b. Next, list whatever it was that kept you attached in a romantic relationship *after* you became involved in cybersex:

4. Look over your previous answers. In a sentence, what effect has the Internet had in each of the following three areas?

Sex:

Romance:

Attachment:

5. What new ideas or activities have you incorporated into these three areas since you became involved in cybersex?

Sex:

Romance:

Attachment:

6. Which changes do you feel good about in these three areas?

Sex:

Romance:

Attachment:

7. Which changes do you feel bad about in these three areas?

Sex:

Romance:

Attachment:

8. Looking back on your experiences and answers to the questions in this excercise, can you create any goals about what you would like in terms of sex, romance, and attachment? Write them in the space below. This exercise will serve as good preparation for the next chapter, and you may find that you will want to refer back to it as you read further in this book.

5
Courtship Gone Awry

WHAT DOES THE TERM "courtship" mean to you? If you are like most people, it's defined as meeting, getting to know, and attempting to gain the affection or love of another person. We would like to suggest that there is a far broader meaning to this term—one that encompasses the process by which we meet and establish all our relationships. In a sense, we "court" our acquaintances, business colleagues, and friends, as well as those with whom we have romantic and intimate relationships. Not all aspects of courtship apply to every relationship, but the basic courtship process is really about creating and building relationships. Keep this wider definition of courtship in mind while reading the rest of this chapter.

We are discussing courtship in this book because we believe that it is one of the most important aspects of being human—and because the Internet is dramatically affecting human interactions and relationships. While the Internet has enhanced communication, it also often contributes to unhealthy patterns of relating to others. Basically, the technology of Internet communication changes the way we relate to others by limiting certain aspects of the courtship process. While there are positive aspects and results in using the Internet to meet and get to know others, there are negative factors that interfere with the courtship process too.

In this chapter, we will introduce you to the twelve components of courtship and explain how the Internet interferes with successfully moving through them. We will also talk about three groups of people who have courtship disorders. The first includes those who have had a lifetime of difficulty beginning and establishing relationships. Their problems with Internet-based relationships are a small part of a bigger problem. The second group includes those who have what we describe as "situational" courtship problems. These people have generally, in the course of their lives, been able to develop good relationships. There are times, however, due to stress or a life crisis, that their relationship and courtship skills seem to fall apart. The third group includes people who have not had courtship difficulties until they became involved with the Internet.

UNDERSTANDING COURTSHIP BEHAVIOR

One of the original pioneers of understanding problematic sexual behavior as a courtship disorder was Havelock Ellis, who referred to exhibitionism in 1933 as a "symbolic act based on a perversion of courtship."[1] Over the years, Sigmund Freud and various colleagues elaborated on the concept of courtship disorder. They specified four general examples of courtship distortion that resulted in paraphilic behaviors; that is, sexual behaviors that are outside of what our culture would consider typical and that have negative consequences. First, they pointed to the process of locating a potential partner that, when distorted, becomes voyeurism. During the second phase, which they called "pretactile interaction," exhibitionism and obscene calls served as examples of disordered courtship. The third phase, tactile interaction, is marked by inappropriate touch, such as deliberately brushing against a woman's breasts in a subway train. Finally, they described rape patterns as a distortion of normal efforts to "effect genital union."[2] The concept of courtship disorders has also been useful in understanding various forms of sexual assault. This courtship model can apply, too, to "nonperverse" behaviors such as sexual compulsivity within marriage, compulsive masturbation, or compulsive prostitution, and it also creates a framework to understand problematic cybersex behavior.

Consider the case of Carrie:

> While growing up, I was sexually abused by my father who fondled me regularly until I was fourteen years old. I was also emotionally and physically abused. At one point, I became pregnant and my parents forced me into an abortion. My mother had the doctor place the fetus next to my head after the surgery so I would "learn a lesson." As an adult, I found it very difficult to allow myself to be sexual with a

man whom I cared for. I was always very anxious and was worried about whether the relationship mattered at all. When I was with men I didn't care about and considered "slime," I was very promiscuous. I also was intensely sexual with myself. I would masturbate whenever I got anxious.

Carrie was tremendously relieved when she finally understood that the abuse she suffered as a child created a disordered sense of courtship in which she was unable to be sexual with a man who really mattered. After all, her father mattered and yet he betrayed her. A further legacy of that betrayal was that unreliable men who did not matter were attractive.

In today's culture, there is no systematic and reliable way to teach the basics of courtship. Did you, for example, ever attend a course that taught you how to appropriately and successfully flirt? Recognizing and understanding the twelve components of courtship make it much easier to look at our own courtship behavior and see where our skills may have gone awry.

THE TWELVE COMPONENTS OF COURTSHIP

1. NOTICING

This is the ability to notice attractive traits in others. With an existing partner, this means staying conscious of the desirable traits in that partner. This dimension also requires the capacity to filter out traits that, while desirable, are not a good match for you. This includes the ability to be discriminating.

We communicate at all times on two levels. The basic level of communication contains the words and content of the message. The second level is known as metacommunication. Messages sent at this level qualify and enhance the basic-level message and are delivered through tone of voice, facial expression, body movement, touch, and other nonverbal means. For example, one person might comment to another, "I'm glad we met, and I'll call you soon." Depending on the metamessage being sent, that sentence could communicate two very different messages—that the person really will call, or that he or she isn't at all interested in the other person and has no intention whatsoever of calling.

Noticing is a critical first step in all relationships. When we meet other people for the first time, we are physically in touch with their appearance. We note how they look; their clothes, smile, body type, physicality, tone of voice, and sense of humor; whether they're shy or effusive; and much more. We often have a physical reaction to them. And we get an almost immediate sense as to whether this is a person we might like to know better. (That first impression may turn out to be inaccurate, but regardless, *everyone* forms such impressions.)

The Internet affects the way we notice others in the sense that it doesn't supply any metamessages. Consequently, without nonverbal cues we have no access to the enormous amount of information we normally use when we first meet and interact with another person. As such, the Internet provides people with a completely new and different way to meet. Meeting by phone is similar, but we still have a kind of physical connection—we can hear the other person's voice. Even telephone conversations, then, give us metamessages such as voice expressiveness, sense of humor, and feelings (excitement, nervousness, or boredom, for example). People can communicate with letters, which also contain some metamessages—the style of one's script and the little personal touches and embellishments created by hand—that give nonverbal information about the writer.

By its very nature, the Internet dilutes individuality enormously. Since it is devoid of metamessages, noticing is severely limited. People who meet online have only words on a stark computer monitor upon which to make judgments. Since we are so used to having these metamessages when we meet another person, we unconsciously try to supply them when they're not available. We want to "fill in the blanks." Particularly in romantic relationships, we tend to fill in the blanks in ways that will meet our expectations of what we want a person and a relationship to be like. That information is necessarily speculative, and what we add is based on our projections of what we want that person to be. We don't have the data to really discriminate, which is a critical aspect of noticing.

Misinterpretation of meaning is another problem in Internet communication. In the business world, such problems are commonplace. For example, let's say that an e-mail is sent and the person receiving it feels put down by the message, although the sender meant nothing of the sort. Text alone seldom supplies enough information for accurate message sending and receiving, even when the writer has been very careful. Over time, these misunderstandings actually begin to inhibit communication because they damage the trust on which the relationship depends.

Confusion arises in situations in which, if carried out face-to-face or even on the phone, the message would be sent and received accurately. We read other people's metamessages—a pause or a questioning tone can indicate misunderstanding—and once we realize what is happening, we can clarify our intent. We might say, "Oh, no . . . don't get me wrong, I was just kidding." Clarification takes just seconds. In person, we can be playful with each other in ways that are simply impossible on the Internet.

When meeting via the Internet, the discriminating process becomes very skewed because we simply don't have the information we need to judge whether the person is a good match for friendship or romance.

2. Attraction

This is the ability to feel attraction toward others and to imagine acting on those feelings. This dimension assumes a functional arousal template in which you select behavior and persons appropriate for you. Attraction involves curiosity as well as desire about the physical, emotional, and intellectual traits of others. In an existing relationship, it means the ability to maintain an openness to change. In quality relationships, the partners continue to "discover" each other. Attraction is passion's starting point and the basis for relationships that endure.

People find the Internet so attractive for meeting others because it offers complete control over the information we give to other people. We let them discover only the things about us that we want them to know. We can even create a fantasy self. This possibility points out another major problem with Internet relationships: how do we know whether what another person is telling us is true? In the physical world, for example, if you move into your neighborhood, drive an old car, don't go to work every day, seldom dress well, and then tell others you are a successful lawyer making $250,000 a year, others might look at your lifestyle and question your truthfulness. On the Internet, however, you could tell others whatever you want and they would have no other information to help them know whether your statement was true. What's more, when we meet physically, we communicate many messages inadvertently or even unconsciously to others. For example, a woman, Louise, meets a man at a party, a man she finds very attractive. Not wanting to appear too excited, she tries to act a bit aloof, but the look in her eyes clearly reveals her true feelings.

Attraction depends on the ability to notice. In order to discriminate and to be attracted to others, we have to be able to notice them. We need to be able to learn about who they are. The discovery process is what makes attraction real. But in cyber-meetings, what we learn about others is limited to text and, perhaps, a photo or video—and they learn *exactly* what we want them to know. The meeting is devoid of metamessages.

3. FLIRTATION

This is the ability to make playfully romantic or sexual overtures to another person. Everyone needs to know how to flirt. Successful flirting uses playfulness, seductiveness, and social cues to send signals of interest and attraction to the desirable person. This ability also includes noticing and accurately reading the flirtation of others. The critical factor in flirtation is knowing when it is appropriate to send and receive it. In addition, the success of long-term relationships requires ongoing flirtation between partners.

Playfulness and flirtation are relevant to all relationships, not just romantic ones. The critical component of healthy flirtation is the difference between the message sent and the message received—you have to know how to send a message so that what you want to convey is what is actually received by the other person.

When flirting online, however, this task is very difficult to accomplish. Once again, the problem is rooted in a lack of "noticing" information available on the Internet. Without these cues, it is easy to misinterpret the message being sent, and flirtation is derailed. Outside the cyber-world, we can, for example, indicate sarcasm simply by using a particular tone of voice while finishing the phrase or sentence with a chuckle. In e-mail, it is impossible to deliver such complex content.

The Internet does make a kind of pseudo-flirtation possible. If you visit a pay porn site and begin interacting with someone, it's really no different from paying a prostitute. The person with whom you're talking will smile at you (if they have a live video feed) and flirt and say you're wonderful, and so forth. Because that person doesn't know you and because you're paying for his or her time, however, this is not true flirtation. In fact, it's even less "real" than if you were actually with a prostitute, because then you would at least have some sense of who he or she is, and vice versa. On the Net, you can pretend that your partner is flirting with you, but in fact he or she is only flirting with his or her camera and your money. At some level, the buyer knows that this person isn't attracted to and doesn't care at all about him or her. It's merely a business transaction.

Once again, trust is the potential victim. Believing another person's flirtation online requires a great deal more trust because we have so little information on which to base a judgment. People can say anything, and they can choose to disappear at any time. The flirtation suddenly becomes nothing more than electrons now randomly dispersed into space.

4. DEMONSTRATION
Sometimes inaccurately described as "showing off," it is in this step where one demonstrates "prowess" (a physical trait, skill, or capability). Sexually, it's the classic "I will show you mine if you show me yours" scenario. There is, in fact, pleasure or eroticism in having a potential partner show interest in your sexuality. Behaviors include demonstrating a skill such as athletic ability, dressing to attract another person, or doing specific sexual acts that further the partner's interest. It is important that you are aware of what you are doing and that you are being appropriate to the context and to the person.

As we have noted, the Internet allows us to create a persona; we are not restricted to who we actually are. The "rich, attractive attorney" had only to *say* (to write, actually) that this was what he did in order to "demonstrate." On the Net, "saying so makes it so." No actual *physical* demonstration is required—or possible—online. Again, so few cues are available online. In real life, someone can say he's a great athlete, but if he's fifty pounds overweight and breathes hard after a two-block walk, we have some pretty good evidence that this just isn't true! Whoever reads a similar claim on the Net will be none the wiser because there's no reality check there.

In courtship, we must be able to verify demonstration. This stage is, by definition, a way to demonstrate that what you say is true, that you are who you say you are. It's really the first test of one's honesty and integrity. In person, we have information, feelings, and intuition on which to base this judgment, but online there is no way to verify that we are who we say we are.

As you can see, each of the steps of courtship build on one another. At this point, it's very difficult to trust "demonstration" if you haven't really been able to move through noticing, attraction, and flirtation. If you don't have the first steps in place, your ability to move ahead in the courtship is limited.

5. ROMANCE

This is the ability to experience, express, and receive passion. Romance assumes the ability to be aware of feelings of attraction, vulnerability, and risk. More important, a lover must be able to express them and have sufficient self-worth to accept the expressions of care from a lover as true. Included in romance is the ability to test the reality of our feelings. Are the people we select as romantic partners consistently appropriate or inappropriate choices? Is what we perceive in the other person accurate, or is it instead a *projection* of what we want to be true? Romance may cause us to see others as we *want* them to be, not as they are.

As we've pointed out, the very nature of Internet communication requires us to project onto others our hopes, desires, and fantasies—what we want to be true about them—because our knowledge of them is based only on what they've told us. So much information that we would generally have in a face-to-face relationship is missing that we feel the need to fill in the blanks. We give potential suitors the attributes that we want them to have.

In addition, we assume (or project) *their* responses to *us* too. "She really likes me and thinks I'm hot," or "He really loves me," or "I'm funny and attractive to her." All of us do this to some extent in our relationships, but the Internet requires us to do so even more because we don't have anything solid on which to base our judgments and assumptions. Reality-based judgments are very difficult because we can't easily grasp reality in an Internet-based relationship. It is this factor that contributes so much to on-line fantasy—and its related problems.

Thirty-nine-year-old Jane describes her experience:

> I had been communicating with this guy for some months, and I was starting to get serious about him. He was a wonderful writer, very expressive and eloquent. He described himself as good-looking with a high-paying job at a major corporation. We seemed to share many interests and values. It was just fun to converse with him. We had both told each other that we were becoming romantically interested in one another. Finally, I proposed that it was time for us to meet in person. He

seemed to hesitate a bit, but finally agreed. Well, I was so disappointed. He was very nervous and shy and couldn't hold a conversation. He didn't seem at all like the person I'd been e-mailing all this time. We didn't meet again, and now I wonder if he was really even the one who was actually writing to me. I mean, maybe he had someone help him.

6. INDIVIDUATION

This is defined as the process by which we differentiate ourselves from others. In the midst of courtship and romance, healthy people are able to be true to themselves. They feel no fear of disapproval or control by the other person. They tell the truth and do not feel intimidated. They can ask for their needs to be met and they do not have to defer to the other person. They trust and believe that people care for them as they are.

Successful individuation depends on the first five steps for its foundation. Individuation depends on truth, trust, and full disclosure. Internet-based relationships, however, are at best only tentatively grounded in reality. The information we have about the other person is severely limited compared with an in-person relationship, and there is absolutely no guarantee that we were told the truth in the first place.

Deep down, we all want to believe that people are honest. In physical, world-based relationships, we have many tools and cues to help us distinguish whether a person is being honest or not. But the Internet takes nearly all of them away and leaves us far less able to make good judgments about others. So we fall back on the desire to believe that others will not deceive us—itself another projection.

Because the Internet interferes with or inhibits the previous five courtship steps, it is nearly impossible to create a foundation strong enough to hold the rest of the courtship. Without the first five steps solidly in place, the sixth step, individuation, is difficult, if not impossible.

7. INTIMACY

As the exhilaration of early passion subsides, partners enter the "attachment" phase, during which the relationship deepens in its meaning and integrity. Intimacy creates a level of profound vulnerability that is ongoing and more difficult than the exhilaration of discovery during early romance. This is the "being known fully and staying anyway" part of relationships.

Internet relationships are not intimate. Intimacy takes work, time, *and* physical connection and interaction. It's very important to understand that people who are hooked on cybersex, regardless of whether they have lifelong or situationally triggered relationship problems, are avoiding intimacy.

The Internet offers a way to get a quick sexual fix with absolutely no requirement of intimacy. Cybersex demands even less intimacy than the most impersonal physical-world relationship. If, for example, you have sex with a prostitute, some intimacy is still required; at the least, you have to be physically in his or her presence; you have to interact face-to-face and body-to-body. Even people who expose themselves must confront a minimal level of intimacy—they have to actually be in the presence of another human being.

The total lack of intimacy on the Internet is the reason why so many people who are avoiding intimacy in their lives get hooked on the Internet in general and cyber-relationships and cybersex in particular. Not only is the cyber-relationship impersonal but also ending it is easy. In physical-world relationships, when matters get uncomfortable and too intimate with a friend, lover, or even a prostitute, it's harder to leave. Leaving takes time and communication. It can be difficult and painful because we feel an obligation to respond to that person and explain why we are leaving. Intimate relationships require us to respond to the other's needs.

Online relationships ultimately require no such demands or responsibilities because we can leave with no (apparent) consequences or explanation. We don't have to respond to another's needs. With a click of the mouse, the relationship evaporates.

Can there really be true intimacy without physical connection? Or is this merely "virtual" intimacy?

8. Touching

Physical touch requires trust, care, and judgment. It is important and should not be taken lightly. Touching affirms the other person, but is respectful of timing, situation, and boundaries. Touching without permission or sexualizing touch betrays trust. While touch can be seductive and misleading, it can also be extraordinarily healing. Adults who were not touched or who were neglected as children often feel extremely touch deprived. They will sacrifice their judgment and their needs simply to be touched.

When touch isn't available in a relationship, again people tend to turn to their own fantasies to fulfill it. This process can be satisfying in the short term, but not in the long run. Humans simply need to touch and be touched.

We want to reemphasize that touch is essential in all relationships, not just romantic or sexual ones. So much can be communicated by such simple gestures as a pat on the back, a hug, the brush of a hand, or a quick, passing kiss. It's OK to say, "I care about you," "I'm here for you," "I'm thinking about you," and "You matter to me."

In addition, people who spend excessive time on the Internet begin to neglect their own real-world relationships. They have less contact, including the physical contact of touch, and this deprivation can actually bring on depression. Often people involved in cyber-relationships think they're having human contact, but in reality they only have contact with a machine. When we get caught up in cybersex, all other personal relationships ultimately suffer.

9. FOREPLAY

Sometimes referred to as the most important part of sexual contact, foreplay is the expression of sexual passion without genital intercourse. Holding, fondling, talking, kissing, and sexual play build sexual tension and are erotic and pleasurable. As a stage, foreplay includes the verbal expression of passion and meaning. In repeated surveys, most people say it is the best part of sex. Despite this reality, foreplay is often skipped over in our culture because of time pressure and stress.

Cyber-foreplay is necessarily limited to very specific kinds of online behaviors since physical touch is not available online. People think they are having foreplay online by having sex-related conversations and even cybersex, but these activities are really only sex talk. True foreplay must also include other courtship steps such as demonstration, flirtation, and intimacy.

Couples who have had online relationships tend to be sexual more quickly when they meet offline because they feel as though foreplay has already happened. It's not unusual for people who have been "together" online to set out on a date with the intent to have sex. They think they can skip right to this level because they have already formed a relationship—when in fact they haven't formed anything more than a text-connection with one another. And when they do meet in person, many people are surprised at what they discover. Even if both have been honest about themselves, they learn that they are really still in the noticing stage. They don't know one another at all. Jane's experience, described earlier under the "Romance" component of courtship, is a typical example of an all-too-common experience among people who try to establish romantic relationships on the Net.

10. INTERCOURSE

Much more than the mere exchange of body fluids, this is the ability to surrender yourself to passion, letting go and trusting yourself and your partner to be vulnerable. Intercourse, while extremely pleasurable, is also an index of the degree to which one is able to give up control. To give oneself over to passion requires true abandonment of expectations. Many people limit themselves or fail in orgasm simply because of trust and control issues.

By definition, intercourse is the physical connection of two people. The closest approximation to intercourse online is mutual masturbation or phone sex—a pseudo-intercourse that doesn't even include the "exchange of body fluids." And since it lacks any of the components of healthy courtship, it can't possibly compare to the more broadly defined act of intercourse that requires complete trust in the other. Online intercourse requires neither commitment nor connection. It is nothing more than one individual satisfying himself or herself with the aid of an online partner.

11. COMMITMENT

Commitment is the ability to bond or attach to another. Some describe addiction as the failure to bond or of not having the capacity to form a deep, meaningful relationship. If someone matters enough, you honor that relationship by your fidelity to it. Being bonded in meaningful relationships, including nonsexual ones, is true commitment.

People who grew up in families where they learned that they couldn't count on others are continually searching for something that they *can* count on—what many addicts refer to as the "black hole" they are trying to fill. Alcohol, sex, drugs, and high risks always deliver what they promise, albeit briefly and ultimately destructively. This pathological relationship with a mood-altering behavior or drug, however, will not fill the void created by the lack of committed relationships.

While one can commit emotionally online, true commitment to an electronic relationship should be questioned. How do people know their partners well enough to be certain that they are, for example, monogamous? Do they have other online—or offline—partners whom they court? Perhaps what we are committing to online are only brief encounters and the pseudo-relationships that result.

12. Renewal

The capacity must exist to sustain renewal, as well as all the above dimensions in an existing relationship.

Being in a committed relationship does not mean you stop flirting or expressing passion with your partner. There is a difference between being attached to someone out of habit and being devoted because of the meaning that has evolved in your journey together. Successful couples continue courtship, continue to show the other they are valued, continue to make efforts to attract their mate, and continue to express the caring they have for one another. If a relationship is not working, partners take responsibility to change it. If the relationship is not tenable, they leave. In online relationships, renewal is impossible if the previous dimensions cannot be achieved online.

COURTSHIP AND THE TEN TYPES OF
SEXUALLY COMPULSIVE BEHAVIOR

In the original research for *Don't Call It Love,* ten types of sexually compulsive behavior were identified.[3] Over the years, these ten types have been developed as an empirically based model of compulsive sexual behavior. Now that courtship dimensions have been added, there is help for people who have problematic sexual behaviors by identifying specific courtship distortions in each of the ten types of behaviors. This makes understanding problematic sexual behavior as an intimacy disorder, as well as a compulsion or an addiction, much easier.

The following list examines types of problematic sexual behaviors and cybersex from the perspective of a courtship problem—that is, courtship gone awry. If you are struggling with problematic sexual behavior or with sexual compulsivity, there are steps you can take that will offer a new perspective on these problems.

The chart on page 84 summarizes the stages of courtship and the ten compulsive types. It shows how each type of behavior is affected by problems in specific courtship dimensions. For example, people who struggle with voyeuristic behaviors (the second of the compulsive types) have problems in three courtship stages: noticing, attraction, and flirtation. Their problem is rooted in an inability to competently carry out the tasks of these three stages. Likewise, a person struggling with seductive-role sex (the fourth compulsive type) needs help in the courtship areas of flirtation, demonstration, romance, intimacy, and individuation. Studying this chart can help you better understand how compulsive behavior is, in part, a courtship problem. These people's life experiences never allowed the evolution of effective and satisfying courtship skills.

FANTASY SEX
Here, people notice attractive traits in others and feel attracted to them, but don't move beyond this stage. Staying in the fantasy world feels safer than acting on the fantasy. Romance and sex can flourish when there is no reality testing. These people also can become obsessed. Laurie, a middle-aged female physician, for example, sought counseling for multiple cyber-affairs. Laurie was in e-mail contact with a number of physicians on her hospital's medical staff and, in her mind, was having a cyber-affair with each of them—except that nothing was actually going on. It was all a fantasy. Countless chat rooms are filled with romance junkies like Laurie.

Masturbation to fantasies is how we learn about our own desire. When masturbation becomes compulsive, we make it a way to escape loneliness. It is about fear of rejection, fear of reality, and anxiety reduction. It can also be self-indulgent in the sense of seeking comfort as opposed to risking a relationship. Many people who engage in cybersex find refuge in fantasy sex because other forms of sexuality are simply too complicated, risky, or require too much effort. Fantasy sex is a way to disassociate from reality, including relationships. The noticing and attraction parts of courtship become very skewed in fantasy sex.

Fantasy sex fits very well with the Internet because, as we have seen, so much of Internet relationships are fantasy. Cybersex is all about trying to stay in a fantasy world because it is safe and requires no work, unlike real relationships.

Courtship Disorder and the Ten Compulsive Types

Compulsive Types	Noticing	Attraction	Flirtation	Demonstration	Romance	Individuation	Intimacy	Touching	Foreplay	Intercourse	Commitment	Renewal
Fantasy	•	•										
Voyeurism	•	•	•									
Exhibitionism		•	•	•								
Seductive Role			•	•	•	•	•				•	•
Trading			•	•	•	•	•				•	•
Intrusive						•	•	•	•		•	•
Paying						•	•	•	•	•	•	•
Anonymous						•	•	•	•	•	•	•
Pain Exchange								•	•	•	•	•
Exploitive	•	•	•	•	•	•	•	•	•	•	•	•

Figure 5.1

VOYEURISM

Voyeurs are also nonparticipants in the sex game. They, however, do move beyond fantasy by searching for sexual objects in the real or cyber-world. In today's society, it is normal to enjoy looking at others sexually. Most people want to take the next step of participating.

Often, people who are Internet voyeurs are extremely passive participants whose goal is not to be involved in chat rooms or interactive Web sites, but instead merely to lurk and watch. To put it in childhood terms, it's "you show me yours and I'll watch."

Usually voyeurism involves objectifying the other person, so it is not a personal relationship. This is the crucial aspect of online voyeurism: the whole experience is about objectifying. Noticing and attraction are skewed because they aren't mutually experienced. A pseudo-flirtation takes place because the person being watched doesn't know the viewer and is not truly interacting with him or her, either.

EXHIBITIONISM

Exhibitionism is the "I will show you mine" part—a way of introducing oneself in an inappropriate way. It is pleasurable and normal to have others notice you sexually. With a partner, exhibitionism is a significant part of sex play. Those with problematic sexual behavior fixate on just being noticed and have difficulty moving beyond this stage. Eroticism for them is being looked at. For some it involves the power of realizing that they have captured another's attention. For others, it is being angry and aggressive by forcing their sexuality on someone. From a relationship perspective, exhibitionism means introducing oneself in an inappropriate way or seeking attention from others with no intent of going further, which is teasing. Sometimes it is the pleasure of breaking the rules. When exhibitionism is obsessional and compulsive, it is a significant distortion of normal courtship.

Cyber-exhibitionism is commonly played out by men who use live-video-feed camera sites. Their goal is to go online and masturbate while others can watch them. This becomes their primary, and sometimes exclusive, way to relate sexually to others. Some men, particularly those who have actually exposed themselves in public, believe that cyber-exhibitionism is a safer and legal way to be sexual. Granted, this form of acting out does not create victims and generally is not illegal (breaking into teen chat rooms with such photos would, however, be illegal). This "solution" does not, however, allow them to address or deal with the deeper relationship and courtship issues underlying their behavior. It's merely a way to carry out the same behavior in a way that isn't illegal. What's more, these men often eventually move or return to the real world using this behavior.

SEDUCTIVE-ROLE SEX
In seductive-role sex, relationships are about power and conquest. Flirtation, performance, and romance are the erotic keys in this category. These people—most often women—are hooked on winning the attention of others and falling in love. Once they have accomplished this, however, sexual interest usually subsides. While they can quickly gain the confidence of others and be intimate in the early discovery and romantic stage, establishing a deeper relationship eludes them. Others in this group feel trapped and unable to be themselves. So, they have multiple online or offline relationships where they can act in different ways with different people. They have a hard time being themselves or being truthful. Since they fear abandonment, having more than one relationship is a way to prevent the hurt they are sure to receive once the relationship ends.

Online, it's possible to have numerous sexual relationships by taking part in different chat rooms. These online trysts provide a way to feel as though you are in a relationship, but at the same time ensure that you will not really be abandoned—because you're not really in a relationship in the first place. Some women cruise chat rooms to flirt and seduce, but when a man actually becomes interested and suggests a face-to-face meeting, these women immediately run the other way. These women don't want to actually meet men because their game would instantly lose its power. The game's attraction is to get guys so hooked that they beg to meet the woman. This way, the woman remains in control and can refuse the encounter. People in this group are crippled in their ability to form lasting bonds and enduring relationships.

TRADING SEX
Online trading for sex can be carried out in a number of ways. Exchanging pornography is the most obvious example; however, the Internet has been the greatest boon to prostitution since the invention of the telephone. It is

easy to go online to a prostitution service, view the variety of men or women available, choose one, and reserve him or her without speaking to anyone. The Internet makes the whole process easier and "safer," though certainly not legal.

Some sex workers actually do form some attachment to their clients, but typically bartering sex for money is devoid of relationship. The goal is to simulate flirtation, demonstration, and romance. What actually happens in most cases is a replication of childhood sexual abuse in which the child seemingly gains power while being forced to be sexual with a caregiver. If a prostitute is a sex addict—meaning that she or he finds sex more pleasurable with clients than in personal relationships and is "hooked on the life"—the situation represents a significant distortion of normal courtship. Often the money exchanged is a sign of success in the sexual "game." Forging significant, enduring bonds or being true to oneself is not part of the game.

Intrusive Sex

People who carry out intrusive sex, such as touching people in crowds or making obscene calls, are really perverting the touching and foreplay dimensions of courtship. In most cases, they are using others for sexual arousal with little chance of being caught. Their behavior represents both intimacy failure and individuation difficulties. Although their behavior is predatory, they do not see it as such. An implicit anger exists here. They "steal" sex because they believe no one would respond as they want. The goal becomes "taking sex" without the other's knowledge. They become quite expert in their subterfuge. Professionals such as physicians, clergy, or attorneys can fall prey to intrusive sex just as easily as anyone else. For example, they can use their occupation to appear quite compassionate when in fact they use their clients' vulnerability for their own arousal. Sue's story is typical of such abuse:

> I saw Dr. "X," a gynecologist, for the first time because of a Pap smear that showed irregular cells. I chose him because my family physician was concerned about cervical cancer. During his digital exam, this gynecologist, well, he just kept his fingers inside me too long. It felt like something more than just an exam, like he was getting off on it. And then when he talked to me afterwards, he kept touching me. It was

nothing really overt, but I really had an icky feeling when I walked out
of that exam room.

Sue felt "icky" for good reason. This doctor was crossing sexual
boundaries with her. He was exploiting the power he had as a doctor for
sexual gratification in a very covert, yet intrusive, way.

For these types of people, stolen intrusion becomes the obsession, and
ongoing relationship life suffers because of secret shame. These people may
try to enter nonsexual realms of the Internet and make them sexual. They
may go into nonsexual chat rooms like the game room and have sexual conversations. Or people will occasionally enter live video sites that are clearly
nonsexual (such as online "coffeehouses" where the discussions focus on
philosophy, politics, books, and so forth) and try to turn the conversation
to sex or even expose themselves to others with a live video cam. Some men
will go into teen chat rooms, pretend they are a teen, ask for a photo exchange, and then send in photos of themselves naked. This is very intrusive,
and illegal, since they know that the teens are underage.

Some people keep sexually explicit screen savers on their work computers that may intrude on others. Public libraries currently have a problem
with people who view or download and print pornographic material just so
other library patrons will see it. Again, this is intrusive and harassing. It is
intentionally crossing a boundary by confronting people with a sexual
image that they did not agree to see.

Paying for Sex

These people are willing participants in simulated intimacy. They may pay
for sex using a credit card on live video feeds and have someone perform
the sexual acts they want to see. They may pay for porn, often spending
hundreds of dollars a month for membership in many Internet porn sites.
And today there are increasing numbers of prostitution rings online, sites
through which you can schedule the time and place where your offline
meeting will take place. This system bridges the gap between online and offline prostitution, since payment and arrangements take place online, with
the meeting happening offline in the physical world. For those who obses-
sively pay for sex, the costs can be staggering. The income of participants
doesn't seem to matter; all spend beyond their means. The guy with a

$500,000 annual salary will spend $5,000 for a night with a playmate, while the guy making $40,000 a year will continue to do $25-to-$40 deals in the backseat of his car with street prostitutes. There are records of people who've spent $500,000 on prostitutes in just two months. All who pay for sex are focused, however, on the touching, foreplay, and intercourse dimensions while ignoring the work (and ultimately, the benefits) of a relationship.

ANONYMOUS SEX

Perhaps no other medium serves the need for anonymous sex better than the Internet. It provides the ultimate in anonymity. Frequently, part of the attraction for these people is the risk of unknown persons and situations. People go online for the sole purpose of finding someone they do not know to be a sex partner. By definition, anonymous sex is not about being in a relationship. With anonymous sex, you do not have to attract, seduce, trick, or even pay. It is simply sex. Frequently, part of the high for sex addicts is the risk encountered with unknown persons and situations. This stems in part from early sexual relationships that were fearful. Having to experience fear in order for arousal or sexual initiation to occur fundamentally distorts the courtship process. The safety of enduring bonds that allow deeper, profound risks of being known by another is never present.

PAIN EXCHANGE SEX

There are many fetish and S and M sites available on the Internet for people who have an interest in this kind of sex and who find it difficult to play it out in the real world. There is an important distinction to be made between people who are merely playing with roles, and engage in mutually consensual S and M activities that cause no damage to either person, versus people for whom this S and M is the only way they know to be sexual. When arousal is predicated on pain, degradation, or humiliation, it simply does not add to a person's health and well-being.

Unfortunately, such activities can and do escalate quickly once these behaviors become compulsive, and this is when people can be seriously hurt. People who take part compulsively in painful, degrading, or dangerous sexual practices, such as "blood sports" (creating wounds that bleed as part of sex) or asphyxiation, often have significant distortions of courtship. Specifically, touching, foreplay, and intercourse become subordinated to a dramatic story line that is usually a reenactment of a childhood abuse experience. Arousal that is based primarily on the experience of pain is a distortion of sexual and relationship health. People whose arousal scenarios are embedded in high-risk sex find enduring relationships to be difficult. They may be downloading S and M images and video clips, and because the only way they know how to act sexually involves degradation and humiliation, their behavior becomes damaging to themselves and others.

EXPLOITIVE SEX

To exploit the vulnerable is clearly distorted courtship. Sex offenders who rape have deep problems with intimacy and anger. Less obvious are nonviolent predators who seduce children or professionals who sexually misbehave with clients. In the workplace, where there is a differential of power, employees can be exploited. When arousal and attraction are dependent on the vulnerability of another, there is a significant courtship problem all along the courtship continuum. Sex addicts in this category will use "grooming" behavior that is carefully designed to build the trust of the unsuspecting victim. Attraction, flirtation, demonstration, romance, and intimacy are all used to gain the confidence of another for sexual exploitation. These people will go to the extent of professing an enduring bond with a much more malevolent intent. Online, exploitive behavior includes sex offenders who target teens and younger children via the Internet or men meeting women online with the intent of arranging an offline meeting so they can force them to be sexual.

PROCEEDING WITH CAUTION ON THE INTERNET

Our human relationships have evolved over millennia in the physical presence of other humans. Today's sudden development of the Internet offers a new and different way to meet others. Can the Internet serve as a healthy and valuable tool to facilitate meeting others? Certainly. Many people continue to find it a place through which they can meet people whom they may not otherwise have been able to meet. Visiting chat rooms and special interest sites, for example, can be a good way to find others with similar interests and to make valuable connections.

Our experience tells us, however, that the Internet provides only the starting point for friendship or romantic relationships. Too many people try to progress through courtship online only to find soon that it's not working out as they'd hoped. This is because it's simply not possible to progress through the steps of courtship online. All the Internet can provide is a kind of prenoticing—a step zero, if you will. Real courtship can progress only if it includes physical connection and all that it brings. People who have had a long online relationship—for a year or two, for example—do learn quite a bit about one another (assuming that they are both being honest), but no matter how much they know, many relationship elements remain missing. The successful long-term online relationships we have witnessed progressed at some point to the phone, and finally (and carefully!) to an actual meeting. That's when courtship really began.

We all have friendships in which we have become physically separated. Despite being geographically apart, we can still maintain those very close relationships via the phone and Internet. When we see our friend, it can seem as though we've never been apart. This happens, however, because we had already completed many of the courtship dimensions before we were separated.

If many years pass without physical contact, however, even the strongest relationships will wane and some of the closeness diminish in the absence of physical companionship. Again, we need face-to-face contact to reinforce our connection; that is, to reinforce the courtship dimensions. Relationships require being in geographic proximity and actual physical contact.

IS IT REALLY CHEATING?

If you are struggling with online relationships and sexuality, you might be saying to yourself, "Well, if cyber-relationships aren't *really* relationships after all, then what's the problem having them? Cybersex isn't infidelity, so why not do it?"

The answer is that every moment you spend in an online relationship or activity is time you could be spending with the people in your life who matter to you. The more time you spend in cyberspace, the more you neglect those relationships. Regardless of whether cyber-relationships are true relationships, the repercussions of them on you, your partner, family, and friends are exactly the same as an offline illicit relationship. By not addressing this issue, you are also putting off the work you need to do to help yourself have richer and more fulfilling offline relationships.

In the next chapter, we will talk about how you can start to make positive changes in your life and begin the healing process.

6

Boundaries

WE'VE NOW TALKED ABOUT courtship and the relationships we have with others. In this chapter, we will look at another relationship, the one you have with yourself. We will introduce the idea of boundaries—what we define as a relationship with yourself—and look at how the computer and the Internet can foster boundary problems and magnify courtship problems and disorders.

We would like you to begin by imagining that you've cloned yourself. Now you must care for this baby, this miniature version of yourself. How would you raise this child? Exactly the way you were raised? Probably not. It's likely that you would raise this child differently—and better—than you were raised. In reality, you would care for this baby as though you were caring for yourself.

In this exercise of caring for your imaginary cloned child, you would regularly ask what would be the most loving thing you could do for him or her in every situation. And that's exactly how you should care for yourself. Treat yourself with the utmost compassion and never be afraid to ask what is best for you at any given time. Having parental feelings toward yourself is healthy. It is your chance to "reparent" yourself. It presents the opportunity to give yourself some of the love, affection, and guidance you missed when you were growing up. It is learning to love and respect and care for *you* that forms the foundation for building appropriate boundaries in your life. Learning to set appropriate boundaries is also the first step in creating a healthy zone in which to live—a Recovery Zone—an idea we will return to in chapter 8.

SAYING NO

Perhaps the most primitive of boundaries is abstinence itself—saying no to something. Let's look at a couple of examples of non-Internet and non-sexual boundaries. Perhaps you want to lose weight, and to do so you've decided to eat more healthy foods and get some exercise every day. For a few weeks, you maintain your new regimen. Then work and family life get busy and you skip exercising for a few days and stop by some fast-food restaurants for quick lunches. How do you feel about yourself? Probably disappointed and maybe even somewhat disgusted. Perhaps you even want to say, "OK, to heck with it," and you pull into the nearest fast-food joint again on your lunch break and dive right into a couple of fat-laden burgers and a super-size order of fries. In so doing, you've broken a boundary you'd set for yourself.

Another example of boundaries might involve a promise made to better handle your finances. You've set a goal to try to save money and to pay off your credit card debt. You become depressed and go on a little spending spree to cheer yourself up. How do you feel about yourself after doing this? You probably thought that shopping would make you feel better, but instead you ended up feeling worse about yourself than before. The items you bought are a daily reminder that you couldn't afford them, so you don't enjoy them, either. You've broken a boundary you set for yourself and now you feel bad.

If you were taking care of yourself, your greater goal would be to get to a point at which you have happiness, enjoyment, *and* relief from living paycheck to paycheck. You must ask yourself this: Is taking care of myself important enough to me that I will do what it takes to make that happen? Author Robert Bly expressed this concept well when he said, "The making of a man is making your body do what it doesn't want to do."[1] You may not *want* to create boundaries in your life, but doing so is absolutely necessary to achieve what you really want in life.

BOUNDARIES MUST BE TAUGHT AND LEARNED

Very young children have no boundaries.[2] Parents need to protect their children from being abused by others and to respectfully help children learn to put limits on their own behavior. It is through the protection and guidance of parents and other caregivers that we eventually learn to have healthy, firm, and flexible boundaries by the time we reach adulthood.

You can also think of boundaries as a kind of "force field" or safety barrier that surrounds us. Emotional and psychological health requires that we know how to set individual boundaries in times of emotional pressure. It also means that we know how to let them down when we want love and nurturing. We also need to know how to set reasonable limits—boundaries—in our relationship with a partner.

The way boundaries are set varies from family to family. People who have grown up in dysfunctional homes with less-than-nurturing parenting usually have inadequately developed boundaries. They may have no boundaries at all or damaged boundaries. They may also use "walls" instead of boundaries, or they may move back and forth between putting up walls and having no boundaries whatsoever.

WHEN BOUNDARIES ARE TOO LOOSE

When boundaries are too loose, children are exposed to invasive abuse—physical, emotional, sexual, or religious—and experiences from which they should be protected.

Physical invasion takes place when one or both parents physically abuse their children. These children may be physically harmed, locked in their rooms, deprived of food, yelled at, or threatened.

Emotional invasion takes place when a parent or other caregiver expects and teaches the child to attend to that adult's own emotional needs. For example, a father who loves tennis relentlessly pushes his boys into playing tennis more than they want to because it makes him happy and he enjoys it. Emotional invasion also occurs when an adult expects from a child a level of understanding and support beyond a child's capabilities. For example, Dad's primary love is his work, so he is seldom home. Mom regularly says to her son, "I don't know what I'd do without you, Paul; I rely on you so much." Paul's mother has unfairly turned to her nine-year-old son for the understanding and emotional support that should be given by her husband, not her child.

Sexual invasion can occur in a variety of ways. It not only includes various forms of inappropriate touch, but may also occur when children are teased regularly about their bodies, when they're told inappropriate sexual jokes, or when they're otherwise sexually harassed. Actually having sex with a child is the most obvious example of this category. It is important to note that if a child is living in an emotionally invasive relationship with a parent, then virtually any form of physical touching—kissing, hugging, lap sitting—can become erotically charged and is a form of sexual abuse.

Religious invasion occurs when, for example, children get messages from their parents that convince them that they are a mistake in the eyes of God. (This discussion about religious abuse is not intended to make a theological statement; it merely recognizes that these behaviors exist.) For example, Lisa, a three-year-old, slid down a banister and fell off and bumped her head. Her mother responded by saying, "I wonder if Jesus wanted you sliding down that banister. If he did, I don't think he would have let you bump your head."

A BOUNDARY SYSTEM WITH "HOLES" IN IT

People with nonexistent boundaries have no sense of being abused or of being abusive to others. They allow others to take advantage of them physically, sexually, emotionally, or spiritually without clear knowledge that they have the right to say "Stop." Nor do they recognize other people's right to have boundaries, moving through the boundaries of others unaware that they are acting inappropriately.

A damaged boundary system has "holes" in it. People with damaged boundaries can set limits at certain times or with certain people. A person may, for example, be able to set boundaries with everyone but authority figures, his or her partner, or his or her children. These people also have only a partial awareness that others have boundaries. Thus, they may step into certain people's lives to try to control or manipulate them. Damaged boundaries can lead people to take responsibility for someone else's feelings, thinking, or behavior. People may feel shame and guilt because their partners insulted someone at a party.

Some people substitute a system of walls made up of anger or fear for boundaries. These walls give off either verbal or nonverbal messages that say, "If you come near me or if you say anything about such-and-such, I'll explode! I might hit you or yell at you, so watch out." Others are then afraid to approach them for fear of triggering that anger. There are also walls created with silence or with words. People using a "wall of silence" become quiet and just seem to "fade into the woodwork." They prefer to observe others rather than interact with them. On the other hand, people using a "wall of words" talk and talk and talk, even when someone politely tries to contribute to the conversation by making a comment or attempting to change the subject.

WHEN BOUNDARIES ARE TOO RIGID

When parents set boundaries too rigidly, they create a "shell" around the children that overly insulates them from the surrounding world. Little can touch these children, including what ought to—love, care, nurturing, and touch itself in the form of physical affection. Such children feel lost, abandoned, and "on their own."

Physical abandonment occurs when a child doesn't have a sense of physical safety (this may happen to latchkey children, for example) or when the parents leave their children for long periods of time. It also occurs when children receive little or no instructions on how to take care of themselves, such as when to go to bed, how to brush their teeth, or how to eat well. Abandonment also occurs in situations where parents are physically present but pay little or no attention to their children.

Emotional abandonment occurs when children are regularly talked out of their feelings. When children come to their parents to talk about something upsetting and are told, "No, you're not upset; that was no big deal," or "Don't be sad," that is emotional abandonment. Though the child experiences feelings, the parents deny the existence or validity of these feelings.

Sexual abandonment occurs when the child does not receive appropriate modeling or instruction about healthy sexuality. Examples include parents who tell their daughter nothing about menstruation until she actually has her first period; parents who offer no support for their children for events that may be embarrassing (for example, the first time they have to take a shower with other kids after gym class); and parents who do not teach their children about safe sex.

Spiritual abandonment occurs when a child does not receive modeling or instruction in healthy spirituality. Parents may not, for example, give the child any opportunity for religious or spiritual instruction. Religious views may be actively or passively denounced. Children receive no teaching about their responsibilities as humans for the welfare of others and the importance of contributing to the greater good of society.

INCONSISTENT BOUNDARIES

It's not unusual for the same child to experience both loose and rigid boundaries. One parent may generally create loose boundaries, while the other parent is setting rigid ones. Here's an example: a father regularly shouts at and puts down his children (a loose boundary), while their mother ignores this situation even when the kids go to her for help. The children are not being heard, protected, and nurtured as they should be (a rigid boundary).

Children may experience abuse in subtle and indirect ways: "Well, we just don't expect you to be as good as your brother, because your brother is just good at everything he does. He's just naturally smarter than you are."

Many adults who are struggling in their relationships grew up in families in which boundaries were either regularly violated or inconsistently set. It is hard for adults to set boundaries and build healthy relationships when an appropriate model was never provided. Attempt to recall incidents of invasion or abandonment from your past. Your mind will allow you to remember incidents as you are able to deal with them.

THE INNER VOICE

Boundaries are a relationship with ourselves, one in which we seek to hear and follow our inner voice. Have your ever had the experience of being about to do something when you hear a voice inside that says, "No, don't do that," but then you do it anyway—even though you were pretty certain that the outcome wouldn't be good? You didn't listen to yourself and you felt bad about it afterward. When we hear, acknowledge, and follow that voice, we are holding to our boundaries. We are honoring our relationship with ourselves. But don't mistake what we are talking about for narcissism or arrogance. We mean making a real commitment to care for yourself in the way that a good parent would by nurturing, supporting, and protecting yourself. Respecting good boundaries means being able to say, "No, I'm not going to do that, even though I want to, because if I do, I'm going to mess up my life."

Keeping boundaries means more than just paying attention to your conscience. Your conscience simply tells you what's right and wrong. We are referring to a level of discernment that grows out of a caring for self rather than from a worry about what the impact of your behavior might be on another. It means honoring your internal sense of what is the best for you. If you act in a way that always honors yourself, your actions will not harm others.

We all have an inner voice that can positively guide our actions. At times, however, we choose to ignore that voice. The ancient Greeks understood this very well, describing it in the myth of the Sirens. The Sirens were maidens who called out with irresistibly lovely voices to sailors, luring them landward toward shipwreck on rocky, dangerous shores. Because their call could distort all sense of time and weather and danger, countless ships followed the "Siren call" to destruction and death.

The Internet and cybersex provide an easy way to mute that voice. They are like the Sirens' call, a seemingly innocent and harmless beckoning to enter a portal that distorts time, perceptions, and values. Cybersex can override your inner voice and begin to collapse your boundaries, just as the reefs crushed the sailors' ships as they followed the Sirens' call. Cybersex is capable of casting a spell under which you no longer think about what you are doing and distractions fall away as you slip deeper and deeper into the cyber-world.

SETH'S DESTRUCTIVE STORY

Seth, a married fifty-five-year-old man, father of two adult children, tells this story:

> I stopped drinking twenty-three years ago. During my thirteenth year of sobriety, I began treatment for serious problems with my sexual behaviors, which included going to prostitutes, pornography use, and extramarital affairs. After much struggle, I got my life back together and became an insurance claims adjuster. Eventually, I became one of my company's best, often traveling throughout the country to handle the biggest and most complicated claims. I was doing quite well for more

than a decade—so well that I even stopped attending Twelve Step meetings. I felt that the support they had provided for so long simply wasn't necessary anymore. And my life was going well—until I discovered cybersex. I became interested in pornography on the Net. Then I started looking around to see what else the Net had to offer in the sexual arena. Soon I discovered I could book prostitutes via the Net. It was quickly downhill from there. When I started using prostitutes and going to strip bars again, I became so despondent that I started drinking on the sly. Because I was on the road, my wife was not aware what was happening. Eventually, I made a pass at two women, both of whom were involved with claims I was investigating. They reported my inappropriate actions to the company and I was promptly fired. In only three short months of destructive behavior, all that I had worked for and built over many years was gone. My wife was devastated by this turn of events. It came as a complete shock to her. She had no idea that I'd been drinking again, let alone been unfaithful to her. She threatened to walk out on the spot. I was able to talk her out of it at the time, but I don't know what will happen to our relationship in the long term.

Seth had worked diligently for many years to create strong boundaries for his behavior. Here was a man who had a solid and long-term recovery with firm boundaries. After all, he was aware of the situations that could trigger his drinking and sexual compulsions. He knew how to stay away from their antecedents, the actions and situations that could become a slippery slope leading him closer to his triggers. Seth at first thought it was safe to dabble in cybersex. "It's not real sex," he told himself. What's more, it didn't seem like any trigger he'd ever encountered or like any of his trigger antecedents. Internet sex turned out to be very powerful, and by stumbling into the world of cybersex, Seth indeed set off many of his old triggers.

Again we see the power of cybersex. Passing through this portal creates an essential distortion in which there is the loss of self as you enter a trance-like state, mesmerized by the Siren call of the Net. Nothing seems real, which is precisely why the Internet makes it so easy to distort your relationship with yourself—your boundaries. It's so easy to tell yourself you're not really doing anything wrong or destructive to yourself or others. There are no impediments or constraints to going online—you need only a computer and a modem. You don't have to lie. You don't need money. You can be anonymous. You don't have to get into a car. You don't have to do anything more than boot up your computer. Boundaries become distorted and collapse easily and silently, almost without thought. "None of this is real," we tell ourselves. The Internet becomes a kind of sensory deprivation tank in which we float mentally, undistracted and untroubled by a suddenly muted inner voice.

INTERNAL AND EXTERNAL BOUNDARIES

There are two sets of boundaries—internal and external (concrete). External boundaries are marked by motivation that comes from outside of ourselves. Often we set external boundaries because we know there will be consequences if we don't set them. People who acknowledge their problems with cybersex may, for example, set an external boundary by

- keeping their computer on the main floor of the house rather than in a more private home office
- choosing a nonsexual screen name
- using the computer only when at work
- not logging on to sexual sites
- giving the password to a spouse or partner so he or she can check computer usage or history files

External boundaries are very concrete steps that help you contain or control your behavior. They are often steps that a spouse or partner or counselor wants you to set, and they are usually easily measurable or verifiable. Going on a diet involves setting and maintaining external boundaries. Let's say that your doctor has told you that you need to lose weight because of heart problems. At her suggestion, you decide to limit your calorie intake to a thousand per day. You decide to cut back on fatty foods and eat more fruits and vegetables, and so forth. These are concrete and measurable steps, and they're also externally motivated.

Setting external boundaries is often a good place to start when making changes in your behavior, but it is only a first step. (In the next chapter, we will show you exactly how to set appropriate and concrete external boundaries that are the first step in recovering from cybersex behaviors.) Too often, people believe that this is the only step they need to take to get control of a problem. Establishing concrete boundaries, however, is not enough. You also need to establish internal boundaries, which is essentially the process of learning to care for your inner self. Without internal boundaries, you will, in the long run, always find ways around your external boundaries. Having appropriate internal boundaries means taking actions because you inherently know that by doing so, you are caring for yourself and doing what is good for you. This is, as you might recognize, a more difficult and longer-term project.

The good news is that keeping your internal and external boundaries becomes easier over time. A new system emerges. You will begin to build momentum and strength as the weeks, months, and years pass, in much the same way that your problematic behaviors became stronger and more difficult to control over time. As you set and keep boundaries, you'll find yourself feeling good about having met your goals. As time passes, you'll continue to feel better about yourself and your life.

As you know, boundaries are about the relationship that you have with yourself. Relationships with others also require us to establish boundaries. Before you can set any boundaries with others, though, you must have clear and firm boundaries with yourself. You have to be able to hear that voice that says yes or no, right or wrong. You have to understand your own limits and boundaries.

If you have a history of problematic or addictive sexual behavior, it's likely that you have trouble recognizing and trusting your inner voice and that you have weak or even nonexistent boundaries. The Internet has merely provided you with another way to act out.

If, on the other hand, you have become involved with cybersex but have never fallen into anything sexual like this before, it's likely that you can hear and pay attention to your inner voice and that you still have fairly intact internal and external boundaries. The power of the Internet and the lure of cybersex may weaken or bypass your boundaries.

CULTURAL CYBERSEX BOUNDARIES

The struggle so many people are having with cybersex is exacerbated by the fact that our culture has yet to establish clear boundaries with regard to the

Internet. We have barely begun to discuss what is appropriate Internet content and behavior, with the exception of acknowledging the illegality of trafficking in child pornography and advertising for or booking prostitutes online. Even those boundaries, however, are blurred. Software programs are now available that, for example, "generate" people. From an array of photos, users can choose different people's eyes, ears, noses, arms, and so on, and from these disparate parts construct a new photo of a "person," albeit one who doesn't really exist. Some people have been generating pornographic photos of children with this program by taking "pieces" from photos of real children and putting them together to create photos of nonexistent children. Since they technically aren't photos of real children, are these photos pornographic? Is sending them around the Net trafficking in child pornography?

In some of the personal stories we've detailed in this book, you've seen other examples of this cultural struggle. Is an affair on the Internet really an affair? If you're not actually having physical contact with another person, can we say that one has been unfaithful or adulterous? What about exposing one's genitals: it's illegal to do this in public, but is it illegal to do so on the Net from the privacy of your own home?

Because our culture is still struggling to develop boundaries for the Internet, people don't really have much support as they try to develop personal boundaries regarding cybersex. With the Internet, we have created an entirely new way to connect with one another. Thus far, at least, it is one without guidelines and without history. It's uninhibited. It's different from television and radio because of its interactiveness. What's more, the technology developed, emerged, and has been embraced by so many people so quickly that we've been unable as a culture to keep up with the many different ways that people can use the Internet for sexual purposes (such as creating computer-generated photos). Without culturewide consensus, the inner voice that helps keep us safe in other areas is compromised.

The Catholic Church defined virtual sexual relationships as infidelity in 2000. That statement is an example of the culture beginning to sort out and define what is morally acceptable Internet behavior. We can expect more institutions to do likewise so that people have norms and guidelines to follow. In the meantime, however, each of us will have to set our own boundaries.

You might be thinking, "OK, since there aren't really any rules, how can I be breaking any? There's nothing wrong with my behavior." Just because

few cultural boundaries exist doesn't mean that there shouldn't be boundaries, nor does it mean that we should feel free to do whatever we want.
There are internal anchors available to help us determine whether our behavior is right or wrong—our own moral/value system. If you believe it's
wrong, for example, to have an affair, then you can infer that it's wrong to
have a cyber-affair. In addition, you can pay attention to your inner voice.
How would it feel to you, for example, to carry out an online affair unbe-
knownst to your spouse or partner? How would that person feel if he or she
discovered your "affair"? What would be the effect of your online behavior
on others? Would it be any different from a physical-world affair? No. Both
have similar effects on all involved and both cause a breach in trust. You
can also look at the effect of your online behavior on other aspects of your
life. Are they positive or negative? Are they making your life happier and
more fulfilling or are they making things worse?

When people compromise their boundaries, even if they don't realize
that they've done so, they still feel a sense of shame. That feeling of shame is
a signal that you've broken a boundary. It's an indicator that you've done
something that, on some level, you do not feel good about doing. It means
that at some level, you wish that you had not done that behavior. And this
brings you back to not caring for yourself, not knowing what you need to
do to care for yourself, or not listening to what your inner voice is telling
you is best for you. In most people, this feeling arises immediately after
they've broken a boundary. They may say to themselves, "How could I do
that again? I promised myself I wouldn't do that. I don't like myself when I
do that." At a deep level, even if you didn't consciously recognize it, you
have an internal boundary that tells you it is not OK for you to do certain
actions because you know they will hurt you and perhaps another person too.

We want you to ask yourself—to pay attention to—how you feel after
participating in cybersex. Do you feel guilty? Do you feel ashamed? Disgusted? If you're thinking about this now, you might initially say to yourself, "No, this isn't me. I don't have any problem. I feel fine when I've been
on the Internet. I'm just sexually liberated." If you scored high on the
screening tests in chapters 1 and 2, and if you take some time to really think
about this and to pay attention to your feelings, you may discover a different response. And you may realize that what you are doing is causing pain
or shame in your life and sorrow in the lives of the people you love.

CHANGING BOUNDARIES

You may have the impression now that boundaries must be rigid, even absolute, in order to be effective. In fact, boundaries can, and in some cases should, change. To illustrate this idea, let's look at families and the ways they organize themselves into what are called family systems.

A healthy family has the capacity to organize and reorganize itself as it grows and changes—in other words, to develop, set, and change boundaries. Family system models generally recognize four levels of adaptability within families. Each of the four levels represents a range of behavior options.

- Rigid: Rigid families use extremely autocratic decision-making styles in which there is limited negotiation, with strictly defined roles and rules.
- Structured: Structured families mix authoritarian with some egalitarian leadership, resulting in stable roles and rules.
- Flexible: Flexible families use egalitarian leadership, seeking negotiated agreements and making for easily changed rules and roles.
- Chaotic: Chaotic families have erratic and ineffective leadership that results in impulsive decisions, inconsistent rules, and role reversals.

Structured and flexible systems are regarded as the best for optimum family and individual growth. Healthy families move between these two systems depending on various factors. For example, a family with two children under the age of five would thrive in a structured format, given the need for consistency and direction of small children. When the children are older, the same family will shift to a more flexible mode, given the need and ability for the children to handle more autonomy and decision making.

Of course, every family has its moments of chaos and rigidity, but families that remain in the extremes damage their members. For example, children who live in rigid families end up with lifelong struggles with rules and authority—whether it is in excessive rebelliousness or excessive passivity—because of the unreachable expectations of their parents. Chaotic families produce children who have difficulty incorporating a consistent set of boundaries into their own consciences because no one ever showed them how to set boundaries or had any expectation of them to do so. An intriguing aspect of systems is that opposite extremes have similar consequences. Both rigidity and chaos affect conscience formation and boundary-setting ability.

A family's inability to adapt to children's needs becomes extremely important because of the close connection between a child's need to depend on others and compulsive/addictive behaviors. To illustrate, in rigid families, children who ask for help may receive assistance, but with a heavy price in the form of lectures, high expectations, and moralizing about failure. Under those conditions, children quickly learn not to ask for help. In chaotic families, when children ask for help, the assistance is incomplete, inconsistent, or doesn't come at all. Rather than embarrass their parents again and subject themselves to further confusion and disapproval, the children simply stop asking.

Children need to be able to count on—to depend on—their families for survival, nurturing, love, and approval. If the family doesn't provide it, they will look for what they can depend upon, and they find it. Drugs, alcohol, food, and sex always produce a predictable, albeit an ultimately self-destructive, high. If a child develops a reliance on these external sources, pleasurable experiences become the primary relationship upon which he or she relies.

Healthy adults have a range of boundaries covering all areas of their lives, including relationships with family members, work colleagues, legal issues, and so on. And at times, we change our boundaries. If, for example, a man is struggling with online sexual behaviors, we might suggest that masturbation is not an acceptable behavior for a time because that was what he did whenever he felt lonely, angry, or sad. In six months or a year, when he better understands himself and is feeling better about himself and his marital relationship, we might say that it's OK to masturbate. Boundaries can have a fluidity and flexibility to them, depending on what's going on in your life.

The danger, of course, is that we can all be good at coming up with reasons for changing our boundaries. Each of the examples of problematic online sexual behavior in this book shows how somebody rationalized boundary changes. You might, for example, have set a boundary that says you won't use your computer at work for sexual purposes. But, during a particularly stressful day, you might find yourself thinking that just for today, just for five or ten minutes, you will log on to a sexually explicit Web site at work to feel a little better.

THERE IS HELP OUT THERE: NO NEED TO GO IT ALONE

We encourage people who are working to change their sexual behaviors to develop and rely on a strong support group. If you are thinking about changing a boundary in your life, it's important to talk it over with someone in your support group before you change it. And that means talking to a live person, not leaving a message on his or her answering machine, such as, "OK, today I'm changing my boundary about pornography at work. I'm sure this will be OK with you. Good-bye." You need to actually talk it over with another person who will help you to look at why you're thinking about this change and to determine whether this is a healthy change.

Again, we come back to asking what is really best for you—whether an action will support your relationship with yourself. If you cross that boundary at work, how will you feel about yourself when you get home or when you talk with those in your support group and tell them what you did? All the smaller boundaries are tied to this basic one.

Some people have a tendency to react to their problematic or addictive sexual behavior by saying something like this: "OK, so I have this problem. Sex is a problem, so forget it. I just won't have anything to do with sex at all. I'll just stop."

Complete abstinence is not a solution, and this kind of thinking is just a move to an opposite extreme. It's similar to members of a chaotic family deciding to become rigid. As we've pointed out, we should seek the middle ground, which is a healthy sexuality.

Setting appropriate boundaries is critical to building and maintaining healthy relationships, successful recovery, and relapse prevention. It requires a critical restructuring of the relationship to yourself. Intimacy problems start with you and your boundaries. People who struggle with compulsive or addictive behaviors have not experienced or learned normal, healthy ways of nurturing themselves and respecting their own limits. What makes such a person vulnerable to the Net and to cybersex must be repaired in order to develop a healthy sexuality.

In previous chapters, you have explored the components that contribute to problematic Internet sexual behavior. You have taken screening tests and you've learned about arousal templates, the components of courtship, and courtship disorders. In this chapter, we have talked about boundaries and how to set and maintain them. We have looked at ways to determine whether or not you are a person who can and does listen to your inner voice. You've seen how appropriate boundaries are a critical component of healthy relationships and that they play an important role in successful recovery from problematic and addictive online sexual behavior.

As you look at these areas of your life, can you recognize the role boundaries play in your life? Can you recognize a pattern in your sexual behavior? Can you see particular areas that are not going well? If so, you may be experiencing a number of feelings: guilt, sadness, shame, remorse, despair, and hopelessness. If you are, this is a good sign. It means that you are able to look more honestly at yourself and your behaviors. This is the first and critical step in making a positive change in your life.

Be assured that there is hope for successful change. In the next and subsequent chapters, we will help you leave problematic and addictive sexual behaviors behind. We will show you how to develop more healthy relationships and a more fulfilling sex life. We will help you set appropriate boundaries and determine what people in your life can help you through this transition and maintain this new, positive direction in your life.

7
Taking That First Step

AT THIS POINT, YOU MAY BE EXPERIENCING a range of feelings—confusion, concern, frustration, anger—as you begin to look more closely at the situation you're in, feelings of loss and hopelessness. Such feelings are very common. The good news, although it may be hard to believe right now, is that understanding the significance of your problem is really the beginning of the recovery process. In this chapter, we will help you understand the extent of your problem and how, by doing so, you're taking a big step forward in attaining recovery. You've probably had many moments when you resolved to change, control, or stop your cybersex behaviors, but you didn't. That's because you didn't really understand that you had a serious problem. What we're talking about now is how you can get to the point of accepting your situation and as a result make positive changes.

NO MORE CYBERSEX

In the language of Twelve Step recovery, you are beginning to take a First Step. A First Step has two critical components, the first being to acknowledge your limitations. This means acknowledging that perhaps you aren't the same as most other people when it comes to cybersex. When you participate in it, you, unlike many others, can't control your usage. The second component of a First Step is to accept that you need help with this problem and that support may come in various forms such as therapy, medication, spiritual growth, behavioral changes, and personal exploration and growth.

In addition, it's time to recognize and acknowledge that your cybersex behavior is damaging you and others in your life and it can't continue.

We certainly don't advocate that people with compulsive addiction become celibate for the rest of their lives. We instead want to help them find a way to develop a healthy sex life, which is much different from a life immersed in cybersex. Just as an alcoholic must stop drinking completely, so, too, must you stop your cybersex activities. Cybersex is a behavior that some people simply cannot control. There's no middle ground. Cybersex is an activity you can't take part in any longer. "Controlled" use doesn't work because it's just too easy to fall back into compulsive behaviors. There's no room for negotiation.

THE GRIEVING PROCESS

Once you accept the fact that cybersex is an activity you can't take part in because you can't control it, you will begin a grieving process. Initially, this process involves some denial—denial that the problem exists and that there is any need to change. Eventually, we all go through a grieving process when we finally accept that there are limitations in our lives. There's a feeling of loss when you have to accept that there's an activity—drinking, gambling, or cybersex, for example—that other people can take part in that you cannot. Grief is part of addiction, and Twelve Step recovery programs are really a grieving process. We will return to this idea at the end of the chapter.

Your feelings of grief will likely center around the following four areas: (1) realizing that you can't engage in cybersex any longer; (2) the "death" of your sexual fantasy life; (3) the impact of past losses as a result of your cybersex behaviors; and (4) a fear of not knowing who you'll be or what you will do without cybersex because it has been like a "friend" who provides you comfort.

REALIZING THAT YOU CAN'T ENGAGE IN CYBERSEX ANY LONGER
All recovering alcoholics, for example, eventually come to the realization that when they consume alcohol, they just aren't like most other people they know. Try as they might have, often over many years, they simply can't control their alcohol use. Cybersex presents a similar problem for you, and

you have to acknowledge that even though other people you know may be able to dabble in cybersex, you cannot. Occasional or moderate use quickly becomes an obsession.

The Death of Your Sexual Fantasy Life

You, like many people, probably had and still have numerous sexual fantasies, some of them "forbidden." At some point, you discovered sex sites on the Internet and soon realized that you could access any fantasy you ever had, not to mention new ones. You discovered a whole new world where you could have sex with hundreds of partners. Cybersex became the answer to your dreams. But eventually you became so wrapped up in those fantasies that you lost touch with life in the real world. You've discovered that you have to let go of your cybersex life and that there are sexual limitations. In reality, creating a rich, fulfilling relationship with one person is where the real challenge lies. Your fantasy life is nothing more than an imaginary trip beyond your limits, beyond what is really possible. By living in that fantasy world, you are actually preventing yourself from having a relationship that will be truly meaningful. With the realization that you can't have it all, however, comes a profound sense of loss.

The Impact of Past Losses as a Result of Your Cybersex Behaviors

At this point in the recovery process, when people begin to acknowledge what's been happening to them, they suddenly look back on their lives only to finally see the fallout that they've left behind—all the relationships that they've destroyed, the botched jobs, and the lost educational opportunities. The damage assessment begins, and they examine the consequences of their behavior.

You might think of the months or years you were participating in cybersex as riding the crest of a wave that became larger as it accumulated the consequences of your cybersex behavior. But now, time has run out. The wave is coming up against the shoreline of reality and you can't pull off and paddle back out for another ride because it's simply grown too big. As the wave begins breaking, what you're feeling is all those consequences crashing down around you, tossing you like a pebble in the undertow. You see, feel, and are surrounded all at once by all of it.

Suddenly, you feel the pain of all the unacknowledged losses of family, friends, job opportunities, and relationships. The embarrassment of having been discovered by a spouse, partner, or employer comes crashing through. And perhaps you are realizing just how much time you've lost doing cybersex. There may have been countless hours that could have been spent enjoying friends and family, reading, taking classes, exercising, playing sports, achieving greater success and financial rewards at work, and much more.

These are the origins of your grief. It can feel overwhelming when it is with you all the time. Since you were unaware of or denied your losses along the way, you couldn't grieve them at the time they occurred. Now they appear in front of you all at once because you've finally been able to let yourself see them.

As you become more aware of your losses, you may also feel ashamed, so much so that you may be tempted to put a barrier between you and others. While these feelings are natural and common, you should not further isolate yourself. This is, in fact, what you have been doing all along with cybersex. It's only through reconnecting with others that you will begin to heal and recover from your struggle with compulsive sexual behavior on the Internet. Recovery comes only with the support of others. Later in this chapter, we will show you how to build a strong support group.

A FEAR OF NOT KNOWING WHO YOU'LL BE WITHOUT CYBERSEX

Over time, your whole identity became wrapped up in your cybersex use when it became your life focus. Even though you knew at some level that this was unhealthy, your identity became firmly linked with your cybersex use. In a sense, it has defined who you are as a person. You grew comfortable in this identity. Cybersex became your best friend. Now, when you're anxious or upset, it is still your source of comfort. Without it, you feel lost. Shame also became part of your identity. You feel bad about what you're doing, you're incapable of stopping, and you're worried about what will take the place of cybersex and how you'll handle life without it.

THE CRITICAL IMPORTANCE OF A FIRST STEP

The First Step is not an easy one. It's difficult because it brings many emotions to the surface, one of which is fear of the unknown. You may wonder how you can live without cybersex, since it has been your identity and life focus. Being worried about this admission is natural. Many other people have felt exactly the same way. Courageously, they took that First Step and eventually recovered from their compulsive or addictive behaviors to live happy and fulfilling lives.

Taking the First Step is absolutely necessary. It's a prerequisite for everything that follows. Without it, your chances of learning to manage your behavior are slim. Step One is the foundation for future work, and until you create this foundation, none of the other Steps we will suggest will work.

Earlier in the book, we used food and eating as an analogy. In that same vein, when we are cooking, we follow a recipe, either from a cookbook or from one we keep in our memories. In most recipes, there are certain ingredients that can be manipulated or even left out altogether without substantially compromising the result. But there are other ingredients that are essential to each recipe. Step One fits in the latter category. Without Step One, the recipe for recovery will be a flop.

Yes, Step One is difficult and painful. But we want to emphasize again that it is really the beginning of recovery. It is true that life will seem worse before it feels better. But that's because you're eliminating your "medication"—the behavior you've been using to anesthetize the pain of all your losses during the time you've been doing cybersex. It has become an emotional anesthetic, hiding the pain.

If you look back, you can probably find points in your life when you started to feel some of the losses and consequences of your behavior. What did you do then? Did you turn away and flee back into cybersex behaviors? If so, what was the result? Probably nothing changed and your life just kept getting worse.

When you stop these behaviors, you experience your losses and pain. Remember, part of the goal of a First Step is to provide a safe place to begin experiencing this pain. It's OK—even necessary—to let yourself experience all the feelings that have been pent up inside you. In the end, you will feel better. This process is akin to going into a house that's been shuttered and closed for a long time and throwing open the doors and windows to let in the fresh air and sun. You are throwing open the windows on being fully human.

RATIONALIZATIONS THAT INTERFERE WITH THE FIRST STEP

We all have a natural tendency to develop rationalizations to protect our-selves from things that are frightening and painful. When we begin the grieving process, for whatever reason, it's likewise quite natural to develop certain rationalizations to protect ourselves from it.

As you begin your First Step, you will soon begin to see just how misleading and false the following eight rationalizations truly are. In Step One, you will look more closely at the three key tasks of a First Step: recognizing your powerlessness over cybersex behaviors, determining ways your life has become unmanageable because of these behaviors, and examining the consequences of these behaviors. People recovering from problematic cybersex behaviors typically experience some of the following eight rationalizations.

Rationalization 1: It's not real.
Cyberspace isn't real. There are no people. There are no rules. There are no consequences (that are immediately apparent, at least!). I can indulge in cybersex without worrying about it.

Rationalization 2: Cybersex doesn't hurt others.
I'm not having skin-to-skin contact, so it's not sex, and it's not affecting anyone. No one can get a disease. It can't hurt anyone if it's not a problem. I'm not unfaithful because I haven't really done anything with anybody. Even when I'm in a chat room, for example, it's all still make-believe. In re-ality, most of the time, I'm not even who I say I am. There is no direct harm to anybody and there isn't anything I need to be accountable for.

Rationalization 3: Cybersex doesn't hurt me.
I'm just on the computer, so what's the big deal? It's no different from surf-ing other kinds of Web sites on the Internet. There aren't any conse-quences. As long as I don't have skin-to-skin contact, I'm not hurting myself at all.

Rationalization 4: I can stop anytime I want; I just need to turn off the computer.

None of this is real, anyway. I'm not actually going to a strip club, seeing a prostitute, or exposing myself to a real person. Besides, all I need to do is shut down the computer and everything goes away.

Rationalization 5: I've already done a First Step.

People who are already in a Twelve Step recovery program might think, "I've already done a First Step for sex addiction (or for alcohol use, gambling, or another addiction), so why would I need to do another one? Besides, I haven't (fill in the blank) for years."

Rationalization 6: Cybersex doesn't have any consequences.

I can't get a sexually transmitted disease. It's not going to destroy my marriage if others don't have my mailing address or know where I live. Using the computer is so private. No one knows my access codes. When I'm online at work, well, that's no different from taking a short coffee break in the cafeteria.

Rationalization 7: It's just a game—it's virtual reality.

This isn't serious because it's not real. That's why it's called *virtual* reality. It's fun, it's my entertainment, it really doesn't hurt anybody, and it doesn't bother anybody. Who would ever take this seriously? I don't really mean anything by any of this. It's really not any different from a video game.

Rationalization 8: I just use it occasionally. Cybersex doesn't interfere with or jeopardize things in my life.

I'm not on the computer all the time or anything like that. I just go on when I feel like it. It's just something to do. I'm still in a good relationship with my partner, have a good job, and spend time with my kids. It's no big deal!

POWERLESSNESS

"Powerlessness" means being unable to stop your cybersex behaviors no matter how hard you try and despite negative consequences. Have you tried to stop, cut back, set limits on, or change the patterns of your use?

You may, for example, have promised yourself you wouldn't use your computer at work for cybersex, especially after your information services department began monitoring Internet use, yet you continued to do so despite the danger. You might have promised yourself you'd never go to a particular sexual Web site again, but you ended up at a similar one. You may have promised yourself that you'd never stay online past 11:00 P.M. to engage in cybersex activities, but you found yourself online in the middle of the night at least three nights in the last week.

Consider how much you have been preoccupied with cybersex and how much you have been using it as a way to reduce anxiety in your life. How have your thinking and activities revolved around your cybersex use? Planning your day around your use, daydreaming about when you'll be free to participate in cybersex, and becoming anxious and angry when situations arise that prevent you from using are examples of preoccupation and powerlessness.

It's also important to note that any attempt to control your cybersex behavior is an indication that it is already out of control.

Powerlessness Inventory

In the space below or on a separate sheet of paper, begin your own powerlessness inventory. List examples that show how powerless you have been to stop your Internet sexual behavior. Be explicit about types of behavior and frequency. Start with your earliest example of being powerless and conclude with your most recent. Write down as many examples as you can think of. By doing so, you will see the pattern of broken promises emerge and add significantly to the depth of your understanding of your powerlessness over these behaviors.

1.

2.

3.

4.

5.

6.

UNMANAGEABILITY

Unmanageability and powerlessness are closely intertwined. Unmanageability is, in fact, the manifestation of powerlessness. When you lose the ability to control your cybersex behavior, it affects all aspects of your life and soon becomes unmanageable. "Unmanageability" means that your cybersex use has created chaos and damage in your life. These are the consequences of powerlessness.

How do you see your life as unmanageable as a result of your cybersex behaviors?

1.

2.

3.

4.

5.

6.

CONSEQUENCES

When you stop and really look at the results of your cybersex behavior, you will see for the first time just how you and many others have been affected in a variety of different ways. Read and answer each of the following questions honestly. Spend as much time as you need to complete this exercise. Later, you may want to share your answers with others who are helping you in recovery, such as your sponsor or therapist.

SOCIAL LIFE
Have your cybersex behaviors affected your social life? If so, how?

Have you become more isolated from friends? If so, in what ways?

Do you spend so much time online that you're too tired to go out?

List three specific examples of how your cybersex behaviors have affected your social life.

1.

2.

3.

PHYSICAL CONDITION
What impact have your cybersex behaviors had on you physically?

Do you have difficulty sleeping?

Do you find yourself without energy?

Do you find it difficult to exercise as regularly as you once did?

List three examples of how your cybersex behaviors have affected your physical condition.

1.

2.

3.

ECONOMIC SITUATION
What impact have your cybersex behaviors had on your financial condition?

- Overspending?
- Loss of job or job promotions?
- Mismanagement of household funds?

List three examples of how your cybersex behaviors have affected you economically.

1.

2.

3.

JOB OR PROFESSION
What impact have cybersex behaviors had on your work and career? Problems can surface such as

- lowered productivity
- frequent absenteeism
- deteriorating quality of product or decision making
- frequent tardiness

List three examples of how your cybersex behaviors have affected your work and career.

1.

2.

3.

SCHOOL

If you are a student, problems like these may surface as a result of your cybersex behaviors:

- not keeping up with homework assignments
- frequent absenteeism
- lower grades
- social isolation

If applicable, list three examples of how your cybersex behaviors have affected your school-related social activities or education.

1.

2.

3.

EMOTIONAL PROBLEMS

How has your cybersex use affected you emotionally? Emotional problems can include

- depression
- feelings of low self-esteem
- difficulty in getting close to others or in expressing feelings
- extreme feelings of loneliness
- unexplained fears

List three examples of how your cybersex behaviors have affected you emotionally.

1.

2.

3.

FAMILY PROBLEMS
How have your cybersex behaviors interfered with relationships that mean the most to you?

- Loss of closeness?
- A feeling that other family members have lost respect for you?
- Using family members emotionally or financially?
- Extreme feelings of remorse or guilt?
- Withdrawing from family activities?
- Being unfaithful to your partner or spouse?

List three examples of how your cybersex behaviors have affected your closest relationships.

1.

2.

3.

ACCEPTING YOURSELF

Your admission of powerlessness and unmanageability marks the beginning of your recovery. But you must go beyond admission to acceptance—acceptance that your behavior has been compulsive—and come to the realization that you need ongoing help to achieve freedom from its power.

When you finally take time to really look at your behaviors, the result

can be shocking. You're probably saying to yourself, "So I have this problem and it's out of control. What can I do? How can I get my life back together?" Regardless of your worries, take heart, because you are now on
the road to recovery from these behaviors.

MAKING CHANGES

Before we look at specific changes you can make in your behavior, we want
to introduce you to two levels of change—first-order and second-order
changes.[1] These two levels parallel respectively the setting of external and internal boundaries, which we explored in chapter 6. First-order changes are
very concrete actions that are taken to quickly stop a problem and to address
specific consequences. First-order changes can also be well described by the
French aphorism "The more things change, the more they remain the same."
For example, think of Marie, a woman who's been married three times, each
time to an alcoholic. She changed husbands but still found herself in the same
situation. She did not change her life with each marriage. Instead, she continued to marry and live with alcoholics. First-order changes won't help anyone solve compulsive or addictive behaviors *on a permanent basis.* They are
literally about trying harder at things that won't work in the long run.

    It is important to understand that compulsion or addiction of any kind
is a first-order phenomenon. The harder addicts try to stop their behavior
alone and in secret, the more their failure is guaranteed. Only when they
break the rules of compulsion or addiction by seeking help for their addiction will they be able to begin making the second-order changes needed to
free themselves of these behaviors.

    Second-order changes are those steps that you take to actually change
the dynamics of your life and the way you live. Second-order changes for
Marie, for example, would include going to therapy and stopping dating.
During therapy, she learns that she comes from an alcoholic family and that
this background has been the basis for her selection of men.

    Both first-order and second-order changes address the issue of unmanage-
ability. In this chapter, we will offer suggestions for first-order changes, and
in chapter 8 we will look at second-order changes.

    To further illustrate the difference between the two types, let's imagine
that you were hurt in an auto accident. When the paramedics arrive, the

first action they take is to determine if you're breathing. Then they look for and control any severe bleeding that could bring immediate death. They would also immobilize any broken bones at this time. First-order changes are the splints, airways, and pressure bandages used to begin healing compulsive or addictive behaviors. They will stabilize your life in the short run by immediately controlling behavior and consequences.

Let's return again to that "accident." If you have internal injuries, your life will still be in danger. Dealing with such injuries takes more time and care, as well as professional staff in a hospital setting. Treating only the superficial wounds won't save your life. Likewise, you need second-order changes to recover in the long run from your compulsive or addictive behaviors. Second-order changes take more time, but eventually the whole person is healed, inside and out.

You may be tempted to skip over the first-order changes and go straight to the second-order changes. Carrying our analogy further illustrates why this is a bad idea. Focusing only on the internal injuries—with "second-order" care—would not be effective because you'd die of hemorrhage or shock before treatment for the internal injuries could be given. Thus, both first-order and second-order changes are necessary because both play a crucial role in healing.

EXAMPLES OF FIRST-ORDER CHANGES

The boundaries you'll start with may seem rather restrictive. That's because, for the time being, you need external limits and controls that will give you very little room to maneuver. Then, as you get more control over your behaviors and your life, you'll be able to loosen the restrictions and see how well you can cope with more flexibility. The first-order changes you need to put into effect fit into five categories. These categories suggest that you reduce access, reduce anonymity, reduce objectification, make yourself accountable, and develop healthy online habits.

REDUCE ACCESS

- If your computer is in a relatively private setting in your home, move it into a higher-traffic area that is more regularly frequented by family members. Don't, for example, keep it in a home office, in your bedroom, or in an area where you can close a door for privacy. Instead, move it into your family room.

- Don't go online except when others are at home.
- Set limits for when and how long you're allowed to use your computer. In addition, set a curfew for evening use, such as an 11:00 P.M. deadline.
- Use electronic limits to reduce your access. With a sponsor, acquire and run software protection such as Net Nanny, Cyber Sitter, Cyber Patrol, or Guard Dog, which prevent you from getting into the sexual Web sites.
- Switch to a "safe" Internet service provider. A number of family-oriented Internet service providers, for example, carefully screen out sexual sites and often provide better protection than software like Net Nanny. To find one in your area, type "family-oriented service providers" into an Internet search engine such as Google or Yahoo.
- If you were using your computer at work for cybersex, leave your office door open whenever you're using the computer and place your monitor so that others can see it as they walk by.
- Avoid any chat rooms that are at all sexual in nature.

Reduce Anonymity

- Be sure that your e-mail addresses and screen names actually identify you, even if it's only your real first name. No more hiding behind fictitious identities.
- Confide in at least two other people (in addition to your spouse or partner) about your problem. (We'll talk more about finding a sponsor shortly.)

Reduce Objectification

- Regularly remind yourself that those with whom you communicate on the Net *are* real human beings with feelings, hopes, worries, and loved ones, just as you are, and they can be affected by your interactions with them. This Internet is *not* a video game.

MAKE YOURSELF ACCOUNTABLE

- Allow a trusted friend, sponsor, or therapist to monitor your behavior and access. Give this person access to your computer history files. Make yourself accountable to this person for the time you spend online and what you did online.

DEVELOP HEALTHY ONLINE HABITS

It is very important to understand that we are not saying you can't use your computer or the Internet. While that might actually be the best option, the Internet has become such an integral part of many of our personal and work lives that we simply have to have access for many reasons. You can learn to use the Internet for only healthy purposes by developing healthy online habits and accessing supportive recovery online resources. For example:

- Get an online sponsor.
- Develop e-mail buddies who are also recovering from problematic online sexual behavior.
- Find and use Web sites that can support your recovery rather than undermine it.
- Find and visit online support groups. For example, "Today's Thought" at www.hazelden.org will provide you with an encouraging thought each day.

In chapter 8, we will also introduce you to a Web site that has been created exclusively for this book so that you can use it as you progress in your recovery.

FINDING OTHERS TO SUPPORT YOUR RECOVERY EFFORTS

A word of caution: often the people who are involved in cybersex can't be objective enough to decide what they can and can't handle online. For this reason, it becomes increasingly important to seek therapy, join a Twelve Step group or other support group that focuses on this problem, or both. It is also important to find a sponsor (a trusted person with whom you can talk about sex and recovery).

We also encourage you to get an online sponsor, because such a person can truly understand the pitfalls of the Internet. This is another way a therapist and a support group can help—by steering you toward appropriate sponsors who understand the Internet and who will be able to effectively help you monitor your Internet behavior.

Therapists can help you in other ways too. If you're having a problem with online sexual behaviors, it's likely that they are a symptom of deeper, longer-term problems such as depression or issues growing out of your childhood and family of origin. Dealing with depression or anxiety requires help from a professional. Some people also find that medications help them with this problem. For all these reasons, we strongly recommend that you get a comprehensive psychiatric evaluation by a psychiatrist.

You may question whether you really need so much help in dealing with these behaviors. It's important to again acknowledge that you have a problem and that if you'd been able to handle it on your own, you wouldn't be in the spot you're in right now and reading this book for help. Depression and anxiety, for example, have nothing to do with your willpower or how strong a person you are. They often have roots in brain chemistry, and once it is in balance, you will be better able to work through these problems.

We also want to stress the importance of combined therapies. Too often, people seeking help for compulsive or addictive online sexual behavior will select only one source of help, such as a Twelve Step group, group therapy, or seeing a therapist. This strategy can work successfully, but using a combination of therapies increases the likelihood of your success. A comprehensive treatment approach is best. We believe that using individual and group therapy along with recovery groups and medication, if appropriate, is the most effective recovery strategy.

RECOGNIZING FALSE RATIONALIZATIONS

Earlier in this chapter, we presented eight rationalizations that are commonly used to deny or excuse problematic online sexual behaviors. The following four explanations substitute reality for those rationalizations.

Rationalization 1: They're just electrons; they're not real. They're only virtual.

Regardless of the "unreality" of the Internet, real people *are* involved. You're real. The other people online *are* real, even if you can't really see or touch them. Your family is real. Your colleagues are real. Your children are real. Your behavior affects real human beings.

Rationalization 2: Cybersex doesn't hurt others, it doesn't hurt me, and there are no consequences.
Just looking at the lists you made of the consequences of your cybersex behaviors should put these illusions to rest.

Rationalization 3: Occasional use isn't a problem for me. Besides, I can stop anytime I want. I just need to turn off the computer.
You probably often told yourself this, but did you stop? Did you turn off the computer? Did "occasional" use become "using whenever I had the opportunity"? Were you able to stop? And even when you did, did the fantasies stop spinning in your head? How about the desire to go back online? If you could have stopped whenever you wanted, you would have. But you didn't because you couldn't stop.

Rationalization 4: I've already done a First Step; why do another for this?
Regardless of other First Steps you may have done, it is imperative that you do a First Step that focuses on cybersex so that you can recognize powerlessness, unmanageability, and consequences in terms of this particular behavior.

GRIEVING THE LOSS OF CYBERSEX

For a person with problematic cybersex behavior, sex has been the primary relationship—the main source of nurturing in life. The end of that relationship is like a death.[2] The person who stops the compulsive cybersex cycle, which gave meaning and direction to life, suffers a very real loss. For example, the following signs of grief are typical in the beginning stages of recovery:

- confusion about how to act and what to do
- feelings of alienation
- fantasies about how things could have been different
- sadness over unfulfilled expectations and a wasted life
- desire for a quick fix

- feelings of exposure and vulnerability
- failure to take care of self
- uncontrollable emotions
- dark thoughts about death, including suicide
- sudden accident-prone behavior
- fear that the pain will not go away

Severe grief reactions are caused by many types of losses or major changes such as the death of a spouse or child, divorce, loss of job, or change of residence. In all of these situations, the signs of grief are predictable. This same process occurs for the addict in recovery.

One resource for people struggling with out-of-control cybersex behaviors is the Twelve Step program, which helps them through their grieving process. It disrupts preoccupation and obsession with sex and supports grieving over the loss of the pathological relationship. To make the connections explicit, let's explore each stage of the grieving process as it affects the recovering person, focusing on the help Twelve Step programs offer.

With all losses, most bereaved people initially deny reality and isolate themselves. They resent people who urge them to accept their loss, who would rob them of their denial. While living in denial and isolation, those with compulsive cybersex behaviors in particular deny the impact cybersex has had on their lives. Concerned friends, relatives, and professionals make an effort to confront that denial and often encounter extremely defensive behavior.

THE IMPORTANCE OF THE TWELVE STEPS

The First Step of the Twelve Steps adapted for sexual addicts helps with denial and isolation in several ways. It states: We admitted we were powerless over our sexual addiction—that our lives had become unmanageable. Usually, addicts do a methodical inventory of all the ways their addiction proved to be powerful, including all those events they would have done anything to avoid but were powerless to stop. Throughout the inventory, addicts note how life has become unmanageable and intolerable with the addiction. The process helps them own their loss. They admit (to acknowledge powerlessness) and surrender (to acknowledge unmanageability) to the illness and accept their need for help. This is the process you have begun in this chapter.

Once they have acknowledged a loss, most grieving persons become very angry. For addicts, the anger is similar to what people feel when a loved one has died. Often bereaved people feel angry with God, the deceased, and themselves for not having done more. Sometimes the anger is punctuated with moments when the bereaved bargains with God ("If only you change it, Lord, I will . . .") or continues to deny ("Maybe a terrible mistake has been made . . ."). Usually the person experiences alarm or panic that reflects the terror of facing life without the loved one.

You will also become angry. You may feel angry at God for letting this happen, anger at the compulsion and addiction, anger for loss of it, and anger at yourself for not having done something sooner. Bargaining and denial ("Maybe I'm only a partial or weekend addict . . .") provide relief for the pain. By taking the Second Step (Came to believe that a Power greater than ourselves could restore us to sanity) and Third Step (Made a decision to turn our will and our lives over to the care of God as we understood Him), you perform a significant act of trust, acknowledging a Higher Power who can help you regain sanity. You then turn your life over to your Higher Power. This leap of trust requires acceptance of the fundamental dependency of the human condition. You can then create meaning out of the experience, as did author Viktor Frankl during his time in a Nazi concentration camp during World War II. Like Frankl, you may discover that suffering has meaning in a spiritual context.

Those who suffer losses and pass through the stages of denial and anger come to accept themselves through letting go of the loved one. For those with compulsive or addictive behaviors, however, letting go does not repair all the damage the addiction has done to them. The enormity of the addictive patterns and the years of self-degradation overwhelm them. Steps Four and Five will help you bypass shame and gain self-acceptance. Step Four (Made a searching and fearless moral inventory of ourselves) asks you to make a thorough inventory of personal strengths and weaknesses, including all the ways you have not lived up to personal values. This careful look at yourself may cause sadness and remorse.

Step Five (Admitted to God, to ourselves, and to another human being the exact nature of our wrongs) invites you to share your inventory with another person. In sexual or cybersex recovery programs, this is usually a chaplain or pastor, although it may be another member of the fellowship.

The experience of relating all that history to someone else exposes you to an extreme level of vulnerability. Being so exposed, and yet being affirmed and accepted, creates healing of the highest order. The spiritual skills of the clergy may play a key role in self-forgiveness and self-acceptance. In effect, you can feel restored to the human community. Often, great joy and relief occur after the Fifth Step has been taken.

As in all grief, the struggle does not subside with self-acceptance. Bereaved people have moments during which they intensely search for the lost relationship. You will experience pangs of loss when your sadness and desire for the old way returns. This is a time for "slips," loss of courage, euphoric recall, and testing limits. Once again, the program provides a framework to help with this hanging on to grief. Steps Six and Seven ask you to be ready to let go of the defects of character that could bring back the active compulsive/addictive life. Again, part of letting go requires trust in a Higher Power and trust in the existence of a healing process. With Steps Six (Were entirely ready to have God remove all these defects of character) and Seven (Humbly asked Him to remove our shortcomings), you identify your compulsive "friends"—those beliefs, defenses, attitudes, behaviors, and other issues that supported your behavior when it flourished. For example, you may see how self-pity serves as a gateway back into the addiction. Since self-pity was very much part of it, in recovery it simply adds to the grief reactions. Now you must learn to stop giving in to these so-called former friends of the addict.

As the grieving process evolves, a new sense of identity emerges. With restored confidence, the bereaved seek reconciliation with people they had pushed away. For you, the renewal of identity takes concrete form in terms of celebrating your progress. Marking anniversaries (for example, at one, three, and six months; one year, two years; and so on) becomes extremely important.

When you build on this renewed sense of self, your shame will no longer prevent reconciliation with friends and family. With Step Eight (Made a list of all persons we had harmed, and became willing to make amends to them all) and Step Nine (Made direct amends to such people wherever possible, except when to do so would injure them or others), you list those people you have harmed and make amends to them in hopes of healing the breach in the relationship. Making these direct efforts brings comfort through further restoration of self and, in some cases, forgiveness.

All who suffer great losses reach a point where they must establish their renewed identity and recognize that life goes on. It is not true, however, that when grief subsides, pain goes away entirely. In effect, although the sadness never leaves, it is transformed, becoming incorporated into our beings as part of that suffering that brings wisdom and depth of feeling to all of us. One simply learns to adjust to life in order to carry the suffering.

Step Ten (Continued to take personal inventory and when we were wrong promptly admitted it) encourages a daily effort to take stock of your life using the principles of the first nine Steps. Step Eleven (Sought through prayer and meditation to improve our conscious contact with God as we understood Him, praying only for knowledge of His will for us and the power to carry that out) suggests that spiritual progress results from a daily effort to improve conscious contact with a Higher Power. Step Twelve (Having had a spiritual awakening as the result of these steps, we tried to carry this message to others and to practice these principles in all our affairs) asks you to tell other addicts about the power of the program. They, in turn, pass on what they have received.

These last three Steps help addicts integrate the program principles into daily life, and the program thus becomes an intervening system that disrupts the addictive system and provides ongoing support for the lifelong process of surviving the loss. In effect, you will join a community based on healing principles validated over time. The Twelve Steps consolidate these common principles into a discipline for living daily with suffering and loss. Although their simplicity can mislead the unknowing, these Steps require great courage and can result in profound experiences.

The table on page 132 summarizes the impact of the Twelve Steps on the loss of the cybersex relationship.

Those with compulsive or addictive sexual behaviors are particularly vulnerable to using preoccupation with these behaviors as a way to cope with the sorrow of loss and the sadness of life. Unlike alcoholics or compulsive gamblers, they cannot avoid the object of their addiction—their sexuality—so the compelling forces that were a part of their compulsion or addiction will always be an integral part of their lives. Consequently, the tendency toward grief remains immediate, and the Twelve Step program becomes even more vital as a path to return to sanity.

Codependents use the Twelve Steps, as well. (We will talk much more

The Loss of the Cybersex Relationship

Typical Grief Reactions to Loss of a Loved One	Typical Grief Reactions to Loss of Cybersex Relationship	Steps	Therapeutic Tasks
Denial and isolation. Blame for those who press for acceptance.	Denial and isolation. Defensive around behavior.	1	Admission (powerlessness) and surrender (unmanageability)—acknowledge need for program.
Anger. Bargaining. Alarm reactions.	Anger and rage about loss of compulsion/addiction. Slips into denial about being addict to prevent loss. Efforts to bargain—the "partial" addict. Terror at life without compulsion addiction—"Will I die?"	2, 3	Trust, mistrust issues worked through, including accepting Higher Power.
Acceptance of self.	Struggle to get past enormity of compulsive/addictive patterns and self-degradation.	4, 5	Bypass shame; self-acceptance.
Search for the lost relationships. Pangs of loss.	Time for slips, loss of courage, euphoric recall, testing limits.	6, 7	Identify the "friends of the addict."
Emerging new identity. Reconciliation.	Pride in progress; anniversaries and straight time important.	8, 9	Comfort with new sense of self. Reconciliation with old/new friends. Restoration and forgiveness.
Establish and maintain continuity.	Integration into lifestyle and behavior.	10, 11, 12	Establish network for new identity.

Figure 7.1

about the role of spouses and partners in chapter 10.) They have experienced the loss of a loved one to the compulsion or addiction. They, too, have a need to cut through their denial, replace anger with trust, alleviate their shame, and renew their sense of identity. The processes are the same, since the compulsive/addictive and codependent systems parallel each other so closely.

This "simple" Twelve Step program reaches far and touches many. Based on the commonality of human experience, the Twelve Steps can work for everyone.

Taking a First Step means admitting that you have a problem, that you can't use cybersex like other people can, that you admit your powerlessness to control your cybersex use and that your life has become unmanageable as a result, and that you examine the consequences of your cybersex behavior. As you move through this process, you will begin to grieve all that you've lost as a result of your uncontrolled cybersex use. You will also feel grief because you can no longer use cybersex. We have introduced you to the Twelve Steps as one way to work through this process of self-discovery and grief, and we strongly encourage you to attend a Twelve Step group or work with a therapist as you move further into recovery. In addition, as you read on in this book, you will find additional help for dealing with your grief and for strengthing your recovery.

8

Changing the Way You Live

YOUR INVOLVEMENT WITH CYBERSEX and its effect on your life and the lives of those close to you may now be bringing up overwhelming feelings of fear, worry, confusion, sadness, anger, and guilt. The road to healing may seem difficult, even impossible, but don't give in to despair. There is hope. Perhaps you have reached that quiet moment of surrender, realizing that you have a problem with cybersex and that you really do need to do something about it. Or maybe you're not yet sure about your commitment to changing your cybersex behaviors. You may be wondering whether it's really worth the trouble and the effort. Whatever stage you are at, it is important to acknowledge your feelings and move on.

Our work with thousands of people who are recovering from compulsive or addictive behavior has shown us that there are predictable stages people pass through as they descend into more and more problematic compulsive and addictive behaviors and as they recover from these behaviors. While we can't say for certain what you will experience in recovery if you follow the steps we lay out, you will be able to relate to these commonly shared experiences.

SECOND-ORDER CHANGES — ON A PATH TO LONG-TERM CHANGE

In the previous chapter, we discussed first-order changes—the concrete actions taken to quickly stop a problem and to address specific consequences. We will now introduce you to second-order changes—those steps that you take to actually change the dynamics of your life and the way you live. The following chart shows the difference in attitudes during the first-order and second-order change processes and the requirements of each.

First-Order Change Attitudes	Second-Order Change Attitudes
I don't have to tell others.	There are no secrets.
I can change behavior by myself.	I am powerless to change without the help of others.
I can always figure out or force a way to handle problems.	Sometimes there are events that I can't seem to control.
I work best alone.	I need contact with and the help of others.
No one is hurt by what I do.	Damage has rippled through the lives of people I know.
I have not been hurt by what I have done.	My behavior has disconnected me from myself.
I must operate in secrecy.	I must make a full disclosure.
I must isolate from others.	I must create support networks.
I cannot give anyone the whole story.	Trustworthy people get the whole story.
A double life is the only way to get my needs met.	Integrity must become the way I get my needs met.
Chaos is the norm.	I have a plan to reduce chaos and seek the help of others.

First-order attitudes are the stumbling blocks on the path to second-order changes, and it is important to address them as you move toward making second-order changes. Second-order changes will set you on a path to long-term change. While your situation may feel quite hopeless or even desperate—and the struggle quite unwanted—those who have traveled this path before you have found that over time, a completely new way of living can emerge. This new life, you will discover, will be well worth the pain and effort of the work you're in the midst of right now. Though it may be nearly impossible to imagine, you may eventually come to see this struggle as a treasured gift, one that has given you a new life that is more rich and fulfilling than you ever imagined possible.

In making second-order changes, you will find that deeper tasks will emerge. The first-order changes of the previous chapter have enabled you to get a temporary handle on your problematic behavior, but now you need to look at the deeper issues that a lifelong solution will require of you. Surely more work and pain will be part of this journey, but if you commit to this process, you will not be disappointed with the result.

Some aspects of recovery address basic developmental issues, and these issues take time to heal. How much time depends on each person. For some, it may be a year or two, while for others it may be longer. The process is not identical for everyone. Some people have great difficulty stopping their behavior. Be aware that there are critical factors that help the process and others that undermine it. Before we describe these factors, we will first explore the six stages that people with compulsive or addictive behaviors go through as they succeed in their recovery.

The Developing Stage

Jeremy was an executive responsible for some of the largest and most important accounts for his high-profile ad agency. He had it all—money, prestige, authority, responsibility—*and* a secret cybersex life. Jeremy initially began using the Internet for sex when he discovered online strip clubs. Jeremy tells his story:

> I'd often gone to real strip clubs in the past, but as my responsibilities in the agency increased, I just didn't have time to go anymore. The online clubs turned out to be a great substitute. In some ways, I enjoyed them even more than the real thing. I could "visit" whenever I wanted, right from my office, and I could actually request specific women and activities. Eventually, I also discovered that I could find and book prostitutes online, too, which I did from both my work and home computers. My life was one of extremes. On the one hand, I managed ad campaigns for women's health care products and, on the other, I abused women through my use of prostitutes.

One doesn't have to be a high-powered executive to have the addictive pride that says you can manage the unmanageable, that you can do things others can't. It is this arrogance that pushes aside realities like AIDS, family commitments, and work priorities.

Things come apart, however, no matter who you are. For Jeremy, life began unraveling when his wife stumbled across one of the prostitution booking sites in his computer's history file. Confronted by this undeniable evidence, Jeremy confessed but minimized the problem, saying that he'd gone to the site only to see if one could really hire a prostitute online. He swore to his wife that he'd been faithful and to himself that he'd change his ways. Jeremy even talked about seeing a counselor, but he had not accepted that he had a problem—or at least one he couldn't handle.

Jeremy was, at this point, in the developing stage. Unmanageability and powerlessness forced him to acknowledge his problem, but he continued his problematic sexual behaviors nonetheless. True recovery begins only after this stage, which can sometimes last two or more years. For Jeremy, it took over a year, and, like many others, he made efforts to curtail his activities but his compulsive cybersex behavior continued.

Key characteristics of the developing stage include

- seeking help but discontinuing it or deciding it isn't useful
- a growing appreciation of the reality of the problem but a tendency to counter this realization by minimizing the problem or thinking you can handle it by yourself
- temporarily curtailing or stopping the compulsive behavior or substituting other behaviors (Jeremy delved into sexualized online chat rooms)
- having the fear that stopping cybersex activities would mean stopping sex altogether

For most people struggling with compulsive or addictive sexual behaviors, these behaviors are seen as closely connected to survival. The behavior has until now been a "trusted friend," relied upon for some time. This "friend" has always delivered what it promised, but at a price. As the price grows intolerable, addicts prepare to face the fact that something in their lives has to change.

CRISIS AND DECISION

It was three months after Jeremy gave up his cybersex activities when he felt that life was once again under control.

> One afternoon at work after everyone had left the office for the day, I went online to hire a prostitute. When my colleague's phone rang, I decided to answer it. I left my computer with the "order" information

and a photo on my screen. While I was away, my boss returned un-expectedly for some papers he'd forgotten for a meeting. Noticing that the light in my office was still on, he stepped into my office to say hello, but was greeted instead by my computer screen with the prostitution booking service on it—in full view. Caught a second time, and con-fronted by both my wife and my boss, I agreed to seek counseling. Since neither could be conned or forced to budge, I finally had to be honest with myself.

Jeremy had entered the crisis and decision stage, the stage at which a commitment to change is made. This stage can occur within a single day or it can take some months; in any case, it marks the real beginning of recovery. Reaching this stage can happen in many ways. For some, there is a growing consciousness that something needs to be done. Others are frightened into action by the escalation of their behavior. Still others are so overwhelmed by their behavior that they will do anything to fix it.

Most people struggling with compulsive or addictive online sexual be-haviors are forced to do something by events or by people—family mem-bers, partners, friends, or therapists. Because of their denial, the pressure may have to build up over a long period of time.

Shock

This stage is a time of emotional numbness, extraordinary disorientation, and efforts to control the damage. It's not unusual to spend some months in shock. It's OK to move ahead slowly. Maybe nothing major will happen for some time, even for as long as a year. Simply entering recovery and dealing with the implications of the problem can be so stressful that undertaking significant change would overload you. Time-honored sayings like "One day at a time" and "Keep it simple" are appropriate prescriptions for this stage of recovery.

The following experiences can characterize this stage:

- disorientation, confusion, numbness, and an inability to focus or concentrate
- periodic bouts with despair and feelings of hopelessness that can become more intense as the sense of reality grows
- angry feelings about limits set by therapists, sponsors, or family members

- in recovery or support groups, experiencing a sense of belonging along with the realization that recovery was the right decision
- feelings of relief and acceptance once the double life has ended

Perhaps the biggest struggle during this period is for people to be honest with themselves about the extent and nature of their problem. Jeremy, like many others, began to bargain and argue about his problem. He says:

> I remember how intellectual I was and how argumentative I was. As I look back on some of the arguments and discussions I had, the only problematic behavior I admitted was the use of prostitutes. All the other stuff—the lying, the deception, the chat rooms, the online strip clubs, and other online stuff—I didn't take responsibility for any of that. The fact that I'd been caught was the problem for me.

With time and support, however, clarity about the problematic behavior will emerge. When you can see and accept reality, you will enter a stage of profound grieving.

GRIEF

Grieving involves denial or bargaining, anger over the losses, acceptance of the reality of your situation, and sadness. Actually, some aspects of grieving, particularly bargaining and anger, first emerge in earlier stages and simply continue in the grief stage. What really distinguishes this stage is the sadness and pain felt when losses are finally acknowledged.

Given the difficulty of this stage, it shouldn't come as any surprise that this is the point when people most often give up and revert to their old behaviors. Those behaviors had long been used to avoid pain, so when the pain becomes overwhelming, those problematic behaviors seem to bring relief, just as an old friend brings comfort and aid. This is a time when you will badly need outside support. You may be tempted to avoid this pain, but in order to heal and to begin a new life without the problematic behaviors, you simply have to pass through it. It is this pain that sets the stage for the next step; without it, you simply can't take that step.

Feelings may include

- continued anger and defiance
- sadness and pain punctuated with periodic bouts of despair
- deep sadness over the losses incurred because of your behaviors

- a sense of profound loss as your problematic behaviors cease to serve as friend, comforter, and high

At this point, Jeremy finally began to see what he'd been doing:

> I realized that my getting caught wasn't just bad luck; I realized that I had set these lessons up. The universe kept putting these lessons in front of me and I'd been unwilling to pay attention to them. So the lessons had to get even more dramatic in order for me to finally say, "OK, I give up. I see the lesson. I'm ready to learn."

When that final acceptance occurs and you allow yourself to be vulnerable—to be human, ordinary, not unique—then significant change can begin. Awareness of your behavior will expand and deepen over the years. Right now, however, it's important that you recognize its broad outlines and understand that your problem was more than just your behavior. It's important to recognize that these behaviors grew out of your beliefs, attitudes, and distorted thinking and were preserved with denial and delusion. With acceptance, you then enter the repair stage.

REPAIR

For Jeremy, the real watershed between grief and repair came when he finally told his wife and his sponsor the true extent of his behaviors and asked from his heart for forgiveness and the opportunity to begin anew.

That is when the chaos stopped and the rebuilding began. Jeremy began to build "sobriety." He no longer sought out prostitutes or used the Internet for sex.

> By this time, I was connected. I was part of a good support group, and I really used the help that they offered daily. We did things socially and I involved myself in meetings—and eventually as a sponsor for another guy who needed help. I immersed myself in therapy, including a weekly men's group. The result was that I was able to set aside my old behavior. I found that my relationship with my wife entered a new and deeply connected level and that I felt for the first time in my life "a sense of spiritual connectedness."

For many, the repair stage is generally marked by the cessation of problematic sexual behaviors, and by intense spirituality and personal growth.

Jeremy likened the steps he'd been taking to building the foundation for a new home:

> It's brick, sunk in the ground, nothing fancy, just gray, cement blocks. And there's the beginning of a house on top that is in three dimensions and color. I'm not exactly sure what the house will look like, but I can tell already that I'm going to like it.

A number of crucial changes characterize this stage:

- a sense of productivity and renewal
- a new capacity for joy
- deepening of new bonds with others
- taking responsibility for yourself in all areas of life, including career, finances, and health
- learning to express your needs, accepting that you have them, and working to meet them
- a focus on completing tasks (degrees, projects, work, and so on) and being dependable (punctual, following through, and responding to requests)
- living less "on the edge and at the extremes"

A common goal at this point is to achieve balance, to learn to live in the Recovery Zone, a concept we will explore in greater detail later. Since life has been out of control for so long, you must now focus on the basics. Working toward completion and staying low-key will feel good after all the unmanageability you've experienced. But the repair stage also requires developing new skills and forging new bonds. You will likely be forced to face fundamental issues that made you vulnerable to the draw of cybersex in the first place. Those behaviors can be stopped, but the deeply personal problems of distrust, victimization, and shame will remain. Few people are successful in dealing with them on their own, and it's for this reason that we strongly urge you to seek therapy and group support.

During this period of repair and personal growth, a greater understanding of your problematic behaviors will continue to grow. Essentially, you will be restructuring your relationship with yourself. You will begin to develop a much better understanding of your behavior and will come to realize what made you vulnerable to cybersex. You will be able to identify the governing themes and scenarios that connect all your problematic behaviors. Once you have a better relationship with yourself, you will be able to trust other people. You may also find yourself beginning to trust in a power greater than yourself, a Higher Power, and at that point a spiritual opening occurs. You will no longer be living in fear. You will acquire a vital perspective on your powerlessness, become more forgiving of yourself, and learn to care for yourself more deeply. And at this level of self-care, you will begin to nurture yourself into the growth stage.

GROWTH

Empowered by recovery, you will enter a stage in which you explore new options and restructure relationships. The changes that have occurred will enable you to open up what has been a closed system. Your problematic or addictive behaviors offered only decreasing options. Recovery creates an open personal system that allows for the expansion of countless options. Even better, once a system is open, it has the capacity to renew itself. Many people experience periods of dramatic personal growth years after their initial recovery.

Relationships with children, parents, and partners can all become richer and more sustaining. Many recovering people talk about being more emotionally present on the job, as well. They talk of more balance and greater intimacy, of an improved capacity to resolve conflict, and of being less judgmental and more compassionate. With the evolution of this new style of relationships, satisfaction with life dramatically improves.

Jeremy experienced these changes too: "The whole addiction was about me, me, me, me, me. In recovery, I turned to the opposite extreme of really taking care of 'me' in a healthy sense. Then I learned to be a conduit to allow this love that I'm receiving to flow through to others." Jeremy was very clear about the importance of creating a solid personal base. Of his relationship with his wife, he says, "It is now two wholes sharing a life together."

Characteristics of the growth stage include

- profound empathy and compassion for oneself and for others
- developing trust for one's own boundaries and integrity in relationships
- feelings of achievement over new milestones in love and sex
- a new ability to take care of and nurture relationships
- transforming or ending old relationships

Another characteristic of this growth stage is a deep abhorrence of one's old behavior. Once people in recovery have enough distance from their old problematic behaviors, they often have extremely visceral reactions when they think about them. Many say they look back almost in disbelief at some of the things they've done.

The growth stage provides a special perspective on the course of recovery in general. It's clear that many people with problematic or addictive sexual behaviors were not always able to stop all their behaviors at once. Most people tend to focus initially on what got them into trouble. Then, as their awareness grows, they see the variations on the theme. Recovery moves them from crisis management to an expanded awareness and a more evolved consciousness. And this evolution takes time.

By the time recovery reaches the growth stage, it no longer involves false starts. Consciousness of sobriety and of richer relationships has brought the person to a new level of being. And it's at this stage that people in recovery often talk about the compulsive or addictive behavior as a gift. They have experienced a depth of humanity that many people never achieve. Their compulsive or addictive behaviors and subsequent recovery have given them a greater perception, compassion, and presence. Not only do they serve as models for other recovering people who follow them, but they also are literally helping our whole society heal.

It is important to keep in mind that in life, nothing happens in neat stages. The eleven-year-old child, for example, often has some adolescent traits along with traits typical of elementary-school children. Similarly in recovery, you can experience shock, grief, and repair in significant ways at the same time. Slips and relapses may slow development or even throw you back to the first stage of recovery. Other factors can impede development and recovery too, and lack of support from family, friends, and colleagues is perhaps the most devastating of all.

HERMES AND HERMES' WEB

A special tool that we find effective in helping people understand the complex nature of compulsive and addictive behaviors—as well as the process of recovery from them—is called Hermes' Web.[1]

Who or what is Hermes? One of the Greek pantheon, Hermes is the connector, the god of the crossroads. All things meet on Hermes' ground—

sexuality, business, ethics, medicine, and criminality. Hermes weaves them together. Hermes has the ability to move in and out of all other worlds freely and is never held captive. He is known for connecting high and low, living and dead, dark and light, and all manner of things. Hermes is an imaginal center in his own right.

Hermes is nonauthoritarian, an equalizer, creating symmetry and equality in relationships and politics. His aim is not power, but imagination and connection. Hermes is the friendliest of gods and works to connect the human and the divine, however estranged they may become. As the Greek god of thieves, borders, and commerce, Hermes is not afraid to combine elements, to take from here or there to put together what works rather than play by the rules and be ineffective.

Hermes seeks to keep life alive, mercurial, and vibrant. Hermes is also the desire for life, the yearning and urge to be alive, to explore, mix, and tangle. His fleetness is his excitement. He brings diversity and friendliness to the world, connecting all its elements.

Hermes' Web is a diagram that shows the interconnectedness of life, both internal and external, and honors the One whose role it is to bring awareness and soulfulness to life. Hermes' Web allows people to visualize their internal landscape and thus facilitate Hermes' work. It is a tool that demonstrates how everything in a person is interconnected, whether conscious or unconscious. Hermes' Web also demonstrates the negative consequences of various degrees of disconnection. You may view a picture of Hermes' Web at the Web site we have designed for this book: www.recoveryzone.com.

You can also view Hermes' Web as a representation of the human personality. As you look at the illustration on page 145, the top point represents the part of you that you like best, the part that best represents who you are. It's the part you "buff up" and show to the world; it's what we call the "ego." The opposite end of the piece represents the part of you that you keep hidden from the world. It's the "shadow" side, the part of you that you don't want others to see, the part of yourself you don't like so well, that you are even ashamed of and seldom acknowledge. The other pieces in Hermes' Web can represent "opposites," or extremes, in your personality. The point on one might represent anger and on its opposite end represent passivity. Another might represent sexually compulsive behavior and its

Hermes' Web

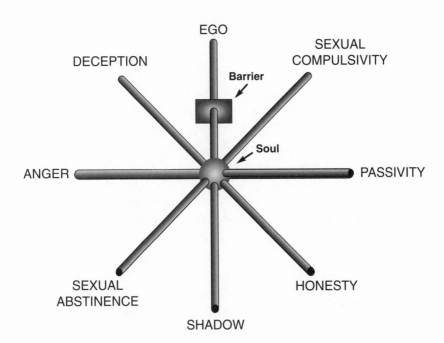

Figure 8.1

opposite end sexual abstinence. For a moment, think about your behaviors and their opposites. Can you see how you tend to live or act at one extreme and then another?

Now notice the section where all the pieces merge and cross paths. This section represents your core, and it "contains" your passion, your spirituality, the very best parts of who you are. The place where all these points come together we call the "convergence of soul." In each of us, ideally, there would be a strong connection between our ego and our soul. In other words, the parts of ourselves that we show the world and how we live in the world (the morals and values that we've learned in life) would reflect the soul, wherein lie our innate goodness and passion and spirituality.

For some people, however, this is not the case. Instead, they begin, often at a very young age, to build a barrier between the parts of themselves they show to others and the convergence point. This happens for a number of reasons, all having to do with information from others—parents, relatives, teachers, siblings, and peers—that is negative. They may be told that they aren't good or worthy of love or wanted. These messages can be conveyed verbally, but often they are given through actions. In the extreme, they are given through physical, emotional, or sexual abuse or neglect.

We take in all messages that we receive about ourselves, be they positive or negative. And when they are negative, we all have to "do something" with them—and that "something" is usually to create an internal barrier between those negative messages and ourselves. It's a barrier between our ego and our core, the soul. As these messages continue to pour in over the years, they begin to accumulate. The "pile" grows larger and larger; the barrier between our outer self and our core grows more and more dense, making it more and more difficult for us to connect to our soul. Over time, we begin to lose touch with our passion, our spirituality, our soul.

When children living in chaotic or abusive settings create such a barrier, it is, ironically, a healthy process. They need to protect themselves. To stay sane, literally, requires that they create a thick barrier between their ego and their inner self as a way to avoid dealing with a difficult environment. Children who don't have the ability to erect such barriers actually can and do go insane. While this coping mechanism is useful and effective for self-protection in childhood, this is not the case once we are adults. These strategies become counterproductive and interfere with having relationships and with living a rich and fulfilling life.

COPING AND COMPARTMENTALIZATION

When you have been keeping secrets, you become like a volcano: the part of yourself that is visible above ground is serene, calm, and beautiful, even majestic and unthreatening, like the cone of the volcano. Underneath the surface, invisible to others *and* to yourself, are all the experiences and feelings you have kept hidden for many years, just as deep below ground under the volcano lies a mass of molten lava, heating and building pressure, month by month, year by year. By stuffing experiences into that barrier and out of sight—by keeping secrets—you've learned how to live a double life.

This "skill" is known as compartmentalization. You have seen examples of compartmentalization in the lives of public figures, but perhaps have never put a name to these actions. Presidents, ministers, politicians, and others create a public persona, a "self" that they show to the world. But too often there is another side, a shadow side, and occasionally, that shadow side is revealed to the world when news of sexual misconduct or financial misdealings, for example, splashes across the media and into our lives. These people have used compartmentalization to deal with the duality of their lives. Can you begin to see how secrecy, compartmentalization, and the private, hidden world of cybersex are all connected?

Over time, all the thoughts and experiences and feelings that you put into the core begin to build up, and the older you are, of course, the more stuff you have buried. Deep under that volcanic peak, enormous pressures have been building for many years. Eventually, enough pressure builds up that an explosion, or a "flip," occurs and some of that hidden stuff is thrown out into the world. It may take the form of a violent crime, using alcohol or other drugs, or the compulsive use of cybersex. This acting out is a way to relieve the pressure that's built up in your core.

At the moment when the flip occurs, you also reveal your true self—your soul. That soul, however, is completely encrusted by all the "garbage" that you've piled on it for so long, while the person you consider yourself to be, that buffed, kind, moral person, is not there on the other side.

But the flip doesn't last long. Soon you flip back, denying to yourself and others what you've done. We call this a "truthful lie."[2] A person may deny having been drunk at the office party or having molested a child or having had sex with someone he or she met via the Internet. Because the part of us that we identify with—the ego on top—*couldn't* have done those acts, we deny them. Unconsciously, we tell ourselves that it was the part of us we *don't* identify with that did them. And that is the truthful lie.

Compulsive and addictive behaviors are a sure sign that there is a major barrier between the ego and the inner self and that we are feeling a great deal of pressure and stress. We are desperate for a way to relieve some of that pressure, and the three quickest ways to get some relief are sex, alcohol, and other drugs. We are trying to find a way to open ourselves up, and for a brief moment, these seem to do the trick. Other compulsive behaviors, such as gambling and overeating, may also seem to serve this purpose. But the relief is only temporary—very temporary. We feel alive and free, but before we know it, we crash. Eventually, the pressure builds up and again we act out. Soon we are in the midst of a cycle of compulsive/addictive behavior, one we return to over and over because we don't see any other option.

LIVING IN THE EXTREMES

In this state, we are living in the extremes, not in the convergence zone of the soul. Research has shown that people who have lived with a great deal of anxiety or fear—stemming from dysfunctional families, child abuse, sexual assault, trauma, or other causes—can actually experience an alteration of the brain that causes them to process information in the extremes. They tend to see life in terms of "all or nothing," "black or white," "all one way or all the other way." And when they turn to alcohol, other drugs, food, or sex, for example, to relieve the pressure and to fill the void they feel, they go to the extreme. They do not know that a middle way exists, that it's possible to have appropriate boundaries or to control their impulses. They stay in the extreme—extreme sex, extreme drinking, overeating, and so on. Perhaps, for example, they've been sexually abused as a child, and one of two things happens when they grow up: they either act out sexually or shut down sexually. Likewise, individuals who have experienced violence when they were children will, without help, either become victims or perpetrators of violence. Other people find themselves caught up in binge-purge cycles. They will binge on something such as alcohol or food and then go to the opposite extreme by trying to purge this behavior from their lives. They'll act out sexually and then decide to become celibate. In either case, these people don't know how to live a balanced life.

The answer to this predicament isn't just to go to the opposite extreme; abstinence, for example, is not the answer to problematic sexual behavior. Likewise, the answer is not, as too many people initially assume, to make the barrier even stronger. Doing so may seem to work, but if you take this course, you're actually just creating a very large "pressure cooker" that will eventually explode. Your next flip, and there *will* be a next one, will be even more dramatic with even greater negative consequences. All the stuff you've been trying to hide will come out despite your best efforts to hide it.

The task of recovery is essentially to dismantle the barrier you've created over the years and to reconnect with your shadow side—*and* with your soul. Once you start to take down that barrier, you will have to address all the issues and experiences and consequences that you stuffed inside it. With this opening comes pain and grief. This is also the most likely point at which you'll relapse and turn back to your old behaviors. It's for exactly this reason that we have urged you to put your first-order changes in place. Having a support group, a therapist, boundaries for your computer use, and so forth will also help you get through this difficult time with less chance of a major relapse.

RELAPSING AND THE RECOVERY ZONE

If you do relapse, it's not the end of the world. Others, too, have relapsed. This doesn't mean you can't recover or that you should give up. It's just part of the process. In the next section of this chapter, you'll find more help for your journey into recovery.

At this point in recovery, it's easy to focus on the ability to become abstinent and to control your sexual behaviors. The real challenge, however, is to learn how to approach and work with deeper personal issues. It's about learning to deal with what Carl Jung called the "shadow self." It's not really the Internet or cybersex that has been casting a shadow over you; rather it's that you've been in the shadow of yourself. Once the barrier is down, you will start on a journey that will help you expose your shadow self and see who you really are. People who have been in recovery for a long time will tell you that one of the easiest tasks in recovery is abstaining from the problematic or addictive behavior. The more difficult task is to look at your relationships with other people and your relationship with yourself and to explore your life—past and present.

You will begin to move toward the center, what we call the Recovery Zone. When there is no longer a barrier between the parts of yourself, you can begin to develop an ongoing connection with your core—with your soul. With the barrier gone, your creativity and passion can flow throughout your life. Your life can become a reflection of the beauty of your inner self. You experience continual growth and expansion. You are living in the zone of the convergence of the soul.

MAKING SECOND-ORDER CHANGES

Second-order changes are the actions that will help you find the path to the deepest parts of yourself. They are the steps that will enable you to develop a new life in recovery. As you have seen, this is a difficult journey, one that often requires a number of interventions, including therapy, support groups, and spiritual guidance. It also takes time. It may help you to have more patience if you remember that it took you some time to get into the situation you're in and it will likewise take some time and work for a change to take place. To achieve sound and tested guidance for sustainable recovery, consider the following tools:

Finding and Working with a Good Therapist

There is a difference between going to therapy and actually being in therapy. "Going to therapy" means minimal involvement. It's basically showing up, sitting down, and waiting for the therapist to take charge. You don't voluntarily open up, share problems, or take any initiative. "Being in therapy," however, means that you come to each session with concerns and issues to work on. You have a commitment to being there mentally and emotionally, not just physically. You're there to take charge and to take responsibility for what happens. Therapy is not something your therapist "does" to you. Rather than resisting therapy, acknowledge your need for help. Open yourself up to the struggle and pain involved in recovery rather than trying to do everything you can to avoid it.

Once your therapist has helped you contain your behaviors, he or she can help you begin to look at the deeper issues that lie behind your compulsive and addictive behaviors, such as family-of-origin experiences, past trauma, and your relationship with your partner. Since working in therapy is a second-order process, this task will take time.

Finding and Using a Sponsor

Again, there is a difference between getting a sponsor and using a sponsor. "Getting a sponsor" is merely the act of finding someone who will agree to sponsor you. Your connections are brief and somewhat perfunctory; you don't really ask for help and you don't take advantage of all that a sponsor can do for you. "Finding and using a sponsor" means connecting with a person who is willing to know everything about you—the whole dark side, the below-the-surface part of the volcano. A sponsor should be a person with whom you can discuss anything you want, someone who will support you without necessarily colluding with you, and someone who will be honest with you and who can confront you on any issue. Your sponsor may be someone who has already walked this road before. Or you may want to choose a close friend or colleague. We strongly urge you not to choose your partner as a sponsor, however, since partners are not only too close to the problem but often have also become part of the problem. Once you have a sponsor, allow this person to help you. Having and using a sponsor is fundamentally about letting yourself be known. You must be willing to surrender to feedback regarding what it will take to get your life under control. And that means you have to let this person know how bad things really are right now, so he or she can see how best to help you.

Finding and Using a Support Group

As with therapy and sponsorship, there's a difference between going to group and using a group. If you are forcing the group members to work to get through to you, if you're trying to keep as much of your life as hidden as possible, then you're just "going to group." "Using your group" requires that you let down the barriers and allow others to know who you really are. This includes sharing when you're in trouble, taking chances, trusting the group, and asking for help.

Participating in Twelve Step Meetings

Many people have found tremendous support for recovery from a variety of compulsive and addictive behaviors—problems with alcohol, other drugs, bulimia, gambling, sex, and more—through attending Twelve Step meetings. As with support groups, you can go to meetings and just sit in a corner and people will pretty much leave you alone. Or you can go to meetings, listen, introduce yourself, socialize with people afterward, tell your story— your *whole* story—and talk and contribute at each meeting you attend. It may take some trial and error to find a meeting that feels right for you, but when you do, make a commitment to it. Remember, you're trying to build a support network, and meetings are a great way to begin this process. These people will understand you because they have been where you are now. And they know how to help and support you because they were helped and supported by those who came before them.

WORKING A PROGRAM

The phrase "working the program" grew out of the Twelve Step tradition. It means to actively participate in a Twelve Step program. While Twelve Step programs can be very effective, we are using the term "program" more broadly here. By "working the program" we mean that you need to make a firm commitment to participate in whatever recovery program or process you choose. That program may differ from a Twelve Step program in that it has different assignments and goals or is behaviorally oriented. Each therapy and recovery program looks a little different, but that's really not important. You could go to any number of different programs and still find help through each, as long as you are committed to the process of working that program. Conversely, you could go to the best program in the world and not be helped at all if you aren't committed. It's not so much the content of the program you attend that's critical as it is your willingness to open up and be known. Commitment to the process is the key to success. You truly need to "work" the program.

WATCHING OUT FOR THE BOUNCE EFFECT

Be aware of what we call the bounce effect. This happens when people begin working a program and attending support groups. They initially make big disclosures as they tell their stories and having done that, they feel better—and then they stop. They don't take further steps. They rarely call their sponsor. They merely attend meetings; they don't participate in them. They have failed to understand that change, growth, and healing are *ongoing* processes and that they need to share continually what is happening in their recovery and lives. Opening up to others is not a onetime event or simply an end in itself. It is the first step in sharing who you are and who you are becoming. This kind of openness needs to become a way of life if you are to succeed in recovery. Our research with thousands of recovering people who have participated in Twelve Step programs has shown that those who committed to and followed the program through Step Nine rarely relapse.

The goal of treatment and recovery is not to immediately jump all the way to the other extreme—to make an enormous and dramatic splash at a meeting and to your sponsor and then be done with everything else. Instead, seek the middle ground. Begin the process and then continue it. Participate in your therapy groups, work the steps of your program, and begin to do service to others. You won't, at this point, know where this will all end, but have faith in the process and continue. Go on sharing your life and your problems and your challenges and your failures with others in your therapy program or recovery group and with your sponsor—and keep coming back week after week, month after month, and year after year. Recovery is not an event; it is an ongoing process, a process that will, over time, become far less focused on recovery from problematic sexual behaviors and more focused on personal and spiritual growth.

MAKING SOCIAL CONNECTIONS

Reestablishing social connections is one of the most important steps you can take in recovery, particularly if you have problems with sexual behavior on the Internet. If you've been involved in cybersex, your "social relationships" have atrophied to the point where you have only one, and that's between you and your computer. Although there are some useful ways to develop and refine recovery with the Internet and to find support on the Internet, if that's as far as you take recovery, it means that your primary relationship is *still* between you and a computer. It is simply imperative that you begin to develop face-to-face contacts with other human beings, and the only way to do so is through actual social activities. Enroll in a photography or foreign-language class, join a church group or bike club, volunteer at a community organization, or take advantage of one or more of the countless other opportunities to meet people. One of the keys to breaking your link with the Internet is simply being with people in person. You need to have real, as opposed to virtual, interactions and relationships. You need to be out in the world interacting with people rather than sitting at home, isolated and alone with your computer. Through these social experiences, you'll meet people with whom you can become a companion and friend, and you'll find the opportunity for deeper relationships in your life. Developing good social support can, in fact, be just as important and effective for your recovery as finding a good therapist.

INVOLVING FAMILY AND FRIENDS

It's important to seek support from as many places as possible. Some people are comfortable talking with others in their lives, such as appropriate colleagues, good friends, and family members; while others find it enormously difficult to tell even one person. Those in the former group, however, have the best chance of achieving successful recovery.

A word of caution, however. When you begin to talk about your life, you may find that there are some people who don't really need to know what you have been through and for whom hearing your story would be painful and difficult. Hence, you need to respect the needs of others and to think about the consequences of revealing your story before doing so. It may not be appropriate, for example, to tell all your co-workers or your boss, if for no other reason than that you may be fired. It may also not be appropriate to tell your parents or other extended family members. This is really an example of working to develop good boundaries.

So start slowly. Find one or two people you can truly trust, get a sponsor, contact a good therapist, and then, with the help of this support group, slowly decide whom else you should include. Over time, you will find that the more people you can include in your support group, the stronger your recovery will be.

We can't overemphasize the importance of involving your partner early in the recovery process, because his or her involvement will dramatically increase your chances of success. It's also important that your partner have a therapist, too, and that you, your partner, and both your therapists be involved in this process, especially for help in determining how much detail you reveal to others. You should reveal only information that will not be abusive to your partner. Disclosing every detail of everything you've ever done may simply be hurtful and unnecessary.

A SEXUAL HEALTH PLAN

For some time now, your life has been dominated and driven by your sex life. As you now recognize, this has not been particularly appropriate or useful. You may be tempted to say, "Forget sex. It's been a destructive thing in my life and I'm just going to quit doing it." While that is a common and understandable feeling, it's not a particularly good choice. Once your first-order changes are in place and you've begun working on your second-order changes, you'll see more clearly that your choice is not between complete abstinence or complete out-of-control sexual behavior. At this point, you need to begin exploring what it means to make sex an appropriate part of your life. It is possible for sex to be wonderful and exciting rather than awful. Having a sexual life that's based on discovery, openness, and intimacy is possible. You can't have good personal relationships until you know and like yourself. This is why it is important to work on yourself and develop new friendships and other social contacts. As you can see, it will take some time to see how your sexuality can appropriately fit into the rest of your life.

You can begin to develop a sexual health plan by using what we term the Circle Plan.

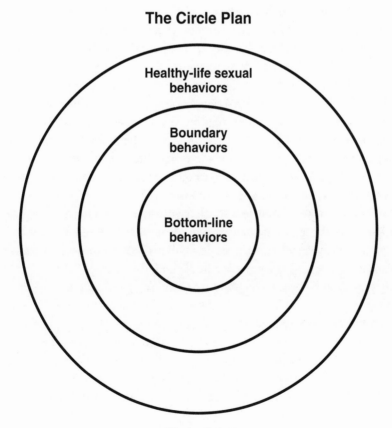

The Circle Plan

Healthy-life sexual behaviors

Boundary behaviors

Bottom-line behaviors

Figure 8.2

The center circle will contain your "bottom-line" sexual behaviors—those behaviors that you simply cannot do any longer. For someone who's been using cybersex compulsively, a bottom-line behavior would be, for example, to never engage in sexual conversations in a chat room nor to visit pornography Web sites.

The "boundary behaviors" in the middle circle are more difficult to define or classify: they may be acceptable or unacceptable, depending on your state of mental and emotional health, and they include behaviors that you are not sure are appropriate for you. For some people, for example, masturbation is never appropriate because they can't control it once they start. For others, it's fine unless they are hungry, angry, lonely, frustrated, tired, or in some other state of heightened anxiety. If so, masturbating can send them back into negative and compulsive behaviors. If, on the other hand, their life is in balance, masturbation may be acceptable. The behaviors in the middle circle are those that often literally require some kind of boundary.

The outer circle includes healthy sexual behaviors—those positive sexual behaviors that you are working to make a part of your life. These behaviors parallel second-order changes and can include such steps as sharing your inner life, including your sex-related hopes and worries, with your partner and establishing and maintaining more social connections. This circle includes behaviors that you, your sponsor, your therapist, and others supporting your recovery agree are always acceptable. Sexual health plans are unique to each individual, and we strongly suggest that you develop your plan with the help of a therapist and sponsor.

It's important to recognize, too, that your plan will change over time. Your sexual health plan one or two years from now will be different from your plan in early recovery. At first, you will probably find many behaviors in the center circle and fewer in the middle and outer circles because, at this point, you won't be able to handle much. As your recovery becomes stronger, your center-circle behaviors will decrease and the middle- and outer-circle behaviors will increase.

How do you decide when you can move behaviors out of the center and middle circles? This decision is not one you should make alone; always do this with the help of your sponsor, therapist, and support group. This should not be only one person's decision, and if there are disagreements among you and your support group members, no change should be made. These decisions require consensus.

SPIRITUAL DEVELOPMENT
Spiritual growth and development is an individual matter. How you pursue the spiritual aspects of your life can involve a variety of means, including meditation, membership in a religious organization, exploring Eastern spirituality, or practicing yoga, to name just a few. Involving someone else as a spiritual coach or mentor can be useful, as can joining a spiritual community with which you can readily identify. Your spiritual growth can become a tremendous source of support for your recovery.

To optimize your recovery, we strongly suggest that you embrace both the first-order changes laid out in the previous chapter and the second-order changes we addressed in this chapter. First-order changes are meant to be stopgap measures. If you stop with them, you will experience some healing, but the likelihood of falling back into your old behaviors will remain high. Keep in mind that first-order changes are only surface measures; they will not enable you to address the causes of the problem, which are deeper and take more time to work through. They will, however, help you quickly get your life under control and set the stage for the deeper work to be done with the second-order changes. As you can see, second-order changes help you build a strong support group. It's also likely that you'll be surprised to discover that this isn't a journey you have to take by yourself. In fact, it is a journey that you really *can't* take alone.

SUPPORT IS NEARBY—AS CLOSE AS OUR INTERNET WEB SITE

We'd like to offer you the opportunity to make the Internet a positive therapeutic experience. We have developed a site (www.recoveryzone.com) specifically to support you, the readers of this book. You will find that it has information and articles about problematic sexual behavior, research on what works and what doesn't work for recovery support, and a number of exercises you can do that will give you a safe and positive computer and Internet experience, one that can enhance your recovery efforts.

One of the exercises you'll find there will help you look at your behavior extremes, as did the exercise earlier in this chapter. In addition, it will help you find and explore your Recovery Zone—that space in which your behaviors are in balance and safe. It will help you be clearer about the boundaries you need to establish in your life. Finally, it will help support your recovery and lessen the likelihood of relapse.

That brings us to the topic of the next chapter: relapse prevention. There you will find information based on the experiences of many others who have struggled with problematic sexual behaviors.

9

Preventing Relapse: Maintaining the Changes You've Made

FOR ALL OF US, making changes in our lives can be difficult. Each year in late January or early February, for example, we hear stories from friends about New Year's resolutions that have fallen by the wayside. Stories about failed diets or exercise plans are ubiquitous. You, too, have likely made promises to yourself about changing your cybersex behavior, only to find you've been unable to keep them.

Making life changes happen takes more than a promise to yourself. Yes, it is often difficult, but the lives of countless people who have done so is proof that it's possible. That's what this chapter is about: learning how to maintain the changes you've decided to make in your life.

It will help you to look more closely at the process of change. In the book *Changing for Good,* authors James Prochaska, John Norcross, and Carlos DiClemente state that there are six steps, or stages, that everyone goes through when making changes in their lives, regardless of what their goal is.[1] For example, if you think about a specific problem that you have resolved, chances are you will recognize immediately that its resolution didn't happen all at once. Perhaps for a while you ignored the problem; then you considered tackling it; after that, you may have made definite plans to change. Then, once you had garnered your forces—mental, physical, and social—you acted and began to struggle with the problem. If you succeeded, you worked at maintaining this change. If you failed, you probably gave up for a time, went back to the drawing board, and then tried once more.

Each of these steps is a predictable, well-defined stage: it takes place over a period of time and includes a series of tasks that must be completed before moving on to the next stage. Each stage doesn't inevitably lead to the next; it is possible to become stuck at one stage or another. However, by understanding these stages, you can gain control over the cycle of change and move through it more quickly and efficiently and with less pain.

As you read through these stages, we suggest that you keep in mind some changes that you've made, or tried to make, in your life and try to see how these stages apply to them.

STAGE 1: PRECONTEMPLATION

In this stage, it's not that you can't see the solution; it's that you can't see the problem! People at this stage usually have no intention of changing their behavior and typically deny having a problem. Although their families, friends, neighbors, doctors, or co-workers can see the problem quite clearly, the typical person in this stage can't.

Most people in this stage don't want to change themselves, just the people around them. Often they come to therapy because of pressure from others—a partner who threatens to leave them, an employer who threatens to fire them, or judges who threaten to punish them. Their first response in therapy is often, "How can I get others to quit nagging me?" When all else fails, they may change, but only as long as there is constant outside pressure. When that's gone, they quickly return to their old ways.

Precontemplators resist change. When their problem comes up in conversation, they shift the subject. They lack information about it and they intend to maintain ignorant bliss at all costs. Denial is characteristic of precontemplators, who place the responsibility for their problems on factors such as genetic makeup, family, society, or whatever, all of which they see as being out of their control. Precontemplators also tend to be demoralized as well. They don't want to think, talk, or read about their problems because they feel the situation is hopeless.

So how can you change if you don't want to? The answer is in the approach; even precontemplators will progress toward change if they have the proper tools at the proper time.

STAGE 2: CONTEMPLATION

"I want to stop feeling stuck." These words are typical of contemplators. In the contemplation stage, people acknowledge that they have a problem and begin to think seriously about solving it. Contemplators struggle to understand their problem and to see its causes, and they wonder about possible solutions. Many have indefinite plans to take action within the next six months or so.

In this stage, you have become aware that something is amiss in your life. You've begun noticing that some "difficulties" have arisen. Your work supervisor recently had a meeting with you specifically to talk about those missed deadlines and the fact that you've been late getting to work more and more often. You know that both situations are due to your increasing cybersex involvement. The thought occurs to you that perhaps cybersex is a "bit of a problem." You contemplate making some changes, putting some controls on your use, and cutting down a bit.

The nature of contemplation can seem puzzling: you know your destination, and even how to get there, but you are not quite ready to go yet. Many people remain in this stage for a long time. Many spend years telling themselves that someday, they'll change. When contemplators begin the transition to the preparation stage, their thinking is clearly marked by two changes. First, they begin to focus on the solution rather than the problem. Then they begin to think more about the future than the past. The end of the contemplation stage is a time of anticipation, activity, anxiety, and excitement.

STAGE 3: PREPARATION

Most people in the preparation stage are planning to take action soon, often within the very next month, and are making the final adjustments before they begin to change their behavior. An important step now is to make public the intended change. But although people in this stage are committed to acting and may appear ready to do so, they have not necessarily resolved their ambivalence. They may still need to convince themselves that this is what is best for them. People in the preparation stage may already have instituted a number of small behavioral changes, such as cutting their cigarette intake or counting calories. Awareness is high, and anticipation is palpable. People who cut short this stage—for example, waking up one morning and deciding to quit smoking cold turkey—actually lower their chances of success. It's better to make use of this time by planning carefully, developing a firm, detailed scheme for action, and making sure that you have learned the change processes you need to carry you through the process.

You might be asking yourself questions like, "Do I need to get rid of the computer altogether?" "Do I need to put limits on how much time I spend on the computer or where I use it?" "What do I need to be cautious of?" "What is it exactly that I need to change?" In other words, what preparations do you need to make to effect the change?

Often anxiety is the impetus for finally taking action. While anxiety is often seen as a negative state, in this case, it has a positive effect in that it can impel us to finally move out of contemplation and into preparation and action. Without anxiety, there is often no change. If life is comfortable, why rock the boat? Concern and discomfort push us to take action to relieve anxiety.

STAGE 4: TAKING ACTION

The action stage is the one in which people most obviously change their behavior and their surroundings. They stop smoking cigarettes, remove all tempting desserts from the house, pour the last beer down the drain, send all the pornography to the dump, or confront their fears. In short, they make the move they've been planning.

The danger in this stage is that many people, including professional therapists, often mistakenly equate action with change, overlooking not only the critical work that prepares people for successful action but also the equally important (and often more challenging) efforts to maintain the changes following action.

It's important to recognize that the action stage is not the only time you can make progress toward overcoming your problem. Although modifying your behavior is the most visible form of change, it is far from the only one: you can also change your level of awareness, emotions, self-image, thinking, and so on. And many of those changes take place in the stages that precede action.

Furthermore, any movement from one stage of change to the next represents considerable progress. If, after years of avoiding a problem, you consciously begin to acknowledge that it exists and think seriously about changing it, the transition from precontemplation to contemplation is no less significant than from preparation to action.

STAGE 5: MAINTENANCE

There are great challenges at every stage, and the maintenance stage is no exception. It is here that people must work to consolidate the gains that they have made during the previous stages and struggle to prevent lapses and relapse. Change never ends with action. Although traditional therapy sees maintenance as a static stage, in fact it is a critically important continuation that can last from as little as six months to the rest of one's life. Without a strong commitment to maintenance, there will surely be relapse, usually to the precontemplation or contemplation stage. Programs that promise easy change—crash diets, one-day smoking-cessation sessions, or whatever— usually fail to acknowledge that maintenance is a long, ongoing process.

STAGE 6: RELAPSE

While Prochaska and his associates described this change process in a linear sequence—precontemplation, contemplation, preparation, action, maintenance—life is not so clear-cut and simple. Most people do slip up at some point, returning to earlier stages before renewing their efforts.

Relapse means slipping back into the behaviors you've decided to leave behind. Prochaska and many others who help people make changes in their lives strongly emphasize several points about relapse. First, relapse is a normal part of the change process. Making changes is not like flipping a light switch—as in, "yesterday I did such and such" and then, "click, and now today I do it differently and that's that." The average successful self-changer relapses several times.

Needless to say, the feelings relapse evokes are not pleasant. You may feel like a complete failure, embarrassed, ashamed, and guilty and may believe that all of your hard efforts at change have been wasted. Demoralization sets in, and you may want to give up entirely on changing. You may slide all the way back to the precontemplation stage.

After several setbacks, you may feel as though you are going in circles. But you're not. Think of the change cycle not as a circle, but as an upward spiral. You may be in the contemplation or planning stage again, but this time you can draw on the lessons you've learned from your previous efforts. Relapse, or recycling, gives you the opportunity to learn. Viewed in this way, relapsing into old behaviors is not seen as a failure, but rather as a learning experience. You've prepared and taken action. Then, when you slip up, you simply move back to stages 2 and 3 to reevaluate what you're doing, how you slipped, and what you can do to minimize the chances of future relapse. Your goal is to learn from your slip. Prochaska and his associates say we can always expect some level of relapse to occur, particularly if the change is a difficult one like dealing with cybersex. Taking action and slipping is much better than taking no action at all.

You may find that you will cycle through these stages in various areas of your life at different levels for many years. Let's say, for example, that you've come to grips with your cybersex behavior. It's no longer a problem. Then, however, you notice that the relationship between you and your partner isn't all that you want it to be . . . so you apply the change process to this issue.

In its broadest sense, this change and recovery process is really a way of living life more fully and consciously. It's not something that you do for a few days, weeks, or months and then say, "Great! That's done. Time to move on."

Again, although we are applying these stages to the problem of cybersex, people move through these stages whenever they make changes in their lives. They are not just applicable to dysfunctional behaviors.

We have found that, when people are recovering from problematic sexual behaviors or cybersex addiction, there is a particular point when they are most likely to relapse. In the previous chapter, we explored the six stages that people with problematic or addictive behaviors go through as they move on in their recovery, and it is in the third and fourth stages, shock and grief, respectively, that relapse is most likely. Why then? Relapse normally occurs when people are most emotionally vulnerable. It is in these stages that people finally begin to be honest with themselves and to truly look at their behaviors and consequences for the first time. This is a wonderful point in recovery, but it is also a time when strong emotions surface. In the face of this emotional tempest, it's easy to revert to old dysfunctional behaviors for "comfort." This does not, however, mean failure. On the contrary, it means that we've taken another major step forward in recovery because we've been more honest and open with ourselves.

To help you better understand the place of relapse in recovery, let's look at the experiences of two people, Rudy and Linda.

Rudy is a thirty-five-year-old male, blue-collar worker who engaged in cybersex online. He used pornography chat rooms and other cybersex while masturbating. He felt tremendous guilt over this behavior because of his religious beliefs. As a result, Rudy entered treatment for problematic (offline) sexual behavior, in particular, for exhibitionism. Eventually during treatment, Rudy did admit that cybersex was a serious problem in his life too. Rudy participated in treatment by engaging in the minimum requirements of the program. There wasn't any reason to dismiss him from the group, but it was clear that Rudy never truly engaged in the therapy process. His counselor realized that Rudy was on a path toward relapse when he began to attend their sessions only infrequently while experiencing a series of stressful situations at work and within his family. Rudy clearly had applied first-order changes with regard to his cybersex behaviors by selling his computer and engaging in the minimum requirements of recovery. But Rudy had never made any second-order changes. Consequently, when stress in his life increased, he had no strategies or support in place to help him cope. His relapse included carrying out sexual activities online by using his brother's computer during the day, when his brother was at work. The only reason Rudy stopped his relapse behaviors was that he was caught.

Linda is thirty-eight years old, married, and the mother of two young children. Once her children were both in school, Linda began to log on to chat rooms to relieve her loneliness. Soon she developed several romantic online relationships with men there. On several occasions, she agreed to meet partners offline for sexual escapades. After one year, her husband discovered her online and offline affairs and demanded that they stop.

Linda entered treatment and began a solid recovery program by acknowledging that both her online and offline sexual behaviors were out of control. After two years of treatment and attendance in a Twelve Step group, Linda felt her life was back on track. She continued her counseling sessions and began to tap into painful childhood memories and childhood trauma that she had never dealt with. Her parents had been alcoholics and Linda had suffered neglect and emotional abuse. She began to realize for the first time that her family was not all that she had thought it was and that she really didn't have much support.

Not long after this, Linda's relationship with her husband became strained, finances grew tight, and she began to feel entitled to a better life. Feeling very vulnerable, Linda once again turned to the Internet. She logged on to one of her old chat rooms and found some of her old "friends" still there, ready to once again hook up sexually. Acting out brought on a great deal of guilt and shame, but Linda continued in her relapse for several weeks. She then realized that she was in trouble and needed to return to treatment.

The experiences of Rudy and Linda are examples of the two types of relapse: first-order and second-order. And yes, they parallel first- and second-order changes. People who have first-order relapses have been impelled to go to treatment primarily because of external factors. Perhaps a spouse or partner threatened to leave if they didn't enter treatment, or they may have been ordered into treatment by the court. As such people "contemplate" their situation, they do not consider the deeper issues that have created the situation in which they find themselves. Instead, they are only thinking about what will happen to them if they don't accept treatment. They often see treatment participation as a way to "get the heat off" for a time while they figure out how to carry on in the future without getting caught. Their "preparation," "contemplation," and "action" steps don't grow out of an admission that they have a serious problem. Their focus is instead on developing tactics that will enable them to continue their cybersex behaviors without once again suffering the consequences that landed them in treatment. Theirs is a reaction to outside forces rather than action taken as a result of self-examination and inner growth. Still narcissistic, they are worried only about what will happen to them. They go through the treatment process, but remain disengaged. They never really decide to give up their cybersex behaviors.

In Rudy's case, it's apparent that his was a first-order relapse, since he never really became engaged in the recovery process. He hadn't really moved beyond the contemplation stage, nor did he ever truly resolve to give up his cybersex activities.

Second-order relapse happens to people who, like Linda, have made both first- and second-order changes and who are working their program. Linda reached a point in recovery at which she was emotionally vulnerable. She had finally begun to experience all the feelings that come with more self-awareness, including fear, remorse, anger, and pain. Though she relapsed, Linda recognized the problem on her own and decided, also on her own, to return to treatment. The impetus for this decision was not the result of outside forces. Had Linda planned for this time in her recovery, however, she may have been able to avoid her relapse.

The following chart summarizes the characteristics of and differences between first- and second-order relapses.

<u>Relapse Characteristics</u>

First-Order Relapse	*Second-Order Relapse*
Makes only first-order changes	Makes both first- and second-order changes
Is not truly committed to treatment	Is committed to treatment and healing
Denies extent of problem	Accepts extent of problem
Is unwilling to look honestly at behaviors and consequences	Attempts to look honestly at behaviors and consequences
Sees treatment only as a means of "getting the heat off"	Views treatment as a means of self-healing and personal growth

SUDS: SEEMINGLY UNIMPORTANT DECISIONS

Relapses tend to be seen as a matter of impulse—as a moment of weakness when someone lets down his or her guard. Research has shown us, however, that this is not the case. Stress, coping strategies (or lack thereof), and decision-making skills all play a role, as do SUDS—seemingly unimportant decisions.[2] Relapse is really the culmination of a chain of events that starts days, weeks, or even months in advance of its actual occurrence. Often, the actual relapse act can't be carried out immediately because of situational constraints such as, in the case of cybersex, unavailability of computer and Internet access or the lack of privacy. The desire for immediate gratification may be temporarily put off and instead be redirected to secret planning or fantasies about cybersex. Because of the potential for conflict and

guilt associated with these secret schemes and plans, people are likely to engage in rationalization or denial, or both. These two distorted ways of thinking can then combine to influence certain choices or decisions as part of a
chain of events leading ultimately to a relapse.

We believe that people who are headed for a relapse make a number of
mini-decisions over time, each of which brings them a bit closer to the brink
of the triggering high-risk situation. An example is the abstinent drinker
who buys a bottle of sherry to take home, "just in case guests drop by." Or
the ex-smoker who decides it would be fine to choose a seat in the smoking
section of a restaurant. Or the recovering gambler who expands a vacation
driving trip to California to include a visit to Lake Tahoe, which is just a
few miles down the road from the gambling mecca of Reno, Nevada.

The term "SUDS" describes these decisions. It is as though people
slowly begin to set the stage for a possible relapse by making a series of
SUDS, each of which moves them one step closer to relapse. A final advantage in "setting up" a relapse in this way is that people may be able to avoid
assuming responsibility for the relapse episode itself. By putting themselves
in an extremely tempting, high-risk situation, they can claim that they were
"overwhelmed" by external circumstances that made it "impossible" to resist the relapse.

Stress can be a powerful relapse trigger too, one that should not be un-
derestimated. Consider this scenario: over the past few weeks, one of your
children has been having problems at school. This has taken extra time from
you and your spouse. In addition, your spouse has been worrying about an
impending visit from her parents. The result: There's a lot more tension
around your house than normal, and it's been building up for a few weeks,
wearing you down. You've been thinking more and more about how good it
would be to jump online for a little dose of cybersex, just like old times.
You've resisted this temptation with the help of your sponsor. But now it's
Friday evening, and you're home by yourself . . . with your computer.

One of your primary relapse prevention goals is to become aware of the
behavior chains that can lead you to relapse. If you can recognize them,
then you can take action long before you get to the point of relapse. In the
example above, talking with your wife about the stress you're feeling and
your concerns about the end result would be a positive step in breaking the
chain. Once you recognize your behavior chain, you can begin planning for

ways to substitute new, positive, and supportive behaviors to prevent re-lapse. You realize that when life gets stressful at home, you need to spend time with a friend, for example, or talk with your wife about it, or get some exercise. Essentially, you need to do whatever seems to help relieve the stress before you feel the need to turn to cybersex for relief.

The concept of behavior chains and our power to change them points out another important difference between a first-order and a second-order relapse. People who have first-order relapses always think that the cause of the relapse is something outside of themselves. The cause is external, something over which they have no control. They might say, for example, that it was their spouse's nagging that caused the relapse, or an argument with a relative, or a boss who is pressuring them. On the other hand, people who have made second-order changes would talk about this relapse in terms of their own responsibility: "I have been fighting with my wife a lot lately" or "I haven't really been responsible at work lately." These people realize that *they* are responsible for their behavior.

The concept of behavior chains and our power to change them also shows the importance of identifying your relapse triggers and determining ways to avoid them. We already have numerous procedures in our society that require us to prepare for the possibility (no matter how remote) that various problematic and dangerous situations may arise. For example, fire drills help us be prepared in case a fire breaks out in public buildings or schools. Anyone who has been on a cruise ship is familiar with lifeboat drills to teach the passengers what to do in the event that the ship encounters trouble at sea. Certainly no one believes that requiring people to participate in fire drills increases the probability of future fires; on the contrary, the aim is actually to minimize the extent of personal loss and damage should a fire happen. The same logic applies in the case of relapse prevention.

Include a "relapse drill" as part of your prevention strategy. Learning precise prevention skills and related strategies is more helpful than relying on vague suggestions to "work your program." Think of situations that you know could trigger a relapse for you. Begin with the scenarios that would be less likely to do so, and then move on to ones that would place you at higher risk until, finally, you list the situation that would be the most dangerous for you. For each of these situations, then, think of ways you could react that would enable you to escape the "fire" without being burned. As the intensity and risk of relapse increases with each situation, your escape plan will need to be better planned. List at least six to ten relapse-threatening situations. Finally, choose three—one that is quite low risk, one that presents a more moderate risk, and a high-risk situation—and write down your escape plan for each on an index card. Keep those three cards with you at all times. You may also find that referring to them occasionally will help remind you of your goals in recovery. Several popular slogans emphasize these ideas: "Forewarned is forearmed," "An ounce of prevention is worth a pound of cure," and "Be prepared!"

TRIED-AND-TRUE RELAPSE TRAPS

First, we'll introduce you to five problem attitudes that we call tried-and-true relapse traps: entitlement, resentment, self-reliance, deprivation, and stress. Getting them out in the open helps you avoid relapse. Then we'll give you some solid suggestions for preventing relapse.

ENTITLEMENT
People who fail at some task, who are struggling with problems, or who feel put upon often feel so much self-pity that they believe they are entitled to some kind of reward for their struggles. Conversely, people who are very accomplished and overreach themselves can likewise feel that they deserve some reward for all their hard work. Many people who struggle with compulsive and addictive behaviors stretch their lives to the extreme. Often they have a difficult time saying no to others' requests and find themselves overcommitted. Ministry and medicine, for example, are two professions that reinforce overcommitted behaviors. The people who are drawn to these professions are often very good at them and committed to helping others, repeatedly giving in positive ways, but often they also do a poor job of taking care of their own needs. It then becomes easy for them to think that, because they work so hard for others, they are entitled to some reward, and some rewards, such as cybersex or affairs, can be very self-destructive. Their feelings of entitlement don't derive from a sense of narcissism; instead they grow out of an inability to say no to the needs of others. Sadly, their attempts at self-care are counterproductive. The struggles and hard work of recovery can also lead people into feelings of entitlement.

RESENTMENT

During the recovery process, it's common for feelings of anger and resentment to surface. These feelings may come from many sources: resentment about difficult predicaments, losses suffered, past and future consequences of out-of-bounds behavior, family-of-origin issues, and so on. It is important to acknowledge and address these feelings with a therapist or sponsor. If they remain unaddressed, they can lead to ever stronger feelings of self-pity and entitlement—and eventually to relapse.

SELF-RELIANCE: "I CAN HANDLE THIS"

Once people have progressed in recovery, they can reach a point at which it is tempting to say, "I can handle this," while dabbling in the problematic behavior. An alcoholic may say, "I've been sober for quite some time. I've finally got this drinking issue under control. It's now safe for me to have a drink once in a while." The same can be said for someone who's been engaged in cybersex.

"I had been in recovery from cybersex for nearly two years," said Terrence, a prominent lawyer. "One of the steps I'd taken was not to have the password to my computer. After this amount of time, I really felt I didn't need this safeguard any longer and convinced my wife to reveal it to me. Sad to say, within six months, I was back in trouble with cybersex again."

Don't fall into this trap. This kind of thinking is really no more than bargaining with your compulsion—"I'll give up nearly all these behaviors, but not all"—in an attempt to avoid the feelings of grief and loss over truly letting go of your problematic behaviors. This trap is really an attempt to find ways that you can actually do the cybersex behavior without totally losing your sobriety. When you truly admit that you can't handle cybersex, then you will have to deal with painful feelings about losing that activity in your life.

DEPRIVATION: ABSTAINING FROM ALL THINGS SEXUAL

In recovery from any problematic sexual behavior, it is tempting to say to yourself, "That's it, I'm just going off sex. It's caused me so much trouble, and I don't seem to know how to handle it in a healthy way. I'm just going to quit." The problem is that you can't quit being sexual, and, more important, you don't have to. Trying to abstain will only set you up for a relapse.

Many people who are on food diets experience similar problems. They diet carefully, denying in the process all the foods they really like. The result? Inevitably they leave their diet behind, only to fall into eating binges and regaining the lost weight. "Entitlement" thinking plays a key role here too. It's easy to tell yourself that you've been good for so long and you've deprived yourself of the foods you love for so long that you're now entitled to engage in the "forbidden" loves. That's relapse. If you live in a state of deprivation, you will be more vulnerable to feelings of entitlement.

People who successfully lose weight instead learn how to eat healthfully. They also take time and effort to look inside themselves to see what emotional needs or family issues lie behind their habit of overeating, and they make plans to deal with the cravings that will inevitably arise.

Successful recovery from your dysfunctional cybersex behaviors won't happen through sexual abstinence, but instead through following the steps we have laid out, in particular the second-order changes you make. These steps lead to personal awareness and growth, to an ability to nurture yourself, to intimacy with those you love, and to a healthy sexuality in which you will no longer need your old behaviors to feel good.

Simply stopping problematic or addictive behaviors does not equate with recovery. Again, we are talking about making only first-order changes. Without the introspection and inner growth that come with second-order changes, you are merely setting yourself up for relapse. Feelings of deprivation and entitlement will surely arise. And you may find yourself engaging in compulsive behaviors of another kind, such as drinking or gambling. Until the issues underlying your problematic or addictive sexual behaviors are addressed, there will be no recovery.

STRESS

Higher-than-normal stress levels can quickly increase your risk of relapse. Remember, too, that stress is not always created by negative situations or events. Receiving a long-sought work promotion, moving to a new city, the birth of a child, or a new relationship can all create stress too. If you are unsure about ways to handle the stress in your life, seek out a course on stress management skills, relaxation training, or meditation—and then put these skills to use.

MORE HELP FOR RELAPSE PREVENTION

One of the most useful and important tasks you can do to help prevent re-lapse is to check in each day and see if you are living in the Recovery Zone in the following areas of your life: spirituality, sexuality, work, family, other relationships, feelings, money, food, and alcohol or other drugs.

In each of the following life dimensions, (1) list how you have been living in the extreme; (2) list the behaviors that you allow to be public; (3) list the behaviors that you keep hidden. This will help you see the ways in which you have been living in extremes.

Spirituality:

Sexuality:

Work:

Family:

Other relationships:

Feelings:

Money:

Food:

Alcohol or other drugs:

Next, for each of these dimensions describe behaviors that would be more balanced and centered, that would be in your Recovery Zone.

Spirituality:

Sexuality:

Work:

Family:

Other relationships:

Feelings:

Money:

Food:

Alcohol or other drugs:

CREATING A RECOVERY-ZONE PLAN FOR EACH DIMENSION
In each dimension, create three lists:

1. Bottom-line behaviors: actions that you simply cannot do if you are to avoid relapse
2. At-risk behaviors: actions or activities that you want to avoid because they put you at risk for relapse
3. Recovery-Zone behaviors: goals you are working toward to help you maintain living in the Recovery Zone

Let's use Linda as an example. In terms of cybersex, her bottom-line behaviors, the ones she absolutely must avoid, are online and offline sexual escapades, sexual e-mails, and logging on to chat rooms of any kind. Linda's at-risk behaviors include e-mails to men, e-mails or other contact with former sexual partners or men she's been flirtatious with, use of the computer after 10:00 P.M., and use of the computer in a private space. Recovery-Zone behaviors for Linda would include taking good physical care of herself (eating healthy foods, getting enough sleep each night, exercising regularly), attending Twelve Step groups regularly, staying in contact with her therapist, and fostering healthy relationships. Monitoring these lists daily will help her stay in her Recovery Zone.

All stages of change require a series of tasks, a stretch of time in which to try them, and a certain amount of energy and dedication. Maintenance takes all the required work of the previous changes and builds on it. Difficult as it is, forsaking an undesirable behavior is not enough to overcome it for good. Almost all negative habits essentially become our "friends" over time—in many cases, our "lovers." They play important, sometimes dominating, roles in our lives. Cybersex fulfills many roles: for some, it keeps life from being boring; for others, like Linda, it eases loneliness.

To overcome our problematic behaviors fully, we must replace them with a new, healthier lifestyle. That is why the word "maintenance" can be misleading. You can break old patterns by removing cybersex activities from your life, but doing only that will leave you with a life of longing and deprivation. Lifelong tolerance of this deprivation requires unceasing and powerful acts of will. The "dry drunks" described in alcoholism treatment circles, for example, may be abstaining, but they run a high risk of relapse.

For all of us, former problems, especially compulsive and addictive ones, will hold some attraction for a long time. To remain strong throughout maintenance requires that you acknowledge that you're still vulnerable to the problem even while you're building a life in which the old behavior has no value. Research shows that people who leave behind problematic and addictive behaviors (1) learn to devalue the positive aspects of the behavior, (2) develop confidence in their ability to abstain from it, (3) keep a healthy distance from the behavior, and (4) through development of new habits and behaviors, find few if any temptations to return to it.[3]

STAY ALERT FOR SIGNS OF TROUBLE

Social pressures, internal challenges, and special situations are common threats to maintenance and recovery. Social pressures come from those around you who either engage in cybersex themselves or don't recognize its impact on your life. Internal challenges usually result from overconfidence and other forms of defective thinking, such as those mentioned on pages 170–72 as the tried-and-true relapse traps. While many of the more common temptations will occur for you during the action stage, most people learn to deal with them before moving out of that stage. During maintenance, however, the relatively rarer temptations come into play. They are difficult to anticipate and pose serious threats to your confidence, convictions, and commitment.

ADDITIONAL SUGGESTIONS FOR MAINTAINING COMMITMENT AND RECOVERY

- Write down the difficulties you encountered in your early efforts to change your cybersex behaviors. Next, review the lists you made in chapter 7 in which you described the negative aspects of your cybersex behaviors. Keep both of these lists, look at them periodically, and refer to them at the first sign of slipping.

- Take credit for your accomplishment. This is not the time to criticize yourself for having had problems; instead take both credit and responsibility for change. Use the new year, your birthday, or the anniversary of your change (it doesn't have to be a year; celebrate month by month at first) to reflect on the success you have had and to renew your commitment.

- As you progress in your recovery, you will gradually become more and more comfortable in the presence of certain temptations or situations. But you may not become completely immune to them. Especially during the early months of maintenance, it's best to continue to avoid people, places, or things that could compromise your recovery. Pay attention to the behaviors you need to avoid (found in your Recovery-Zone plan).

- Make a crisis card for your wallet or purse. On it, write a list of the negative consequences of your problem, as well as a set of instructions to follow when you are seriously tempted to slip. The instructions could read as follows: (1) review the negative consequences of the behavior, (2) substitute a positive alternative for the cybersex behavior, (3) remember the benefits of changing, (4) engage in distracting or positive behavior, and (5) call someone (write down a support person's name and phone number).

- Last, but by no means least, seek help and support from your support group, therapist, partner or spouse, and friends. Having someone to call on who has been where you are, who can understand, and who can help is simply invaluable.

Though recovery may seem to be a daunting and endless task, we encourage you to begin thinking in a new way about these changes. If you think of recovery as a burden akin to a diet, it just won't work. Try to view the path on which you've set out as a truly remarkable opportunity, because that is exactly what it is. Once you begin to change, to accept the support others are offering to you, and to live in your Recovery Zone, you will find that you love your new life so much that you don't want to give it up. Gradually, staying in your Recovery Zone will no longer seem like something you have to do (because otherwise your partner will leave you or you'll be incarcerated), but something you *want* to do. You will begin to truly cherish what you've found. This newfound caring for yourself and the pride it creates will build a new feeling of being capable—of self-confidence and self-esteem. This is a hope-filled process.

Even if you are not yet at the point where you have started to experience these feelings, it's important that you know that this place exists. If you've read the book to this point without having done the work we suggested, you're unlikely to understand or believe that this is possible. But by doing the work, you can get there. This is not a fantasy or an illusion. You *can* reach a point where you *want* to be in recovery—a point where your passion for recovery is as strong as your passion for cybersex once was.

10

Family Dynamics and Cybersex

KATHLEEN IS AN attractive, thirty-five-year-old professional woman married to Tom, her second husband.

Our marriage had been somewhat problematic, and I was frustrated because it felt like I was carrying most of the weight in the business that we were in together. For some time, my husband had talked of a fantasy of a sexual threesome with another woman. I didn't really like the idea, but he brought it up so often that I finally agreed. So Tom booked a prostitute via the Internet. She came to our home and we all had sex together. This was a very painful experience for me, but I felt that somehow maybe there was something wrong with me because I didn't like it.

After some months and a number of threesomes with different women, things were just getting worse for me so I sought help from a therapist. The therapist handed me a copy of a book on sex addiction in the first session, and said, "You have a problem, and there's more going on here than you know." I continued therapy for eighteen months, but felt that I just wasn't really making progress. And we still were having threesome-sex occasionally too. During this time, I began to have migraine headaches that kept increasing in severity as the months passed. Eventually, I had to be hospitalized. I just couldn't function anymore. In the hospital, I was medicated constantly with few positive results.

One day, however, I woke up and realized that I was slowly dying.

I was just wasting away in the hospital. And I realized that the migraines were due to the terrible unhappiness in my life because of my sexual relationship with my husband. I finally called my sister, who came and took me out of the hospital and brought me to her home. While living with her, I slowly began to recover. I continued therapy, and after some months, the migraines disappeared. The sexual demands and activities to which I had acquiesced had been so emotionally painful that they had actually caused a physical illness.

Adam and Gordon are professionals in their mid-thirties. Says Gordon:

Adam and I had been partners for four years when I discovered that he had been using the Internet to meet and have sex with other men. I was devastated at this revelation, as you can imagine. But more than that, I was plagued by the feeling that this happened because I wasn't attractive enough to hold his attention—to keep him interested just in me. Now I'm so angry. I don't know how I can trust him anymore. I'm afraid that our relationship will disintegrate. And most of all, I'm furious with him because he got infected with syphilis, and now I have it too.

Cindy and Steve, a Caucasian couple, had been married fifteen years when Steve discovered Cindy had been having an affair with an African American:

When I confronted her about this, Cindy admitted that during the last five years of our marriage, she'd had four affairs, each time with black guys she'd met through the Internet. Needless to say, I was very hurt and angry. Even worse, this situation began eating at me. It wasn't long before I began to pester Cindy for details about these affairs. Then we'd have very aggressive, violent sex. This situation continued for some time, with me wanting more and more details of her exploits with these men. Eventually, Cindy's revelations weren't enough for me, so I turned to the Internet myself and began searching for interracial sex sites. Upon discovering them, I literally spent endless hours at a time on the Net. Cindy didn't like this situation at all, but she didn't feel she had any right to complain because she felt bad about the affairs she'd had. Besides, she told herself, I wasn't having affairs with people; I was just on the Internet. Yet I was spending so much time with it. I just couldn't stop. It was like a drug to me. Next, I began buying "black-and-white" pornography. At that point, Cindy felt so awful that she sought help from a therapist who told her that I was clearly addicted to Internet sex. When she told me this, I told her she was nuts. But soon Cindy's therapist helped her intervene on me and both of us entered treatment. Looking back, it seems so ironic that initially I was responding to Cindy's sexual behavior, but then I ended up ensnared myself by cybersex.

THE CYBERSEX IMPACT

The experiences of these people typify the powerful and adverse consequences to those whose spouse or partner has become compulsively involved in cybersex. The results of a 2000 survey examining the effects of cybersex addiction on the family further describe the serious consequences of cybersex addiction for the partner and children of cybersex addicts.[1] They include feelings of hurt, betrayal, rejection, abandonment, devastation, loneliness, shame, isolation, humiliation, jealousy, and anger, as well as loss of self-esteem. Being lied to repeatedly was a major cause of distress. Cybersex was also a major contributing factor to separation and divorce in couples who took part in the survey.

Among 68 percent of the couples in this study, one or both partners had lost interest in relational sex. Some couples had had no relational sex in months or years.

Partners of cybersex addicts compared themselves unfavorably with the online women (or men) and pornographic pictures, and they felt hopeless about being able to compete with them. These partners overwhelmingly felt that online affairs were as emotionally painful to them as live, or offline, affairs, and many subsequently believed that virtual affairs were just as much adultery, or "cheating," as live affairs.

The impact of cybersex on children was equally distressing. Adverse consequences included

- exposure to computer-based pornography
- involvement in parental conflicts
- lack of attention because of one parent's involvement with the computer, the other parent's preoccupation with the cybersex addict, and breakups of the marriage or partnership

Negative consequences on marriages and partnerships included

- depression and other emotional problems
- social isolation
- worsening of sexual relationship with spouse or partner
- harm done to marriage or primary relationship
- exposure of children to online pornography or masturbation
- career loss or decreased job performance
- other financial problems
- legal problems

A companion online study conducted in late 2000 surveyed forty-five men and ten women, age eighteen to sixty-four, who self-identified themselves as cybersex participants who had experienced adverse consequences from their online sexual activities.[2] When asked about the nature of their online sexual activities, 77 percent of the men mentioned pornography, 46 percent mentioned chat rooms, and 26 percent reported participating in online real-time sexual activities with another person. Among the women, only 10 percent mentioned pornography, while 80 percent reported chatting and 30 percent engaged in online real-time sexual activities. When asked whether their online sexual activities had led to actual sexual encounters, 33 percent of the men said yes, as did 80 percent of the women. In addition, 92 percent of the men and 90 percent of the women stated that they considered themselves sex addicts.

PARTNERS AND CODEPENDENCY

As you can see, partners of people who are compulsively engaging in cybersex find themselves in a very difficult position too, and most have no idea how to react to the situation. They respond in a variety of ways, including

- trying to take responsibility for people, tasks, and situations they're not responsible for
- trying to "be good enough" to earn the love of their partners and others
- reacting to their partners' behavior instead of responding to their own motives

- becoming all-consumed with their partners to the point of putting their own needs on hold
- becoming so emotionally tied to their partners that they can't admit their partners' illness
- losing all sense of themselves, of how they feel and what they need. They become so obsessed with their partners and their problems that they no longer deal with their own lives—their pain, needs, shortcomings, joys, and growth.

THE LOSS OF SELF

In other words, partners often become codependent on their addicted mates. Codependency, or coaddiction, is an illness, too, in which reaction to compulsivity and addiction causes the loss of self. Like the addicts, co-dependent partners lose an essential sense of self. They may put up a front for the world that says everything's fine, but the reality of what is happening proves this to be a lie. The front has little to do with the codependent's true self. It is only an image that shields the reality of what both partners have become. The codependent becomes part of his or her partner's double life.

The preserving of appearances doesn't prevent the erosion of self. Terri, whose husband used the Internet to view pornography and live sex, and eventually to book prostitutes whom he met at home during his lunch hour, was caught in the web of codependency. Upon learning of her husband's activities, Terri obsessed about her husband—about where he was, what he was doing, and whom he was with. She did all the "detective" work, spying on him, checking his computer, and installing Internet-tracking software. She became paranoid about other women, saw them through his eyes, and compared herself with them. She rationalized that he was more liberal and open-minded about sex than she was. She risked disease because of his sexual habits. She felt embarrassed to go out with him because other people knew about his exploits. For a long time, she never questioned whether she loved him, only whether he loved her. "I never thought about being happy, only whether I could keep him with me," she said.

> I never thought about my needs, only whether I could meet his. Feeling less and less, because nothing I did was enough. Thinking there was

something wrong with me that I could not meet his sexual needs. Hating myself for being "weak." Having no pride. Putting up with abusive treatment. Having no interests outside of the relationship. It was a disaster for me, but for a long time, I didn't know how to escape the cycle we were in together.

All codependents experience such feelings. These attempts at accommodation lead to powerlessness and unmanageability. While codependents are powerless to control their partners' behaviors, they continue to try to do so, and as a result, their own lives become unmanageable and they became coaddicts.

THE SIGNS AND CHARACTERISTICS OF COADDICTION

COLLUSION

Most codependents actively support their partners' compulsive sexual behavior by covering up for them in some way. Powerful childhood rules about family image and secrecy have helped make them unwitting partners in the addictive process. Many codependents keep secrets about their partners. Many lie to cover up for their partners' behavior or actively work to present a united front to the world. Another form of collusion is to become "hypersexual" in an effort to join with the partner. In the example on pages 179–80, Kathleen's husband presented the threesome idea in such a way that she felt something was wrong with her if she didn't participate. So she colluded, joining her husband in activities that gave her no pleasure because she believed that if she didn't, she might lose the relationship altogether. Partners can also feel pressure to go along because the images presented on the Net are always those of smiling partners cooperating. Codependent partners may also feel that their mate's behavior isn't so bad if he or she is only doing cybersex, as opposed to going to strip clubs or using prostitutes. If the partner has a history of using strip clubs, for example, the codependent may actually see cybersex as a sign of improvement in the partner's compulsive sexual behavior. To summarize, the characteristics of collusion include

- joining your partner to present a united front
- keeping secrets to protect your partner
- lying to cover up for your partner

- becoming hypersexual for your partner
- feeling cybersex isn't so bad because it's not "real"

OBSESSIVE PREOCCUPATION

Codependents obsess about their partners and their lives. They think constantly about their partners' sexual behavior and motives. Many actually play detective by checking mail, computer history files, Internet bookmarks, credit card and telephone bills, and briefcases. They may also become obsessed with the Internet themselves, working so hard to find out what the partner is up to on the Net that they spend countless hours online too, entering chat rooms or checking out porn sites. This is a trap many partners who install surveillance software fall into. To summarize, the characteristics of obsessive preoccupation include

- focusing totally on your partner to avoid feelings
- constantly thinking about your partner's behaviors and motives
- checking your partner's mail, purse, briefcase, computer history files, and so on
- forgetfulness
- spending time on the Net investigating sites your partner uses

DENIAL

When not obsessing, codependents lapse into ignoring what is really happening in their lives. Many speak of setting aside their intuitive feelings or totally denying their problem. Many try to stay very busy and overextended to avoid the problem. Despite failures, most codependents believe, at least for a time, that they can eventually change their partners. When cybersex is involved, often codependents tell themselves that it's virtual, not real; that if there's no physical contact, nothing's really happening; that at least the partner is going to work and staying at home at night. Characteristics of denial include

- denying your own intuition
- keeping overly busy and overextended
- believing you can eventually change your partner
- totally denying the problem
- telling yourself that it's virtual sex, not real sex

EMOTIONAL TURMOIL

Life for codependents is an emotional roller coaster. They go on emotional binges, sometimes to the extent that their emotions are simply out of control and they experience free-floating anxiety and shame. Many say that they are always facing a crisis or problem. Cybersex involvement can also dramatically accelerate the codependent's emotional turmoil because of how quickly and deeply a partner can be overwhelmed by cybersex and by the range of sexual activities available with so little effort. Everything can be done at home. Codependent male partners are often rapidly overwhelmed emotionally because they just don't know how to handle such a situation. A physician, for example, was filled with self-righteous rage when he discovered that his wife had been having Internet-arranged affairs with ten of his colleagues and friends. To him, everything was her problem, not his. He couldn't see his role in the relationship's troubles. Characteristics of emotional turmoil include

- out-of-control emotions
- going on emotional binges
- experiencing free-floating shame and anxiety
- always having a crisis or problem

MANIPULATION

Codependents become manipulative in their drive to control their partners. They try and fail over and over again to control their partners' sexual acting out. They may use sex to manipulate their partners or to patch up disagreements. Many threaten to leave but never follow through. Almost all codependents see themselves as having played martyr, hero, or victim roles. Before cybersex, spouses and partners tried to keep tabs on their sexually compulsive partner's schedule. With cybersex, codependent partners may actually control computer access. They may become the keeper of the computer's password, or they may install automatic surveillance software to keep tabs on their partners. Manipulation enters even more areas of life. Since there are additional opportunities for acting out, there's more behavior to try to control over more parts of the day (and night). Characteristics of manipulation include

- playing martyr, hero, or victim roles
- using sex to manipulate or patch up disagreements

- failing at efforts to control your partner's sexual acting out
- making threats to leave but never following through
- taking control of the computer via a password in an effort to control your partner's behavior
- installing automatic surveillance software to keep tabs on your partner

EXCESSIVE RESPONSIBILITY

In their obsession, codependents can be extremely hard on themselves. They blame themselves for the problem. They believe that if *they* change in some way, their partners will stop. Codependents now find themselves having to contend with and compare themselves with all the beautiful people on the Net—and with endless sexual variations and opportunities available on the Net. They may also try to take responsibility for their partners' behavior. Many actually seek extra responsibility by trying to create dependency situations where they will be indispensable. Characteristics of excessive responsibility include

- blaming yourself
- believing that if you changed, your partner would stop
- taking responsibility for your partner's behavior
- creating dependency situations to make yourself indispensable

COMPROMISE OR LOSS OF SELF

Codependency involves a constant series of compromises that erode one's sense of self. Codependents can act against their own morals, values, and beliefs. They give up life goals, hobbies, and interests. Many change their dress or appearance to accommodate their partners and even accept their partners' sexual norms as their own. When Kathleen began participating in threesomes, she compromised her own values and betrayed herself, since she did not want to take part in these activities. Characteristics of compromise or loss of self include

- giving up life goals, hobbies, and interests
- acting against your own morals, values, and beliefs
- changing dress or appearance to accommodate your partner
- accepting your partner's sexual norms as your own

BLAME AND PUNISHMENT

Codependents become blaming and punishing in their obsession. They perceive themselves as having become progressively more self-righteous and punitive. Some have affairs to punish their partners and to prove that they are worthwhile and attractive. For example, a woman who has discovered her husband's online affairs may become involved in one herself just to spite and punish him. Other women post nude pictures of themselves after ending a marriage, sending a message to their former husbands that says, "See what you're missing. See how desirable I am!" as an act of revenge. Many see their behavior as destructive to others. Some even admit to homicidal thoughts or feelings. Meredith discovered her husband's online affairs. To strike back at him, she initiated an online affair with him while posing as someone else. At home, she pretended that nothing was happening. She had become so obsessed with his betrayal that she actually became part of that betrayal.

Both partners may also binge on sex outside of the marriage or partnership while staying compulsively nonsexual with each other, as was the case with Stan and Cheryl.

"I had been having sex with people in an adult video bookstore, among other things," said Stan.

> Cheryl was absolutely infuriated with me because of what I'd been doing and that I'd had unprotected sex. She was worried that both of us may have been exposed to AIDS. Cheryl, I later realized, felt very lonely and ignored, since we'd rarely had sex for some time. Eventually, Cheryl started going into chat rooms, where she arranged meetings with men and had unprotected sex with them. I guess she was trying to punish me. So here we were, having lots of sex with others and none with each other.

Characteristics of blame and punishment include

- becoming increasingly more self-righteous and punitive
- being destructive to others
- having homicidal thoughts or feelings
- having affairs (online or offline) to punish the partner or prove worth
- withholding all sex from partner as punishment

SEXUAL REACTIVITY

Codependents go to various extremes in reacting sexually to their partners' behavior. When one partner gets out of control sexually, it's not unusual for the other partner to close down sexually. Many numb their own sexual needs and wants. Codependents may change their clothes out of sight of their partners. They may make excuses not to be sexual. And many rarely feel intimate during sex. Characteristics of sexual reactivity include

- numbing your own sexual needs and wants
- rarely feeling intimate during sex
- making excuses not to be sexual
- changing clothes out of sight of your partner

CYBERSEX CODEPENDENCY INVENTORY

How do you know if you have become part of your partner's compulsive or addictive behaviors? The following inventory can help you determine that. If you agree with eighteen or more of the thirty-five items in the following exercise, you may have a problem with codependency and need to address your own issues with a professional counselor. While you may or may not be codependent, a score of eighteen or more indicates that you might be at risk for codependency problems.

1. I constantly think or obsess about my partner's cybersex behaviors and motives. Yes No
2. I engage in self-destructive behaviors (physically, sexually, or emotionally). Yes No
3. I check my partner's e-mail accounts, computer files, disks, and the like for evidence of sexual material. Yes No
4. I blame myself for all the problems related to my partner's sexual use of the Internet. Yes No
5. I believe that if I changed, my partner would stop acting out sexually on the Internet. Yes No
6. I feel shame as a result of my behavior or my partner's behavior related to cybersex. Yes No
7. I feel anxiety as a result of my behavior or my partner's behavior related to cybersex. Yes No

8. I use my own sexuality as a way to manipulate my partner. Yes No
9. I feel numb to my own sexual needs and wants. Yes No
10. I accept my partner's norms as my own. Yes No
11. I find myself doing sexual things I don't want to do. Yes No
12. I am overly sexual to satisfy my partner. Yes No
13. I take responsibility for my partner's cybersex behaviors and their consequences. Yes No
14. I keep secrets to protect my partner. Yes No
15. I rarely feel intimate during sexual encounters with my partner. Yes No
16. I lie to cover up for my partner. Yes No
17. I totally deny that there are any problems with cybersex. Yes No
18. I always seem to be in the midst of a crisis or problem. Yes No
19. I threaten to leave my partner, but never follow through. Yes No
20. I am giving up my own life goals, hobbies, and interests as a result of my partner's cybersex. Yes No
21. I have changed my dress or appearance to accommodate my partner's wishes. Yes No
22. I believe I can eventually change my partner. Yes No
23. I play martyr, hero, or victim roles. Yes No
24. My life seems increasingly unmanageable. Yes No
25. I go against my own morals, values, and beliefs. Yes No
26. I deny my intuitions. Yes No
27. I am feeling more and more unworthy as a person. Yes No
28. I shut down sexually from my partner as a result of his or her use of cybersex. Yes No
29. I am obsessed with learning more about cybersex through the media, the Internet, and so on. Yes No
30. I am considering engaging in cybersex as a way to make my partner understand my feelings. Yes No
31. I have fantasies about getting revenge on my partner and his or her online "friends." Yes No
32. I am in competition with the computer for my partner's time and attention. Yes No
33. I am irritable with others when I think about my partner's cybersex use. Yes No

34. I neglect important areas of my life because of my partner's cyber-sex use. Yes No
35. I am a cybersex codependent. Yes No

THE EFFECT OF CYBERSEX ON FAMILY LIFE

When a parent is caught in the web of cybersex, one of the primary effects on the rest of the family is the loss of time with that person. In the beginning stages of the cybersex compulsion, codependents often begin to feel that their partners are slowly drifting away and becoming more distant, but they don't know why.

LOST FAMILY TIME

There are only so many hours in each day, and hours spent on cybersex are hours that cannot be spent with your partner or children. In some ways, cybersex is more time-devouring than other forms of compulsive sexual behavior, such as going to strip clubs or using prostitutes. The Internet gives you access to your sexual activities at any time of the day or night for as long as you want—and from your own home. Many couples use the time after children are in bed to reconnect and talk about their day. But when a partner is using cybersex, this opportunity often disappears. Cybersex addiction is easy to hide, so the partner may not have any clue about what's happening but does know that something isn't right. Communication decreases. The sexually compulsive partner becomes more and more unavailable. This can be confusing for children, too, because the sexually compulsive parent may be home but not available to the children, who can't understand why Mom or Dad can't spend time with them.

Al's story is a poignant example of this situation.

> One night I finally realized what I'd been doing to my kids. I was in my home office on the computer when my two children came in and wanted to play. I screamed at them to shut up and go find something else to do and to leave me alone. When I turned back to the screen, it finally hit me. I was screaming at my own children to leave me for cybersex. I finally saw the impact of my addiction and how it was affecting my relationship with them. I wasn't asking them to leave me

alone so I could work or to prepare for a meeting or a community activity. No, I was saying, in effect, "Leave me alone because I'm having sex on the Internet."

Arlene, too, was seduced by cybersex to the detriment of her children.

I was married to a wealthy man. We had four children and a live-in nanny. When my husband died, I became very morose. I didn't know what to do, so I just began living in my bedroom. We'd had a computer and Internet access, though I'd never used it much. But one day, I went online. Somehow I discovered a very curious and interesting chat room. All the participants were philosophical and intellectual. They were always talking about philosophers like Nietzsche, Heidegger, and Sartre. There was also a kind of hierarchy among the forty or so participants. The top guys called themselves silverbacks. It was like a group of philosophizing primates. There was also verbal sparring going on continuously while they were talking. What's more, the whole scene was underlaid with very sexual talk. Very quickly I got hooked. I was pretty depressed at the time, feeling very alone, and it just drew me in. It was intellectually and erotically very stimulating. It was like an online, real-life soap opera. I spent hours and hours there, day after day, hunkered down in my room. I wouldn't get up until 10:00 or 11:00 A.M. I'd get something to eat and then go online and stay online until two or three in the morning. What about the kids? The nanny assumed complete care for them. For a long time, I totally ignored them. I might as well have been dead, too, for all the care, love, or time they got from me.

CHILDREN EXPOSED TO CYBERSEX

Aside from the loss of time with their parents, children living in homes where a parent is participating in cybersex are much more likely to be exposed to sexual images or activities. The problem here is the ease of access children have to sexual information and activities. What's more, such exposures can happen inadvertently because of the way the Internet works. For example, a client told of her ten-year-old doing an astronomy research project on black holes. She typed in the term "black hole" and was greeted by a Web site dedicated to the genitalia of black women and a screen full of black women's vulvas. Another client spoke of how his son wanted to learn more about the president of our country and the White House. He made a mistake when typing "www.whitehouse.gov" into the search engine and ended up in a porn site. Even accidental discovery gives kids access.

If a parent is using the Net for sex, however, the possibility for access and exposure to sexual sites increases. Even a child with limited computer knowledge can stumble into, or deliberately access, the parent's history files and visit any of those sites, not to mention any bookmarks that have been set up. Furthermore, if a parent is regularly using the Internet for sex, at some point a child *will* happen upon him or her in the middle of sexual activity.

Having a sexually compulsive or out-of-control person living in the house also creates a sexualized energy that permeates the entire home. Children may not understand what is happening, but they do sense this sexualized atmosphere, and when they get older, they recognize in retrospect what had really been happening, even though they were never directly exposed to it.

FOCUS ON YOURSELF AS A PARTNER

Recovery from cybersex compulsion or addiction includes three separate, yet interrelated, components: your partner's recovery, your recovery, and your relationship's recovery. We can't emphasize strongly enough that you must let your partner take responsibility for his or her own recovery.

A word of caution: if life with your partner has become truly out of control and he or she is not willing to get help, you may need to consider having an intervention. For recommendations on additional resources for help, please refer to the appendix.

Most codependents beginning recovery feel as if they are running inches ahead of an avalanche of hope and despair. The possibility of a peaceful life and a nurturing relationship seems terribly remote. One codependent told us, "I simply couldn't envision it at the start." Most cannot.

The burning question for codependents as they face their relationship with a sexually compulsive partner is, Should I leave the relationship? Although for some that question will have to be confronted in the course of recovery, it is usually best not to do so at this point. In the first place, it's not in your best interest. You need to work through your codependency issues in order to recover yourself, and that often happens best with your partner's support. The question at this point is not, Should I divorce my partner? Rather it is, How do I start my recovery?

As a codependent, you have a right to receive help. A good analogy is to think of marriage as a "reincarnation" event. The things you do not work out in your current relationship will simply have to be dealt with in the next. Consider this a kind of marital karma. Without help, the probability of ending up in another dysfunctional relationship is almost certain. You must stop running and face the avalanche. Many people will be there to help you.

Recovery requires that you take certain steps. It's not your job to monitor your partner's sexual behavior. It's not your job to keep your partner "sober." It's not your job to ensure your partner's sexual satisfaction. You simply can't guarantee your partner's recovery, and the more you try to help, the more you'll get in the way. Finally, you must take responsibility for your own recovery.

STEPS FOR CODEPENDENCY RECOVERY

Your most immediate task concerns detachment. You need to refocus your life and recovery on yourself—the person who has been lost in the codependency. The following four guidelines will help you to do so.

1. LEARN TO LOVE WITHOUT INTERFERING WITH CONSEQUENCES
By this we mean caring for another person without intervening in his or her life. Disaster at work, financial chaos, arrests—whatever happens because of your partner's addictive behavior is your partner's problem and responsibility, not yours. As part of recovery, sexually compulsive or addicted partners must feel the full brunt of their powerlessness. Any effort to protect your partner diverts energy from your recovery. Extend support, but not help.

2. ACKNOWLEDGE YOUR OWN POWERLESSNESS OVER OBSESSION
In a Twelve Step support group or therapy—or both—you need to acknowledge that you don't have control over your partner's behaviors. You must survey all the ways you obsess about or attempt to control your partner. This includes all the ways you try to influence your partner's recovery. You must reach a point of surrender, which means committing to stop.

3. Acknowledge the Consequences of Codependent Behavior

Part of surrender is to fully comprehend the costs of your codependent behavior. Accepting powerlessness is admitting what did not work. Acknowledging chaotic unmanageability due to consequences is admitting what did happen. Recognizing the costs deepens the commitment to stop.

4. Define a Codependent's Sobriety

Becoming more clear about personal codependent patterns will tell you which of your behaviors are self-destructive and need to be stopped. Sexually compulsive partners aren't the only ones who need to achieve "sobriety." You must also abstain from your obsessional and dysfunctional behaviors. And you must be clear about what constitutes a slip for you.

DETACHMENT AND ITS ROLE IN RECOVERY

As detachment proceeds, you will discover much. You will learn how you can better handle anxiety. You'll see the ways you tried to control your partner's behaviors. You'll work on being able to say what's acceptable and what's not in a way that's not angry or accusatory. You may have felt responsible for your partner's sexuality. Now you'll see that there's no way you can do that.

Recovery requires that you change your expectations of yourself. You'll learn that you're not the one who needs to supply your partner's boundaries, to monitor choices, or to set priorities. It's not unusual for a codependent to have entered a relationship with someone who has a lot of problems. Typically when that happens, the partner's needs absorb all the codependent's time and energy, preventing the person from looking at his or her own problems.

Working on your recovery is extremely important. An invaluable part of this process is to seek help from a good therapist. Unfortunately, many codependents are reluctant to enter therapy because they feel that they are not the ones with the problem. That's correct, but only to a point. No, you don't have your partner's problem, per se, but you do have problems of your own, and they are related to the behavior of your partner. Therapy will help you look at the role you've played in your partner's addictive behavior; doing so can dramatically improve your recovery.

Our research shows that the first six months of recovery will include times of intense emotional turmoil and pain.[3] It is at this point that you may experience health problems. In the next six months, you will likely see significant change and gain. Career, finances, and self-image improve dramatically and continue to improve in the coming years. Significant improvement in communication with your partner and in the overall quality of the relationship is common. And in the second and third years, codependents find themselves much more able to cope with stress and to develop spirituality and friendships. In addition, codependents can expect progress in sexual health and overall life satisfaction.

Our findings also indicate that the stages of progress you and your partner experience will often be mismatched. As a result, you may become impatient with your partner, even though he or she is proceeding at a rate similar to other recovering addicts. You may also prematurely conclude that the relationship cannot be saved. To prevent premature or bad choices, we urge you to commit to your own recovery.

WHAT YOU CAN EXPECT DURING YOUR RECOVERY PROCESS

- Things will get worse before they get better.
- You will need to monitor your expectations.
- There is no magical solution.
- There will be relapses.
- A year of hard work will be needed before you'll feel that recovery has begun to take hold.
- Recovery will be on track when you and your partner are working independently in therapy.
- For your recovery to progress, you will need to
  —develop a plan so you know what to do when a relapse occurs,
  —make decisions with the support of others (a support group, your therapist, or a Twelve Step group),
  —avoid, if possible, making major decisions (divorce, moving, or changing jobs, for example) during the first year,
  —fulfill the tasks asked of you by your therapist,
  —focus during the first year on your individual recovery, not on the recovery of your relationship,

—do couples work while your independent therapy progresses, and
—seek help from Recovering Couples Anonymous (RCA) when you
decide to work on your relationship.

Recovering Couples Anonymous stresses the idea that recovery is a
three-pronged process that includes your recovery, your partner's recovery, and your recovery as a couple.[4] Your recovery as a couple cannot take
place without the individual recovery of each partner. Conversely, while it is
possible for two partners to achieve a solid recovery independent of one
another, that alone will not guarantee the creation of a healthy relationship.
You must learn how to integrate your recovery together with your partners.
Three ideas lie at the root of this issue:

- People who haven't completed certain developmental tasks look to
  their partners to solve them.
- Two shame-filled people make a shame-based couple for whom
  there is no possibility of a healthy relationship.
- The harsh reality is that making individual changes is not enough
  to give you the skills needed to create a fulfilling relationship.

UNDERSTANDING FAMILY DYNAMICS

Each partner in the relationship brings along his or her unique family history. We don't seek to judge or blame our families for the difficulties we're
having in our current relationships. Instead, we seek to understand our family roots and dynamics. Then we can gain a better understanding of the family models each of us brings to the relationship. In addition, we can better
understand the dynamics involved as we try to combine our own family histories into a new family. This is called the "blending of the epics." Each of us
is on a life journey. When we join with another person to create a couple,
these individual journeys take on even greater importance. Two people are
now trying to merge their individual journeys. They are at different stages in
their journeys, each coming from a different background.

Those individual journeys make up each partner's family epic, adding
to the complexity and difficulty of this merger. Every family is really a great,
transgenerational story—of all the many people involved, their personal

struggles, and their ways of interacting, expressing emotion, loving, arguing, and communicating.

Our families help determine the kind of person we look for in a partner. We look for a partner who can help us resolve the problems we experienced when we were growing up. If we become more aware of our family histories, we can become more aware of the reasons we are attracted to particular types of people.

TELLING YOUR STORY

In our culture today, many people have lost or forgotten parts of their stories. Recovery groups such as Alcoholics Anonymous, Overeaters Anonymous, and others encourage people to discover and tell their stories. Partners need to go through this same process together as a couple. They need to tell their stories to each other to begin forming a joint story. When partners share this process, a new truth begins to emerge that is critical to the relationship's success.

First we must discover what happened to us in our families, the ways we learned to deal with feelings, conflict, and anger. Next we need to share that knowledge with each other. Then we can understand why we react to one another and others the way we do. Until we can do this, real communication and intimacy are not possible.

If two people are at varied points in their journeys, they can be mismatched. As mentioned, individuals who haven't completed certain developmental tasks look to their partners to solve them. When people try to solve these developmental issues through their partners, they are not only doomed to fail, but also create further problems.

COUPLESHAME

Living in the midst of the destructive cycle created with intimacy problems, partners find that they aren't honest with each other, they don't communicate, and they either withdraw or fight. Any problem with money, the children, or their social life only serves as further evidence that they and their relationship are a terrible failure.

Because these couples haven't had a source of support, they are operating with family-of-origin problems, and they struggle with intimacy and codependency—all of which leads to feelings of "coupleshame": shame as a couple.

Coupleshame closely parallels individual feelings of shame. Coupleshame appears when two people with core feelings of shame join in a relationship. As in mathematics, adding two negatives together makes an even greater negative. Two shame-filled people make a shame-based couple for whom there is no possibility of a healthy relationship. Sam and Paula's story illustrates this situation clearly.

Sam and Paula had been going to Alcoholics Anonymous meetings for years. Both divorced from extremely dysfunctional marriages right after they began their recovery from alcohol addiction. They had avoided relationships for years, basically because they were afraid.

Sam and Paula met at their meetings and began dating. Soon they had fallen in love with each other and decided to marry. Then they discovered that many of the same issues that had been part of their first relationships were surfacing again in this marriage.

Miserable in the marriage, they began to feel as if the marriage had been a mistake and they'd chosen the wrong partner. Both were also saddened and disillusioned because they couldn't understand how, after all the work they'd done individually in their years of recovery and fellowship meetings, they could so quickly fall right back into the negative and destructive patterns of their first marriages.

Paula and Sam's story exposes the reality that merely making individual changes is not enough to give you the skills needed to create a fulfilling relationship. These skills can be developed only in a relationship. When faced with a situation similar to Sam and Paula's, many couples reach the conclusion that they shouldn't be together and that they deserve to divorce.

It is important to know that you will not solve coupleshame through separation. Nor will relationship difficulties and problems be solved by working separately outside of a relationship. If you do not work on your relationship issues in this relationship, you are doomed to repeat them in the next . . . and the next and the next. Although they parallel individual skills, couple recovery skills develop only in a relationship.

If and when you and your partner reach a point at which it seems right to begin working on the recovery of your relationship, Recovering Couples

Anonymous can be an enormous help. RCA uses the following questions to help couples better understand themselves and their relationship to each other. If you believe that exploring such issues could help your relationship, we encourage you to contact your local RCA group (see appendix for more information). They will be happy to help.

QUESTIONS TO ASK FOR BETTER MUTUAL UNDERSTANDING

GIVING AND PARENTING
- In what ways have we given so much outside the relationship that it was harmful to ourselves or others—for example, spending so much time on community activities, work, or our children that we had nothing left to give each other?
- In what ways has our giving to others been meaningful and satisfying, while maintaining a balance in our time and energy?

ISOLATION/COMMUNITY
- In what ways have we become isolated from other couples and friends, cutting ourselves off from their support and community?
- In what ways have we sought community for our relationship by seeking out other couples and friends?

CRISIS
- In what ways have we handled crises poorly—in our family, relationship, and friendships?
- In what ways have we created a crisis by blowing a situation out of proportion?
- In what ways have we dealt with crises well?

CONFLICT
- How have we dealt with conflict? Have we repeated fights over the same issue? Have we deliberately created conflict over relatively superficial issues to avoid a deeper issue?
- How have we dealt with conflicts so that they were resolved and both of us were generally satisfied with the process and the result?

STRESS
- In what ways have we allowed ourselves to become so mutually depleted of spiritual, physical, and emotional energy that we have nothing left to give anyone?
- What steps have we taken to manage stress so that we could maintain balance in our lives and ensure a continuous reservoir of energy with which to nurture both ourselves and others?

DENIAL/ACCEPTANCE
- What are the issues in our relationship that we pretend don't exist and have avoided dealing with?
- What are the issues we have acknowledged, faced, and talked about?

Though it may seem impossible right now, thousands of couples have reinvigorated and enriched damaged and foundering relationships. Don't give up hope. Seek help from others. They are only waiting for your call. Healthy and fulfilling intimacy is possible. For additional reading and resources, please turn to the appendix.

II

The Web Frontier

THROUGH THE INTERNET, cybersex has begun affecting our society in subtle and profound ways. It is changing relationships and forcing us to examine and reevaluate our ideas about sexuality. More significant, the impact of cybersex has only begun, and its influence will grow for years to come. What its ultimate impact will be, we can only guess. Clues, however, can be found in the experiences of the people who are struggling with problematic and compulsive cybersex behaviors. We have learned from them that while cybersex has positive aspects, its effects can be overwhelming and damaging, both to the people who engage in it and to their partners, friends, family members, and colleagues. People struggling with and recovering from this problem will encourage us, and perhaps force us, as individuals and as societies to be more open and honest about our sexuality and to more closely examine our relationships and the role our sexuality plays in our lives. Their experiences and their recovery will also create a path for others with similar struggles to follow—one that also offers the hope that healing is possible.

People recovering from problematic and compulsive cybersex behaviors are basically trying to define what healthy sexuality means for them. With the easy access to sexual information and activities that the Internet provides, each of us will also need to determine how we will use this technology as well as how much and in what ways we will allow it to affect our sexuality and our relationships.

This process of pursuing and taking on greater personal responsibility can be seen on a much broader scale as we look out across our planet to see the amazing drive for self-determination and self-government among so many cultures and nations. More and more cultures (the Palestinians, the Kosovars, the Maori, the Serbians, and the East Timorians, to name a few) are reaching a point at which they can no longer tolerate domination by authoritarian leaders. In their landmark book *The Paradigm Conspiracy,* authors Denise Breton and Christopher Largent describe this worldwide shift in power from autocratic and authoritarian models to new modes that incorporate shared power, interaction, and interdependence.[1]

The science of ecology is also revealing just how intricately all parts of our planet and its ecosystems are intertwined. Ecologists are showing us that we must be responsible for our actions and that there are limits to what we as a species can do without destroying all that we depend upon for our survival.

And what if one's actions are irresponsible? We have long had laws governing our behavior, as well as penalties for misbehavior. What went on within the family, including spousal and child abuse, however, was long considered outside of society's purview. This is no longer true, as we have now begun to take a stand regarding domestic abuse. Such steps are also being taken with countries at the international level. The multicountry intervention in the Yugoslav state of Kosovo in 1999, in response to the mass killing and deportation of Kosovars by the Serbian government, was an example of nations intervening within another sovereign state not primarily out of self-interest, but to come to the aid of a persecuted and vulnerable group of people.

As individuals, cultures, and countries, humans are struggling with issues of appropriate limits, self-determination, and interdependence. Neither as individuals, countries, nor as a species can we humans do whatever we like. We are all interdependent and all of us must live within limits.

THE HUMAN CONNECTION

If you are using sex compulsively, you know that it can be very isolating. Sex can become your most important need, to the exclusion of the rest of your life. This flies in the face, however, of our human need for connection. Humans live and actually thrive in community.

Heart researcher and internist Dean Ornish, for example, developed a regimen that can not only halt hardening of the coronary arteries but also actually reverse it without surgery. This regimen includes meditation, a low-fat vegetarian diet, yoga, and support group participation. Subsequent research by Ornish revealed that the key factor in the success of his program was support group participation.[2] Mounting evidence suggests that people without close, durable ties to family and friends are at high risk for everything from cancer and heart disease to ulcers and infections. "Love and intimacy are at the root of what makes us sick and what makes us well," says Ornish. "I am not aware of any other factor in medicine—not diet, smoking, or exercise—that has a greater impact."

Similar studies of men and women throughout the world have revealed a similar pattern. Women who say they feel isolated go on to develop and die of breast and ovarian cancer at several times the expected rate. College students who report "strained and cold" relationships with their parents suffer extraordinary rates of hypertension and heart disease decades later. Heart attack survivors who happen to live by themselves die at twice the rate of those who live with others.

What's going on here? How can something as mushy as "social support" affect the growth of a tumor or the function of a coronary artery? For starters, such support helps regulate our behavior. People with commitments to honor are less likely to abuse themselves. They drink less, eat better, and avoid needless risks. Companionship also lets us share feelings that would otherwise fester and modulate our body's response to stress. Again, people, societies, and nations cannot survive, let alone thrive, in isolation.

Seventy percent of all cybersex traffic occurs Monday through Friday between 9:00 A.M. and 5:00 P.M. Millions of Americans are engaging in cybersex activities every day, and much of that activity is happening in the workplace. It might be a key executive or a technology guru or an invaluable scientist who couldn't possibly be fired but whose cybersex compulsion is simply out of control. Or it could be an employee or a colleague who clearly needs help. Business bottom lines are being dramatically affected by losses in time and productivity due to cybersex. As more employers are forced to confront the reality of compulsive or addictive cybersex, more people will begin to understand and accept the reality of sex addiction. Employers will search for ways to help these people. The power of cybersex addiction will put to rest the doubts of skeptics that sex addiction isn't just weird and perverted anomalous behavior taken up by a few mentally ill people. It is a disease with clear roots, an illness that can strike close to home.

Cybersex addiction is already being recognized in popular culture. In his newest book, *The Bear and the Dragon,* one of author Tom Clancy's characters speaks of this problem: "He had considered prowling some Internet pornography sites. For one reason or another the Asian culture made for an ample collection of such things. He wasn't exactly proud of this addiction, but his sexual drive needed some outlet."[3] Here is a best-selling author whose books are read by millions of people throughout the world acknowledging the power and addictive nature of cybersex and the struggle people have trying to control their addiction.

THE POWER OF THE SEX DRIVE

For much, if not all, of human history, societies have placed strict controls on sexual activity. These controls were easily enforceable, since people lived in tight-knit communities where violation of sexual mores could mean ostracism, a terrible and sometimes even fatal consequence.

Today, however, even before the advent of the Internet and cybersex, attitudes toward sexual activity have become much more relaxed. At this point, we must not underestimate the power of sex to influence behavior. A noted laboratory experiment with rats shows this immense power. First, rats were habituated to heroin. Next, an electrode was placed in their brains that, when activated, stimulated the sexual pleasure centers of the animals. The rats were then given two choices: touch a button that would give them heroin or one that would sexually stimulate them. They consistently chose sexual stimulation over heroin, one of the most addictive drugs known, with extremely uncomfortable withdrawal symptoms. In another experiment, rats were deprived of food for a week. They were then put into a cage with their mates and food. Every rat chose to mate rather than eat the food.

Sex is an enormously powerful drive. In a sense, cybersex is enabling people to "mainline" sex whenever they want it. The many vignettes we've related in this book have shown people choosing to put sex above all other life activities. They ignored their families, work, partners, friends, food, and sleep for lengthy periods of time. Sex became their most important need.

They became lonely, hungry, and tired. They knew they needed other people in their lives, yet they found that they couldn't stop their cybersex activities.

TECHNOLOGICALLY ENHANCED SEX:
CYBERSEX IS ONLY THE BEGINNING

We fear, too, that cybersex is only the beginning of what is coming in the way of increased and enhanced sexual activities and opportunities. For many years now, people have used drugs like cocaine, marijuana, and "poppers" to enhance sexual experiences. Ecstasy, known as the "love drug," is now commonly used by high school and college students for this same purpose. Given the incredible advances in molecular biology, it is not at all difficult to imagine a new designer drug that will incredibly alter and expand the sexual experience—one that will be extremely addictive too.

WHY A WAR ON CYBERSEX WON'T WORK

Science fiction writers have for years written of fantastically enhanced sexual experiences and their addictive qualities. Frank Herbert, in his remarkable classic science fiction Dune series, wrote of an order of women who had perfected the art of enhancing the male sexual and orgasmic experience.[4] The feelings and sensations they could elicit in men were so profound as to be instantly addictive—and enslaving. Men would do *anything* for the promise of another experience. In Aldous Huxley's classic *Brave New World,* a group of characters spends an evening at the "feelies," a movie theater in which, by holding special handles on their seats, viewers could feel all the physical sensations the actors felt as they made love on screen.[5] And finally, there's the holodeck in *Star Trek: The Next Generation,* a virtual-reality room that the user can program to produce any kind of experience he or she wants. While the use of the holodeck for sex was only implied in the series, it's not hard to imagine the potential of such a device. Any kind of sexual experience you could ever imagine with real people could be accomplished with no fear of disease or need for a relationship.

In all probability, inventions like these will be developed in the future because there is so much money to be made. Today's video streaming and Webcam technology were developed predominately by the pornography industry because it recognized the enormous potential for profit. That profit potential is always there, waiting for the next innovation. This is why we believe we are seeing only the leading edge of the cybersex and sex addiction problem. It is imperative for society to acknowledge this situation. It would be fruitless, though certainly tempting, to simply stick our collective head in the sand and pretend that nothing like this will happen or to roll our eyes and write off the issue as a fringe problem among a few "perverts."

A more likely and extremely tempting step in dealing with cybersex would be for the state or federal government to set controls on Internet sex. Logically, this would never work. No matter how clever a blocking software might become, people would be able to bypass it. Previous failed attempts at governing people's behaviors include Prohibition and the "war on drugs." Though begun with the best of intentions, Prohibition failed miserably in its goal to stop alcohol use in the United States. In addition, it spawned a sophisticated and powerful network of organized crime that plagues our society to this day.

Our more recent war on drugs has turned out to be equally futile. The United States imprisons a higher percentage of its citizens than any other country in the world except South Africa, and the vast majority are nonviolent substance abusers who can be rehabilitated. Most crimes in this country are either the direct or indirect result of the criminal's drug or alcohol abuse. Current correctional trends toward longer sentences, fewer prison programs, and limited access to drug and alcohol treatment have only served to guarantee a continuation of the massive recidivism rates we currently experience. Billions of dollars have been spent to stop the flow of illicit drugs into the United States (including $1.2 billion given to Colombia in 2000 for drug interdiction) and to stop domestic production. Yet demand and use is higher than ever for many drugs.

Other countries, Switzerland and the Netherlands, for example, have taken a much different approach to the drug problem by decriminalizing its use. In addition, they provide extensive counseling and medical and treatment services at little or no cost to those who have problems with drugs to help them recover from their addictions and live more meaningful and productive lives. These countries have extremely low rates of drug abuse.

What's more, criminal activity associated with drug trafficking and use in these countries is nearly nonexistent.

So often when our society determines that some behavior is wrong or a problem, we enact a law in an attempt to control that behavior. In some cases, this is the wrong approach. Clearly, some people are having problems with the easy access to sex provided by the Internet and are exhibiting behavior that is regarded as wrong, even criminal, in the offline world. Arranging for prostitutes, for example, generally goes unmonitored and uncontrolled on the Net. What's more, minors have easy access to sexual sites and information too. We have already seen attempts to use the legal system, with the threat of incarceration, to regulate behavior or content on the Internet. It will be very hard, if not impossible, however, to enforce such laws. We will not be able to control cybersex, and a war on cybersex that parallels the war on drugs would be similarly ineffective.

Trying to control the Internet by legal means is really an attempt to solve the problem with first-order changes. Just as that is merely a temporary fix on the personal level, it will not work at the societal level, either. The Internet is not inherently good or bad. It enables us to stay in touch with one another from nearly anywhere on earth. It can be used to help people create new and rewarding relationships. It's not the enemy. As a society, we have to view this cybersex problem in terms of second-order changes. We need to ask ourselves what our goals are. What kind of behaviors do we want vis-à-vis the Internet and cybersex? What will make us better human beings? What will contribute to the growth of healthy sexuality and loving relationships?

At issue is how we will learn to control our own sexual behavior given the reality of this new technology and how we will teach others to do the same. Once again, we return to the theme of self-determination. We must look within as a culture to decide what behaviors will be best for society.

When a new technology emerges, its impact on society often forces us to change how we interact with one another. The Internet is doing just that. The impact of instant access to so much information on sex and the opportunities for cybersex are exacerbating the tremendous changes in our gender-related and sexual mores that have been under way for most of the past century. Fifty years ago, for example, only a small percentage of women worked outside the home and the majority of those who did were concentrated in just a few professions, such as teaching, nursing, and secretarial work. Today, men and women work alongside one another in virtually all workplaces and professions. As this change occurred, new rules for interaction between men and women in the workplace had to develop. "Sexual harassment" is not only a relatively new expression; it's a new concept too—one that grew out of the need to more clearly define the behavior of men and women in the workplace.

DISCUSSING SEX OPENLY

The Internet is enabling us to relate to one another in new ways. But as yet we don't really have any rules about how to use this technology. As a society, we are only beginning to develop these rules. What should they be? Who should develop them? And how? Who will have input? And what should the rules be about sexuality? As a society, we tend not to talk about sex openly. Studies continue to show that few American parents talk with their children about sex. We push the topic under the table. The Internet and access to cybersex force us to bring sexuality out in the open in a way we have never done before. The Internet has amplified this process enormously. The media, which use sexual images to sell just about everything, have been pushing this issue for some years, but now we are at a point where we simply must be out in the open with it. As a culture—and as a species—we will have to decide how we are going to deal with this new technology and its relationship to our sexuality.

This is an inevitable struggle that will bring the human race to a higher level. It is a struggle that is affecting societies across the globe because the Internet knows no borders. In many countries in which the population is predominantly Muslim, for example, women are struggling to have the rights that they now know many other women have. Television and the Internet have played a powerful role in exposing them to information about how other women in the world live. Throughout the world, the media are forcing us to look at how we relate to one another in what is a time of extraordinary change.

The problem we face is not cybersex, per se. It is learning new ways to relate to one another and to our sexuality. There is much to be sorted out, and this process will take some time. In another hundred years, historians will likely look back and see that the technology of the Internet created a cultural earthquake and that part of that change was directly related to a vastly more open discussion about sexuality and the relationships between men and women.

THE INTERNET: CREATING A NEW TYPE OF RELATIONSHIP

The Internet created the possibility for a new type of relationship, one for which we had no guidelines. For example, is a cyber-affair really an affair if the two people were never in physical contact with one another? These technology-based relationships are uninhibited and interactive. The technology has developed so quickly that we're unable to keep up with the many different ways that people can use—and abuse—the Internet. We simply lack the cultural anchors needed to deal with this technology.

Without cultural anchors, what do we do? On the one hand, it's easy to think that since there are relatively few rules or laws about the Internet and cybersex, anything goes. Besides, existing laws, such as those against soliciting sex on the Net and exchanging child pornography, are difficult to enforce. Because there are as yet no cultural norms about this area doesn't mean that doing whatever one pleases is a good idea. This book has been devoted to helping people see the devastating results of cybersex addiction in people's lives. Just because there are no societal norms for cybersex doesn't mean there won't be individual consequences for such behavior. We have to do as a society what you are doing as an individual. Without cultural anchors, you have no choice but to turn to your own value system and make some inferences about what is appropriate behavior. You're trying to determine how to live with this new technology without destroying all that is dear to you. You're creating new first- and second-order changes and developing appropriate boundaries in your life. You're learning to live in your Recovery Zone. You as an individual—and we as a society—will make some mistakes along the way. We'll have some slips, but the glimpse of a better life will help us persevere.

We have become a culture that believes not only that "we can have it all," but also that we deserve it. We are constantly inundated by social and media messages telling us that we are entitled to whatever we want: a well-paying, fulfilling job; a great marriage or partnership; two or three cars; closets packed with fine clothes; a large and well-appointed house; perfectly man-nered, talented children; time for golf, tennis, skiing, and the health club; vacations in exotic locales; personal fulfillment; and great sex. The U.S. Army's ad slogan "Be All That You Can Be" might actually reflect society's message to us, but perhaps with this addition: "And Buy All That You Can See."

LIVING IN THE RECOVERY ZONE: MAKING CHOICES

More than twenty years ago, Alvin Toffler, in his prophetic book *Future Shock,* had already foreseen and named this phenomenon; he called it "overchoice."[6] Engulfed by far more possibilities than we can handle, we are discovering that, in fact, we can't have everything we want. Each of us is faced with the task of determining the limits we have to put on our lives. We simply can't experience all that is potentially available to us. Some families, for example, decide to limit the after-school activities of their children in order to preserve family time together. Partners may each decide to forgo promotions—and the new "toys" that could come from higher income—because they want more personal time.

At its most basic level, we are talking about self-determination. We must decide how and where to focus our attention in a way that will let us live the life we want. We must learn what works for us and what doesn't.

Cybersex, called by some "the biggest porn shop in the world," pre-sents this same problem of overchoice. While the good news is that there's more easily accessible information about sex available to more people than ever before—and more and different opportunities to engage in it—we still cannot "do it all." Each of us must determine appropriate boundaries for our sexual activities that allow us to balance all our life goals and needs—those involving work, family, friends, hobbies, and so forth. In other words, we must learn to live within our Recovery Zone.

The limits we set on our lives—the boundaries we create—are based on a relationship with ourselves, one in which we seek to hear and follow our inner voice. These limits enable us to nurture, support, and protect our-selves. As we said earlier, setting appropriate limits also means being able to say, "No, I'm not going to do that, even though I want to, because if I do, I'm going to mess up my life." We take a particular stand because it reflects a belief we have about who we are.

As sex becomes more accessible, less regulated, and more public, it may also become more casual, even to the point of actually being trivial. Given its availability, sex could come to be seen as just another recreational activity, one that, as we know, can become addictive. Sex—an action that can hold tremendous personal and interpersonal significance—may soon no longer be seen as connected to Self, but rather little more than a biological expression having nothing to do with Self. At some point, we have to ask ourselves what sex is and what it means in our lives. If we want to maintain sex as an integral and meaningful part of our relationships, we may find that we simply cannot experience all the sexual choices available to us. We may have to say that sex isn't just another pleasurable diversion. We stand to lose much if an act that can create such profound feelings of connectedness becomes trivialized.

A SPIRITUAL JOURNEY OF DISCOVERY

This is, in the end, a spiritual quest, a spiritual journey to discover who we really are and what we can be as human beings. One of the most important ways we discover who we are is through interactions with other human beings. The Internet and cybersex are leading us to develop a greater awareness of our sexual selves and to discover how our sexuality fits into our lives and our interactions and relationships with others.

Too often in our culture, the relationship of sexuality and spirituality is seen as a war in which one must defeat and destroy the other. This view is futile and counterproductive. The desire to unite through the sexual act can metaphorically be seen as a drive to once again be united with the Divine. This is a yearning for our lost wholeness, a search for our other half, so that we might, if even for only a moment through sexual union, reexperience the lost bliss of our godlike totality. Our sexuality arises out of a sense of incompleteness that is manifested by an urge toward wholeness and a yearning for the One. But what, then, is spirituality? Is it not this same desire, a yearning for the Divine? While spirituality and sexuality are not exactly the same, they are cut from the same cloth. They are, as noted author M. Scott Peck says, "kissing cousins." The sexual and spiritual parts of our being lie so close together that it is hardly possible to arouse one without arousing the other. They are like two snare drums sitting side by side. If you strike one, the other vibrates too.

This is not myth; it's human experience. In Peck's *The Road Less Traveled,* he writes,

> When my beloved first stands before me naked, all open to my sight, there is a feeling throughout the whole of me. Awe! Why awe? If sex is no more than an instinct, why don't I simply feel horny or hungry? Such simple hunger would be quite sufficient to ensure the propagation of the species. Why should sex be complicated with reverence?[7]

Sex is "complicated with reverence" because it is, in fact, the closest many people ever come to a mystical experience. Indeed, this is why so many people chase after sex with such desperate abandon. Whether or not they know it, they are searching for God. The Internet and cybersex enable people to chase all the more frantically and intensely.

SEX AND SPIRIT UNITE

Abraham Maslow, in his studies of self-actualizing people, discovered that they often experience orgasm as a religious, even mystical, event. Maslow made it clear that these people were not speaking metaphorically. With another human in a deeply loving relationship, we can touch the Divine through sex.

Ironically, however, though we need the other to reach these heights, we briefly lose that other at the climactic moment, forgetting who and where we are. Mystics and spiritual teachers through the ages have spoken of an "ego death" as a necessary part of the spiritual journey, even its goal, and the French actually refer to orgasm as the "little death." We have entered the realm of spirit. Sex and spirit become one as we become one with All.

Sex does, however, complicate relationships. It is the search for God in human romantic relationships that lies at the root of the problem, says Peck. We look to our spouse or to romantic love to meet all our needs and fulfill us. This never works, or at least not for long. We can live in the bliss of new love perhaps for a few months, a year, or several years if we are lucky. But after a while, we change or our partner changes or everything changes—and suddenly it's all up for grabs. Throughout this long journey, however, we learn a lot about vulnerability, intimacy, love, and our own narcissism. It is natural for us humans to want a tangible God, but the Divine is not ours to possess. Instead, we must learn to accept that we live within the Divine or, as some describe it, within "the one in whom we live and move and have our being."

The common denominator of sex and spirituality is the search for meaning. Sexuality and spirituality connect through meaning. As we deepen our understanding of ourselves, of others, and of our planet and all its myriad life, we heighten both our spirituality *and* our sexuality. As M. Scott Peck is fond of saying, "I distrust any religious conversion which does not also involve an intensification of one's sexuality." The deeper and more meaningful our sexuality, the more we touch the mystical.

We need to recognize that we are part of a much larger whole. When people are unable to make this connection, they turn to relationships with objects—the false gods, in the biblical sense, of alcohol, money, sex (including cybersex), food, whatever seems to fill the void inside. While still searching for meaning, this path leads to addiction and an unmanageable life.

Despite its novelty, allure, and power, and no matter how intense and momentarily wonderful and fulfilling the experience, cybersex is no different. For all the reasons we've mentioned, it is ultimately an emotionally and spiritually empty and isolating experience.

CHOOSING HOW TO LIVE LIFE

Here is a critically important point. The choice is not to be in control or out of control; the choice is *how* we will live without control. We can "lose" control by admitting that there are larger forces at work in our lives and that we are part of a Divine plan. This will, in fact, bring us closer to our true selves and the Divine. Our other choice is to lose control via compulsive and addictive behaviors. This brings pain, misery, and ultimately self-destruction.

Through prayer and meditation, we seek conscious contact with a Higher Power, a connection that we strengthen as we learn to accept nurturing, to be open to our senses, to trust ourselves and others, and to become more centered within ourselves. As we do this, we are better able to enter into healthy relationships with a partner. Our search for meaning weaves the strands of relationship, self, spirit, and sensuality and sexuality together.

The information, suggestions, and guidelines we've provided can help you start on the road to recovery. Yes, you *can* change. You *can* create better relationships and live a richer, more fulfilling life. Remember that you *can't* do this alone. And you don't have to. Reach out to others for strength, support, and encouragement. All that you need will be given to you.

$\mathscr{A}$ppendix

The Twelve Steps of Alcoholics Anonymous*

1. We admitted we were powerless over alcohol—that our lives had become unmanageable.
2. Came to believe that a Power greater than ourselves could restore us to sanity.
3. Made a decision to turn our will and our lives over to the care of God *as we understood Him.*
4. Made a searching and fearless moral inventory of ourselves.
5. Admitted to God, to ourselves, and to another human being the exact nature of our wrongs.
6. Were entirely ready to have God remove all these defects of character.
7. Humbly asked Him to remove our shortcomings.
8. Made a list of all persons we had harmed, and became willing to make amends to them all.
9. Made direct amends to such people wherever possible, except when to do so would injure them or others.
10. Continued to take personal inventory and when we were wrong promptly admitted it.
11. Sought through prayer and meditation to improve our conscious contact with God *as we understood Him,* praying only for knowledge of His will for us and the power to carry that out.

---

* The Twelve Steps of AA are taken from *Alcoholics Anonymous,* 3d ed., published by AA World Services, Inc., New York, N.Y., 59–60. Reprinted with permission of AA World Services, Inc. (See editor's note on copyright page.)

12. Having had a spiritual awakening as the result of these steps, we tried to carry this message to alcoholics, and to practice these principles in all our affairs.

The Twelve Steps of Alcoholics Anonymous Adapted for Sexual Addicts*

1. We admitted we were powerless over our sexual addiction—that our lives had become unmanageable.
2. Came to believe that a Power greater than ourselves could restore us to sanity.
3. Made a decision to turn our will and our lives over to the care of God as we understood Him.
4. Made a searching and fearless moral inventory of ourselves.
5. Admitted to God, to ourselves, and to another human being the exact nature of our wrongs.
6. Were entirely ready to have God remove all these defects of character.
7. Humbly asked Him to remove our shortcomings.
8. Made a list of all persons we had harmed, and became willing to make amends to them all.
9. Made direct amends to such people wherever possible, except when to do so would injure them or others.
10. Continued to take personal inventory and when we were wrong promptly admitted it.
11. Sought through prayer and meditation to improve our conscious contact with God as we understood Him, praying only for knowledge of His will for us and the power to carry that out.
12. Having had a spiritual awakening as the result of these steps, we tried to carry this message to others and to practice these principles in all our affairs.

Contact List for More Information

A recovery-supporting workbook designed and written specifically to accompany *In the Shadows of the Net* is also available. For more information about this workbook, access www.sexhelp.com or www.recoveryzone.org.

---

* Adapted from the Twelve Steps of Alcoholics Anonymous with permission of AA World Services, Inc., New York, N.Y.

For information on both inpatient and outpatient treatment services, contact the Meadows at 1-800-MEADOWS.

For more information about Dr. Patrick Carnes and his speaking engagements, access his Web site at www.sexhelp.com or call him at 800-708-1796.

For information about Dr. David Delmonico and his speaking engagements, contact him at Duquesne University at 412-396-4032.

For information about Elizabeth Griffin and her speaking engagements, contact her at the American Foundation for Addiction Research at 952-915-9454.

For information on training for counselors and other helping professionals, call the Meadows Institute at 800-420-1616 or access the institute via the Internet at www.itad.org.

Resource Guide

The following is a list of recovery fellowships that may be helpful to you in your particular situation.

Adult Children of Alcoholics
310-534-1815
www.adultchildren.org

Al-Anon
800-344-2666
www.al-anon-alateen.org

Alateen (ages 12–17)
800-356-9996
www.al-anon-alateen.org

Alcoholics Anonymous
212-870-3400
www.alcoholics-anonymous.org

CoAnon
www.co-anon.org

Cocaine Anonymous
800-347-8998
www.ca.org

Co-Dependents Anonymous
602-277-7991
www.codependents.org

Co-Dependents of Sex Addicts
612-537-6904

Debtors Anonymous
781-453-2743
www.debtorsanonymous.org

Emotions Anonymous
651-647-9712
www.mtn.org/EA

Families Anonymous
310-815-8010
www.familiesanonymous.org

Gamblers Anonymous
213-386-8789
www.gamblersanonymous.org

Marijuana Anonymous
212-459-4423
www.marijuana-anonymous.org

Narcotics Anonymous
818-773-9999
www.na.org

National Council for Couple and Family Recovery
314-997-9808

National Council on Sexual Addiction and Compulsivity
770-989-9754
www.ncsac.org

Nicotine Anonymous
www.nicotine-anonymous.org

Overeaters Anonymous
www.oa.org

Recovering Couples Anonymous
314-830-2600
www.recovering-couples.org

Recovery Online
www.onlinerecovery.org/index.html

Runaway and Suicide Hotline
800-621-4000

S-Anon
615-833-3152
www.sanon.org

Sex Addicts Anonymous
713-869-4902
www.sexaa.org

Sex and Love Addicts Anonymous
781-255-8825
www.slaafws.org

Sexual Addiction Resources/Dr. Patrick Carnes
www.sexhelp.com

Sexual Compulsives Anonymous
310-859-5585
www.sca-recovery.org

Survivors of Incest Anonymous
410-282-3400

Books of Related Interest Authored by Dr. Patrick Carnes

The Betrayal Bond: Breaking Free of Exploitive Relationships (Deerfield Beach, Fla.: Health Communications, 1998).
In a savage psychic twist, victims of abuse and violence often bond with their perpetrators to the stunning point that they will die rather than escape. Carnes's breakthrough book focuses on how betrayal intensifies trauma and illuminates the keys to escaping destructive relationships.

Contrary to Love: Helping the Sexual Addict (Center City, Minn.: Hazelden, 1989). This sequel to *Out of the Shadows* traces the origins and consequences of the addict's faulty core beliefs. Building upon his earlier work, Carnes describes the stages of the illness and lays the groundwork for potential recovery.

Don't Call It Love: Recovery from Sexual Addiction (Phoenix, Ariz.: Gentle Path Press, 1991).
This landmark study of one thousand recovering sex addicts and their families explores how people become sex addicts and the role of culture, family, neurochemistry, and child abuse in creating addiction.

A Gentle Path through the Twelve Steps: The Classic Guide for All People in the Process of Recovery (Center City, Minn.: Hazelden, 1994).
A guidebook for people in recovery that helps them understand their own stories and begin planning a new life of recovery. With more than 250,000 copies sold, it holds invaluable insights for beginners and old-timers alike in any Twelve Step program.

Out of the Shadows: Understanding Sexual Addiction, 3d ed. (Center City, Minn.: Hazelden, 2001).

The groundbreaking book that first identified and defined sexual addiction. A must for anyone looking to understand the illness, it's an expert and in-depth look at the origins of sexual addiction and the addictive cycle.

Sexual Anorexia: Overcoming Sexual Self-Hatred (with Joseph M. Moriarity) (Center City, Minn.: Hazelden, 1997).
The devastating mix of fear, pain, and betrayal can lead to obsessive sexual aversion. Tracing the dysfunction's roots in childhood sexual trauma, neglect, and abuse, Carnes explores dimensions of sexual health, targeting key issues that let recovery proceed.

Videotapes by Gentle Path Press

For more information or to order videotapes from Gentle Path Press, call 800-708-1796.

Addiction Interaction Disorder: Understanding Multiple Addictions
Few addicts—about 17 percent—have only one addiction. More commonly, assorted compulsions combine in a complex systemic problem called addiction interaction disorder. This tape outlines how to screen for the disorder (a major factor in relapse) and explores the role of addiction as a "solution" to trauma.

Contrary to Love: Helping the Sexual Addict
A twelve-part PBS video series in which noted addiction psychologist Dr. Patrick Carnes discusses the spectrum of compulsive-addictive behavior and its treatment. The titles of the twelve parts are
  "Our Addictive Society"
  "Cultural Denial of Addiction"
  "Am I an Addict?"
  "Interview with Three"
  "The Addictive Family"
  "Interview with Melody Beattie"
  "Child Abuse"
  "The Twelve-Step Recovery Process"
  "Healthy Sexuality and Spirituality"
  "Finding a Balance in Recovery"
  "Coping in a World of Shame"
  "The Ten Risks of Recovery"

Trauma Bonds: When Humans Bond with Those Who Hurt Them
Victims often cling to destructive relationships with baffling desperation. In this riveting videotape, Dr. Patrick Carnes analyzes how trauma bonding develops and outlines strategies for breaking free from its compulsive torment.

Audiocassettes by Gentle Path Press

For more information or to order audiocassettes from Gentle Path Press, call 800-708-1796.

Addiction Interaction Disorder: Understanding Multiple Addictions
Sexual Abuse in the Church
Sexual Dependency, Compulsion and Obsession
Toward a New Freedom: Discovering Healthy Sexuality
Trauma Bonds: When We Bond with Those Who Hurt Us

For Further Reading

The following list contains books referenced in this book, in addition to further readings that may be helpful.

Co-Sex Addiction Recovery

Beattie, Melody. *Codependent No More: How to Stop Controlling Others and Start Caring for Yourself.* New York: Walker, 1989.

Calof, David L., and Robin Simons. *The Couple Who Became Each Other and Other Tales of Healing of a Master Hypnotherapist.* New York: Bantam Books, 1996.

Carnes, Patrick J. *The Betrayal Bond: Breaking Free of Exploitive Relationships.* Deerfield Beach, Fla.: Health Communications, 1998.

Fossum, Merle A., and Marilyn J. Mason. *Facing Shame: Families in Recovery.* New York: Norton, 1989.

Friel, John, and Linda Friel. *Adult Children: The Secrets of Dysfunctional Families.* Deerfield Beach, Fla.: Health Communications, 1988.

Schaeffer, Brenda. *Is It Love or Is It Addiction?* 2d ed. Center City, Minn: Hazelden, 1997.

Schneider, Jennifer. *Back from Betrayal: Recovering from His Affairs.* New York: Ballantine Books, 1990.

Schneider, Jennifer P., and Burt Schneider. *Sex, Lies, and Forgiveness: Couples Speaking Out on Healing from Sex Addiction.* Center City, Minn.: Hazelden, 1991.

Family

Bradshaw, John. *Bradshaw on the Family: A Revolutionary Way of Self-Discovery.* Deerfield Beach, Fla.: Health Communications, 1988.

———. *Family Secrets: What You Don't Know* Can *Hurt You.* New York: Bantam Books, 1996.

Evans, Patricia. *The Verbally Abusive Relationship: How to Recognize It and How to Respond.* Holbrook, Mass.: Adams Media Corporation, 1996.

Love, Patricia. *Emotional Incest Syndrome: What to Do When a Parent's Love Rules Your Life.* New York: Bantam Books, 1991.

Mellody, Pia, with Andrea Well Miller and J. Keith Miller. *Facing Codependence.* San Francisco: Harper San Francisco, 1989.

Key Recovery Works

Beattie, Melody. *Journey to the Heart: Daily Meditations on the Path to Freeing Your Soul.* San Francisco: Harper San Francisco, 1996.

Bradshaw, John. *Healing the Shame That Binds You.* Deerfield Beach, Fla.: Health Communications, 1988.

Breton, Denise, and Christopher Largent. *The Paradigm Conspiracy: Why Our Social Systems Violate Our Human Potential—and How We Can Change Them.* Center City, Minn.: Hazelden, 1996.

Bryan, Mark, and Julia Cameron. *The Money Drunk: Ninety Days to Financial Sobriety.* New York: Ballantine Books, 1993.

Cameron, Julia. *The Artist's Way: A Spiritual Path to Higher Creativity.* New York: Putnam, 1995.

Covey, Stephen R. *First Things First.* New York: Fireside, 1996.

———. *The Seven Habits of Highly Effective People: Powerful Lessons in Personal Change.* New York: Simon & Schuster, 1989.

Hope and Recovery: The Twelve Step Guide for Healing from Compulsive Sexual Behavior. Center City, Minn.: Hazelden, 1994.

Milkman, Harvey B., and Stanley Sunderwirth. *Craving for Ecstasy: The Chemistry and Consciousness of Escape.* New York: Free Press, 1987.

Millman, Dan. *Way of the Peaceful Warrior: A Book That Changes Lives.* Tiburon, Calif.: Kramer, 1984.

Mundis, Jerrold. *How to Get Out of Debt, Stay Out of Debt & Live Prosperously.* New York: Bantam Books, 1990.

Nouwen, Henri J. *Reaching Out: The Three Movements of the Spiritual Life.* Garden City, N.Y.: Doubleday, 1986.

Peck, M. Scott. *People of the Lie: The Hope for Healing Human Evil.* New York: Simon & Schuster, 1985.

———. *The Road Less Traveled.* New York: Simon & Schuster, 1997.

Sex Addiction

Adams, Kenneth M. *Silently Seduced: When Parents Make Their Children Partners.* Deerfield Beach, Fla.: Health Communications, 1991.

Answers in the Heart. Center City, Minn.: Hazelden, 1994.

Earle, Ralph H., and Gregory Crowe. *Lonely All the Time: Recognizing, Understanding, and Overcoming Sex Addiction, for Addicts and Co-Dependents.* New York: Pocket Books, 1998.

Ellison, Marvin M. *Erotic Justice: A Liberating Ethic of Sexuality.* Louisville, Ky.: Westminster John Knox Press, 1996.

Hastings, Anne S. *From Generation to Generation: Learning about Adults Who Are Sexual with Children.* Tiburon, Calif.: Printed Voice, 1994.

Kasl, Charlotte. *Women, Sex, and Addiction.* Harper & Row, 1989.

Nouwen, Henri J. *The Return of the Prodigal Son: A Story of Homecoming.* New York: Doubleday, 1994.

Sexual Health

Bechtal, Stephen. *The Practical Encyclopedia of Sex and Health.* Emmaus, Pa.: Rodale Press, 1993.

Berzon, Betty, ed. *Positively Gay.* Berkeley, Calif.: Celestial Arts, 1995.

Covington, Stephanie. *Awakening Your Sexuality: A Guide for Recovering Women.* Center City, Minn.: Hazelden, 1991.

Diamond, Jed. *Male Menopause: Sex and Survival in the Second Half of Life.* Naperville, Ill.: Sourcebooks, 1997.

Eisler, Riane. *The Chalice and the Blade: Our History, Our Future.* San Francisco: Harper & Row, 1987.

Hastings, Anne S. *Discovering Sexuality That Will Satisfy You Both: When Couples Want Differing Amounts and Different Kinds of Sex.* Tiburon, Calif.: Printed Voice, 1993.

Klausner, Mary A., and Bobbie Hasselbring. *Aching for Love: The Sexual Drama of the Adult Child.* San Francisco: Harper San Francisco, 1990.

Maltz, Wendy, ed. *Intimate Kisses: The Poetry of Sexual Pleasure.* Novato, Calif.: New World Library, 2001.

————, ed. *Passionate Hearts: The Poetry of Sexual Love.* Novato, Calif.: New World Library, 1997.

Maltz, Wendy, and Suzie Boss. *Private Thoughts: Exploring the Power of Women's Sexual Fantasies.* Novato, Calif.: New World Library, 2001.

Renshaw, Domeena. *Seven Weeks to Better Sex.* New York: Random House, 1995.

Sex and Religion

Elinor, Burkett, and Frank Bruni. *A Gospel of Shame: Children, Sexual Abuse, and the Catholic Church.* New York: Viking Penguin, 1993.

Laaser, Mark. *Faithful and True: Sexual Integrity in a Fallen World.* Grand Rapids, Mich.: Zondervan, 1996.

———, ed. *Restoring the Soul of a Church: Reconciling Congregations Wounded by Clergy Sexual Misconduct.* Collegeville, Minn.: Liturgical Press, 1995.

Rossetti, Stephen J. *A Tragic Grace: The Catholic Church and Child Sexual Abuse.* Collegeville, Minn.: Liturgical Press, 1996.

Sipe, A. W. Richard. *Sex, Priests, and Power: Anatomy of a Crisis.* New York: Brunner/Mazel, 1995.

Trauma Resolution

Bass, Ellen, and Laura Davis. *The Courage to Heal: A Guide for Women Survivors of Child Sexual Abuse.* New York: HarperCollins, 1994.

Courtois, Christine A. *Healing the Incest Wound: Adult Survivors in Therapy.* New York: Norton, 1996.

Crowder, Adrienne. *Opening the Door: A Treatment Model for Therapy with Male Survivors of Sexual Abuse.* Philadelphia: Brunner/Mazel, 1995.

Davis, Laura. *Allies in Healing: When the Person You Love Was Sexually Abused as a Child.* New York: HarperCollins, 1991.

Dolan, Yvonne. *Resolving Sexual Abuse: Solution-Focused Therapy and Ericksonian Hypnosis for Adult Survivors.* New York: Norton, 1991.

Fossum, Merle A., and Marilyn J. Mason. *Facing Shame: Families in Recovery.* New York: Norton, 1989.

Hunter, Mic. *Abused Boys: The Neglected Victims of Sexual Abuse.* New York: Fawcett, 1991.

Maltz, Wendy. *The Sexual Healing Journey: A Guide for Survivors of Sexual Abuse.* New York: HarperCollins, 1991.

Maltz, Wendy, and Beverly Holman. *Incest and Sexuality: A Guide to Understanding and Healing.* Lexington, Ky.: Lexington Books, 1987.

Miller, Alice. *For Your Own Good: Hidden Cruelty in Child-Rearing and the Roots of Violence.* New York: Farrar, Straus, Giroux, 1990.

White, William L. *The Incestuous Workplace: Stress and Distress in the Organizational Family.* Center City, Minn.: Hazelden, 1997.

Hermes' Web and the Web Sight Program

Hermes' Web

- is an innovative new tool for working with difficult clients
- helps communicate essential psychological concepts
- demonstrates treatment dynamics
- compensates for learning and comprehension difficulties
- helps build the connection between intention and behavior
- meets clients where they are—dubbed "the equalizer"

- works on multichannels: visual, tactile, abstract, spiritual
- can be used with many treatment models and modalities

Hermes' Web, Ltd., also offers the Web Sight Program, which incorporates the use of the Web. The Web Sight Program is unique—it combines ten essential and difficult components that, when brought together, have the capacity to reach, work with, and affect the most difficult clients.

The following are the components of the Web Sight Program:

1. Presenting problems and disorders
2. The Web
   - Ego/core
   - The flip
   - Black box
   - Mirroring
   - De-repression
   - Dismantling the victim identity
   - Tracking the perpetration
   - Incorporating the Web into your program
3. Interactive drama
   - Principles of drama therapy
   - The interactive strategy
   - The repertoire of characters
4. Process psychology
   - Group process skills
   - Conflict work
   - World work
   - Racism and privilege
5. Violence prevention
   - The roots of violence
   - The criminal mind
   - The holocaust self
6. Real sexuality
7. Guild philosophy
   - The new ethic
   - Democracy
   - Spirituality

8. Rights of passage
   - Moving from adolescence to adult—the essential lessons
9. Reading contemporary culture
10. Firebelly work
    - Movement
    - Rhythm
    - Team movement/working in unison on body level

For more information about Hermes' Web or the Web Sight Program, contact

Jerry Fjerkenstad
Hermes' Web, Ltd.
235 Bedford Street SE
Minneapolis, MN 55414
Phone: 612-623-3982
Fax: 612-362-9310
E-mail: jrfnh@aol.com

Jerry Fjerkenstad, M.A., licensed psychologist, is executive director of MASC (Minnesotans Actively Seeking Community) and the Dream Guild Theatre, a non-profit corporation providing educational and violence and crime prevention services as well as contemporary theater. Fjerkenstad is employed as senior clinical supervisor at Project Pathfinder, an outpatient sex offender program in Saint Paul, Minnesota. He created Hermes' Web, the Web Sight Program, and the Interactive Drama approach to violence prevention. He is also a writer, actor, pianist, and drummer.

$\mathcal{N}otes$

Chapter 1: The Shadow Side of the Net

1. Lynn Townsend White, *Medieval Technology and Social Change* (Oxford: Clarendon Press, 1966).

2. Alvin Toffler, *Future Shock* (New York: Bantam, [1970] 1991).

3. Al Cooper, David L. Delmonico, and Ron Burg, "Cybersex Users, Abusers, and Compulsives: New Findings and Implications," *Sexual Addiction and Compulsivity* 7, nos. 1 and 2 (2000).

Chapter 2: Do I Have a Problem with Cybersex?

1. J. P. Schneider, "Sexual Addiction: Controversy in Mainstream Medicine, Diagnosis Based on the DSM-III-R and Physician Case Histories," *Sexual Addiction and Compulsivity* 1, no. 1 (1994): 19–44.

2. David Delmonico, published on the Internet at www.sexhelp.com (1999).

Chapter 4: What Turns You On? The Arousal Template

1. John Gage, "Old Brains, New Tricks," *Time*, 7 August 2000, 70.

2. Helen Fisher, "Lust, Attraction, Attachment: Biology and Evolution of the Three Primary Emotion Systems for Mating, Reproduction, and Parenting," *Journal of Sex Education and Therapy* 25, no. 1: 96–105.

3. John Money, *Love Maps: Clinical Concepts of Sexual/Erotic Health and Pathology, Paraphilia, and Gender Transposition in Childhood, Adolescence, and Maturity* (Amherst, N.Y.: Prometheus Books, 1989).

Chapter 5: Courtship Gone Awry

1. Havelock Ellis, *Psychology of Sex* (New York: Harcourt Brace Jovanovich, [1933] 1978).

2. K. Freund and R. Watson, "Mapping the Boundaries of Courtship Disorder," *Journal of Sex Research* 27, no. 4 (November 1990): 589–606.

3. Patrick J. Carnes, *Don't Call It Love: Recovery from Sexual Addiction* (Phoenix, Ariz.: Gentle Path Press, 1991).

Chapter 6: Boundaries

1. Robert Bly, *Iron John: A Book about Men* (New York: Vintage Books, 1992).

2. Pia Mellody, *Facing Codependence* (San Francisco: Harper San Francisco, 1989).

Chapter 7: Taking That First Step

1. Paul Watzlawick, John H. Weakland, and Richard Fisch, *Change: Principles of Problem Formation and Problem Resolution* (New York: Norton, 1988).

2. Patrick J. Carnes, *Contrary to Love* (Center City, Minn.: Hazelden, 1989).

Chapter 8: Changing the Way You Live

1. The use of Hermes' Web as a tool for addiction recovery was developed by Jerry Fjerkenstad. (See appendix for more information.)

2. The phrase *truthful lie* was first used by Jerry Fjerkenstad, Hermes' Web, Ltd.

Chapter 9: Preventing Relapse: Maintaining the Changes You've Made

1. James O. Prochaska, John C. Norcross, and Carlos C. DiClemente, *Changing for Good* (New York: Avon Books, 1995).

2. G. Alan Marlatt and Judith R. Gordon, eds., *Relapse Prevention: Maintenance Strategies in the Treatment of Addictive Behaviors* (New York: Guilford Press, 1985).

3. Prochaska et al., *Changing for Good.*

Chapter 10: Family Dynamics and Cybersex

1. J. P. Schneider, "Effects of Cybersex Addiction on the Family: Results of a Survey," *Sexual Addiction and Compulsivity* 7, no. 1 (2000): 31–58.

2. J. P. Schneider, "A Qualitative Study of Cybersex Participants: Gender Differences, Recovery Issues, and Implications for Therapists," *Sexual Addiction and Compulsivity* 7, no. 4 (in press).

3. Patrick Carnes, *Don't Call It Love: Recovery from Sexual Addiction* (Phoenix, Ariz.: Gentle Path Press, 1991).

4. Patrick Carnes, Debra Laaser, and Mark Laaser, *Open Hearts: Renewing*

Relationships with Recovery, Romance, and Reality (Phoenix, Ariz.: Gentle Path Press, 2000).

Chapter 11: The Web Frontier

1. Denise Breton and Christopher Largent, *The Paradigm Conspiracy* (Center City, Minn.: Hazelden, 1996).

2. Dean Ornish, *Love and Survival* (New York: Harper Collins, 1999).

3. Tom Clancy, *The Bear and the Dragon* (New York: Putnam, 2000).

4. Frank Herbert, Dune (New York: Ace Books, 1999).

5. Aldous Huxley, *Brave New World* (New York: HarperPerennial, 1998).

6. Alvin Toffler, *Future Shock* (New York: Bantam, [1970] 1991).

7. M. Scott Peck, *The Road Less Traveled* (New York: Simon & Schuster, 1997).

$\mathcal{I}ndex$

About the Authors

PATRICK CARNES, PH.D., is a clinical director for sexual disorder services at the Meadows in Wickenburg, Arizona. Dr. Carnes is a nationally known speaker and writer on addiction and recovery. He is author of *Out of the Shadows, Contrary to Love, A Gentle Path through the Twelve Steps, Don't Call It Love, Sexual Anorexia,* and *Open Hearts.* He is editor-in-chief of *Sexual Addiction and Compulsivity: The Journal of Treatment and Prevention,* the official journal of the National Council of Sexual Addiction/Compulsivity.

DAVID L. DELMONICO, PH.D., is an assistant professor in the Department of Counseling, Psychology, and Special Education at Duquesne University in Pittsburgh, Pennsylvania. He is a graduate of Kent State University with degrees in community counseling, psychology, and counseling and human development services. He has worked and published numerous articles in the area of sexual addiction for ten years.

ELIZABETH GRIFFIN, M.A., is a licensed marriage and family therapist with more than fifteen years of experience treating sexual disorders. She has worked in outpatient, inpatient, military, and prison settings. She lectures nationally on the assessment and treatment of sexual disorders as well as cyber-sex issues relating to those with sexual disorders. She is currently chief operating officer for the American Foundation for Addiction Research, a non-profit organization dedicated to fostering scientific research and understanding and disseminating knowledge of the nature and causes of addictive disorders.

JOSEPH M. MORIARITY, B.S., B.A., has worked for twenty years as a freelance writer with a primary focus in the fields of health care, addiction and treatment, science, and education. He has previously written two other books for Hazelden, *Winning a Day at a Time* with John Lucas and *Sexual Anorexia* with Dr. Patrick Carnes.